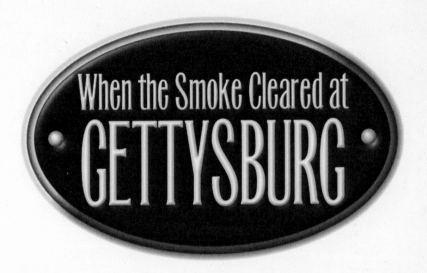

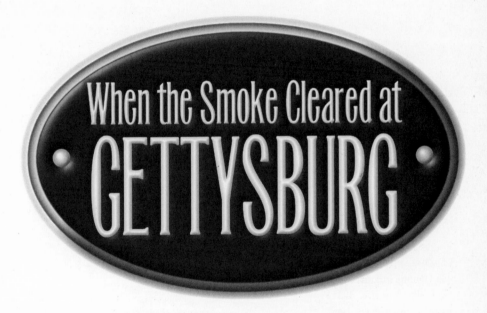

When the Smoke Cleared at GETTYSBURG

The Tragic Aftermath of the Bloodiest Battle of the Civil War

GEORGE SHELDON

CUMBERLAND HOUSE

NASHVILLE, TENNESSEE

Copyright © 2003 by George Sheldon

PUBLISHED BY
CUMBERLAND HOUSE PUBLISHING, INC.
431 Harding Industrial Drive
Nashville, Tennessee 37211
www.cumberlandhouse.com

Cover design by Gore Studio, Nashville, Tennessee.

Library of Congress Cataloging-in-Publication Data.

Sheldon, George, 1951–
    When the smoke cleared at Gettysburg : the tragic aftermath of the bloodiest battle of the Civil War / George Sheldon.
        p.   cm.
    Includes bibliographical references and index.
    ISBN 1-58182-343-6 (pbk. : alk. paper)
    1. Gettysburg, Battle of, Gettysburg, Pa., 1863. 2. Gettysburg, Battle of, Gettysburg, Pa., 1863—Influence. 3. Gettysburg, Battle of, Gettysburg, Pa., 1863—Social aspects. 4. Gettysburg (Pa.)—History—19th century. I. Title.
E475.53.S55 2003
973.7'349—dc21

                                                                        2003009775

Printed in Canada

2 3 4 5 6 7 8 9 10—06 05 04 03

This one is especially for Paul Eugene Adams III, but I know him as "Petey." He is an exceptionally fine grandson.

CONTENTS

PART 4: REMEMBERING AND COMMEMORATING

PREFACE

THIS IS A STORY about ordinary people. They were regular Americans living commonplace lives who abruptly found themselves in the middle of an extraordinary event. Three days in July 1863 changed their lives forever.

This book is not about the momentous battle that occurred at Gettysburg in the summer of 1863. The strategies of the generals, the positioning of troops, and the bravery of the soldiers made Gettysburg historical and unforgettable. This book, however, does not attempt to explain or decipher the impact of military movements or weaponry. It is about the people who lived in and around the town of Gettysburg during the maelstrom. This is their story of what happened after the smoke cleared and the armies departed Adams County. The story also includes those who traveled to Gettysburg to help the wounded, search for loved ones, or possibly profit from the misfortunes of war.

Still, this story begins long before a Union soldier fired the first shot just west of town on the morning of July 1, 1863. It started nearly two years before, when Pennsylvanians responded to Abraham Lincoln's call for troops to quell the rebellion. The people of Adams County—Pennsylvania Dutch farmers and an urban, prosperous population within the growing borough of Gettysburg—answered the president's call by dispatching the town's militia.

Because of the town's close proximity to Southern-sympathetic Maryland, the fear of Rebel attack hung over the community from 1861 until it was realized in late June 1863. As the farmers' fields began to show an abundance of crops, the Confederate army invaded Pennsylvania. The Southerners' goal was to capture a Northern capital and force Lincoln to recognize the Confederate States of America as a sovereign nation. While the Confederate army moved north, the Federal army was not far behind.

Rumors became fact, and the residents of Adams County nervously waited. Their apprehension turned into solemn reality when the Army of Northern Virginia marched boldly and unopposed into Gettysburg in late June.

As an army band celebrated the invasion of the North by playing "Dixie" in the center of the town for all the residents to hear, the Union army moved closer. Within days the two armies collided in Adams County at Gettysburg. For three days they waged a great battle. When it ended, more than twenty-one thousand injured men lay on the field along with thousands of dead comrades. Robert E. Lee's battered army retreated, and the victorious Federals followed.

After the din of fighting ceased, the townspeople and farmers of Gettysburg emerged from their cellars or returned to their scarred homes. For three days the town filled to overflowing with the wounded from the battlefield; surgeons commandeered public buildings and converted them into operating rooms and hospitals. Now, in the wake of the armies, there were shortages of food and supplies, massive mounds of battle debris, and thousands of maimed and wounded men.

A herculean task fell on the people now staring in shock at the shambles around them. Most were women and old men. The town's young men were gone—serving in the army. Many prominent citizens had fled the area to escape capture. Merchants had moved what few goods they had from their stores and warehouses to prevent confiscation by the Confederates. The relatively few young men still in town were surgeons who worked until they collapsed of exhaustion. It was a dreadful, miserable time for everyone.

Within a short while, the town was soon invaded again—by thousands of visitors. Many searched for loved ones, hoping to find them only wounded and mending in a hospital. Some found them in shallow graves; others were never found. Amid the thankful and the heartbroken were gawkers and sightseers, drawn to witness the ghoulish aftermath and the dead. Finally, there were those trying to offer assistance.

A third invasion occurred at the dedication of the cemetery to honor the fallen. The visitors included Lincoln. His modest words became hallowed and as important to Americans as the words of the Declaration of Independence and the Constitution. It was here that the citizens heard their president call for the rebirth of their nation.

Throughout these ordeals, the citizens of Gettysburg and the surrounding area demonstrated tremendous courage and resourcefulness. Their perseverance through the brutal fighting and what followed exhibited remarkable endurance. Human nature being what it is, this dreary time of horrendous combat and the immediate aftermath elicited the best people had to offer and sometimes the worst. Citizens showed compassion and caring; others were greedy and motivated with the promise of profit. Local politics sometimes governed their actions, sometimes disregarding the right thing to do.

While others have written so much about the battle and the men who fought at Gettysburg, little has been said about the people who lived here before, during, and after the conflict. Books, songs, magazine articles, poems, newspaper stories, and speeches told the story of the military men, but few words have been used to describe the children who had their formative years interrupted by the gore and reality of war. Without any formal training or education, housewives became nurses and doctors under the worst possible conditions. Farms that were once the source of many livelihoods became unusable because of the carnage and debris that polluted the fields. Shallow unmarked graves dotted meadows and pastures, and for decades to come, routine plowing unearthed the remains of many soldiers.

Fortunately, many of the people so deeply involved in the Gettysburg experience set down their eyewitness accounts to writing. Their stories were recorded in letters and diaries. Some produced book-length manuscripts for publication. Some waited until the twilight of their lives to compose the history they observed, and certainly their memories had fogged over time. Local newspapers also recorded the details of what happened as it happened, but without the insight time affords such events.

In 1863 Gettysburg was a thriving yet isolated hamlet in the rolling hills of the lush farmland of south central Pennsylvania. For three days approximately 163,000 soldiers engaged in ferocious fighting that resulted in 51,000 casualties. Here is the story of the people who were present when the smoke cleared at Gettysburg.

ACKNOWLEDGMENTS

NO BOOK IS CREATED without the help of others. This book is not an exception, and I want to try to thank those who have so graciously contributed to this result. Although I used various resources from the Internet, I am reluctant to cite Web sites because Internet links constantly change—a recurring problem that I encountered during my research and writing. Interested readers should use a search engine to find more information based on the general information listed here. At the same time, I cannot thank the countless Internet writers who provided bits and pieces of information. Many times a notation on a Web site directed me to more information.

Many fine people at different places along the trail of information helped me dig for the facts used in this book. Special thanks to the staff at the library of the Gettysburg National Military Park.

I also want to thank Terry Neimer of the National Civil War Museum of Medicine in Frederick, Maryland.

Some of the many people who aided me include the staffs of the Pennsylvania State Library in Harrisburg, the Pennsylvania State Archives, the Military History Institute in Carlisle, the Adams County Historical Society in Gettysburg, the Lancaster Public Library, and the Cortland (New York) Public Library.

I am indebted to several people who engaged in lively discussions on the Internet. In particular, I want to thank the wonderful people who participate in the Gettysburg Discussion Group.

I am also most grateful to the many residents of Gettysburg who recorded their recollections and memories.

Numerous people provided me with nuggets of information, advice, and input along the way. Many I have not personally met, but thanks to e-mail, our communications went well, and they filled up my mailbox with great information. One of them was Robert E. Nale, from Sandpoint,

Idaho. He provided some keen insights into the Thirty-sixth Pennsylvania
Infantry Volunteers.

I also received terrific background information and thought-provoking
e-mails from Barbara Jones of Moscow, Idaho. I especially found her knowledge of Gen. John F. Reynolds refreshing and quite in-depth. The general
was from my hometown, but BeeJay's knowledge rivaled many other sources.

Jennifer Shaw of Cherry Hill, New Jersey, provided background and
information about the life of Matilda J. "Tillie" Pierce Alleman.

Paula Gidjunis of North Wales, Pennsylvania, offered insight and
direction, both of which were quite helpful.

I want to especially thank Sister Betty Ann McNeil, Archives and
Mission Services, Daughters of Charity, Province of Emmitsburg (USA).
Sister Betty Ann always responded to my requests and assisted me with my
many questions.

I also want to thank the Saint Joseph's Provincial House 7-5-1-2, #8,
Daughters of Charity in the Civil War. Through the courtesy of the
archives of the Daughters of Charity in Emmitsburg, I was able to include
some interesting information about the service of the Daughters of Charity
at Gettysburg.

I also want to thank Ron Pitkin, president of Cumberland House. I
greatly appreciate his enthusiasm for this book. I would also like to thank
Bruce Gore who designed the book's cover. I think it looks magnificent!
And thanks to everyone else at Cumberland House who helped to get this
book to you, the readers. I appreciate their hard and dedicated work.

Very special thanks and warm recognition to Charles W. Byrd of Hershey, Pennsylvania. Until the sun goes out, I shall always remember his
early support, helpful critiques, but most important, his warm encouragement that kept me going.

And, of course, last, but never and in no way least, a very special thank
you to my much adored wife, Gloria. Without her, there would not be a
book. Her constant support, edits, suggestions, typo corrections, careful
eye, and numerous critiques helped throughout the book. She was kind
enough to trek along to the countless dusty sections of libraries. She pored
over the manuscript, helping to make it a better work.

When the Smoke Cleared at
GETTYSBURG

A SMALL TOWN IN PENNSYLVANIA

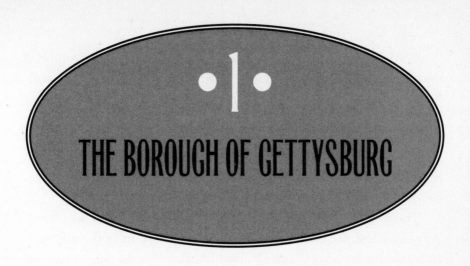

THE BOROUGH OF GETTYSBURG

They were "armed to the teeth" with old, rusty guns and swords, pitchforks, shovels and pick-axes.

TILLIE PIERCE

FOR MANY MONTHS BEFORE July 1, 1863, cries of "The Rebels are coming!" echoed in the streets of Gettysburg. They were words the residents of Adams County had heard many times before.

Two years earlier, in the early morning hours of June 22, 1861, the townspeople gathered at the train station, situated a short distance north of the town square, or what locals called "the Diamond." They were there to bid farewell to the local militia company known as the Gettysburg Blues. Just two and a half years earlier, on December 16, 1858, the same train station had been the scene of the largest celebration the town had ever witnessed. The revelry marked the opening of the station. Sixteen and a half miles of track connected Gettysburg to Hanover. From there, passenger service was available south to Baltimore or east to Philadelphia through a connection at Harrisburg. The railroad also meant that the goods produced in Adams County could be easily shipped to nearby markets.

Gettysburg was growing. The latest technologies of the day infiltrated the town. Telegraph service was available. There were doctors and a dentist. Since the town was the county seat, there were seven practicing attorneys. Local politics were well entrenched, too. Within the borough limits, the Republican Party was firmly ensconced. The rural residents and farmers favored the Democrats. Three weekly newspapers reflected their editors' political opinions. And in 1861 locomotive power was available and being used to send the community's young men to answer the call of duty.

The seventy-seven men of the militia company known as the Gettysburg Blues boarded the train with the rousing support of the citizenry. Under the command of Charles H. Buehler, they departed their hometown for war. Confederates had fired on Fort Sumter in South Carolina just two months earlier.

That same summer evening after the militia had left, a single man on an exhausted horse galloped into town, circled the Diamond, and shouted a warning: "The Rebels are coming!"

At the same time, city leaders were in a meeting one block away at the courthouse, discussing a proposal to raise a home guard to defend the community. Because of the proximity of Gettysburg to Southern-sympathetic Maryland, precautions of guarding the town against Confederate attack were necessary. Two men burst into the meeting and yelled, "The Rebels are burning Hanover, and Gettysburg is next!"

The calm of the meeting gave way to mass pandemonium. The town's supply of arms and ammunition had left with the Blues. Fear that the Confederates might torch the town paralyzed the community. News of what had reportedly happened at Hanover spread like a wind-whipped forest fire. Residents poured into the streets for more details of the approaching Southerners. Many fretted. They grabbed axes and shovels and prepared to defend their town.

"They were 'armed to the teeth' with old, rusty guns and swords, pitchforks, shovels and pick-axes," Tillie Pierce recalled.[1]

The town leaders dispatched riders to nearby communities to spread the word. Someone decided they should send the locomotive down the tracks to Hanover and survey the situation. Around midnight the train engineer fired up the engine, and the steam-driven beast rolled out of the station toward Hanover. The residents remained vigilant with garden hoes, axes, shovels, and clubs. Shortly before daybreak, the locomotive chugged back into town with the news.

The reports of the burning of Hanover were false. The Confederate army was nowhere near the area.

Calm returned that summer night.[2] This was the first but not the last time the townspeople would hear that the Rebels were coming.

In 1863 the town of Gettysburg was seventy-seven years old. Although it will forever be known in American history for its Civil War legacy, Gettysburg was a thriving, tranquil, tiny market community in rural Pennsylvania prior to the arrival of Robert E. Lee's and George Gordon Meade's armies.

One hundred years before the great conflict, the same land was home to some Iroquois tribes. In 1736 William Penn's family purchased the land from the Native Americans, and the area was farmed by European settlers. The northern part of the county, toward Carlisle and Harrisburg, was settled by Scotch-Irish families who had left northern Ireland to escape English persecution. German families traveled beyond Lancaster and York and moved into the southern areas of the county. Within a few short years, more than 150 families worked the land of this lush frontier.

As a frontier settlement, Gettysburg was attacked and white settlers were massacred by war parties. In 1756 there were fewer than one hundred men—exclusive of the provincial forces—fit to bear arms west of the Susquehanna River. Fear had driven them from the frontier. The situation, however, was changing. Over the next two decades their number would grow to three thousand. Still, the area knew its share of unrest. On May 29, 1759, "Dunwiddie and Crawford, shot by two Indians, in Carroll's tract" was noted on a long list of recorded captures and massacres.[3]

Another record entry shows that on April 5, 1758, one man was killed and ten were taken near Black's Gap on South Mountain. On April 13 one man was killed and nine were taken near Archibald Bard's at South Mountain. The war parties seized the settlers as prisoners, plundered the house and barn, and burned the buildings.

The early settlers of Adams County did not stand idly by as their neighbors were butchered, however. Capt. Hance Hamilton raised and commanded a force of two hundred men. They were the ancestors of many of those who left Adams County in 1861 to fight for the Union.

In the early years everyone called the central region of Adams County the Marsh Creek area, named after its main tributary. Samuel Getty, one of those early settlers, established a farmstead in Marsh Creek. In 1761 he opened a tavern. After the Revolutionary War, Samuel's middle son, James, purchased a 116-acre tract from his father's 381-acre farm. By 1786 he had laid out a community of 210 lots around a central square, which still remains the center of town, the Diamond. The newly available home lots surrounded the original Getty tavern. Thus the town of Gettysburg was born.

This area of Adams County was once a part of York County, and prior to that, Lancaster County. A trip to the county seat at York, however, took a full day. Add to that the differences in nationalities and religions of these eastern settlers, and it's not difficult to fathom how these elements led the independent-minded settlers to establish their own county government.

The first Pennsylvania Frame of Government established local governments in 1776, and the U.S. Constitution later followed in 1787. As a result, the growing and prospering population of the area chose to separate from York County. In 1800 the state legislature approved a new county of approximately 618 square miles. It was named for the president of the United States at that time: John Adams. The county seat was placed at the small, prosperous town of Gettysburg.

Strategically situated at a major crossroads between larger Pennsylvania and Maryland cities, Gettysburg grew steadily as a small rural hub along a primary agricultural transportation corridor between south-central Pennsylvania and Baltimore. Ten roads from other farm settlements, boroughs, hamlets, and villages connected and intersected at Gettysburg. Workers improved three of the pikes leading to Gettysburg, making them hard surfaced. An early map of these farm roads, pikes, and principal roads resembled the spokes of a wagon wheel, and Gettysburg was clearly at the center.

The first half of the nineteenth century witnessed the establishment of educational and religious institutions in the town, including the Gettysburg Lutheran Theological Seminary and Pennsylvania (now Gettysburg) College. A growing light-manufacturing industry supplemented the county's growing agricultural economy, which included a viable cart-, carriage-, and wagon-making industry. As the community thrived, a bank opened. A fire insurance company and two drugstores also set up their businesses in the town. There was a separate savings institution and boarding houses. Bakers offered freshly baked goods. There were the usual merchants, doctors, taverns, and large homes incumbent on a county seat.

In the June 27, 1863, edition of the *Star and Sentinel*, a listing for a local hotel hinted at the prosperity of the town's businesses: "Proprietors of the Eagle Hotel on Chambersburg Street have announced the latest improvements in the hotel with the installation of oil lamps in every room and the new tavern and restaurant now serving meals in the first floor lounge. Every attempt has been made to satisfy the needs of the traveler and businessman."

The town of Gettysburg had grown to twenty-four hundred inhabitants. It provided key services for the Adams County area and northwestern Maryland. At the time of the 1863 battle, there were about 450 buildings in the immediate vicinity. With deep lots, workers built the houses with no front yards and rather close to the street.

Twenty-two Gettysburg residents listed their occupation as shoemaker or cobbler during the 1860 census. With the tanneries in town, it is likely that some bought leather and assembled crude shoes or boots for their own use. As their skill at assembling shoes developed, they likely sold shoes for profit to neighbors and others. Although there was a thriving carriage-manufacturing industry in Gettysburg, there was no established shoe-manufacturing industry in Adams County.

Long before the battle, residents John Culp and Alex Cobean sold hats, boots, and shoes from their store on Chambersburg Street.[4] Cobean & Culp's shop was easily identified by the sign of "The Big Red Boot." Their advertisement was:

> We are constantly adding new supplies to our already large and fashionable stock of hats, caps, boots, and shoes.
> We have every style of spring and summer hats, which is quality and prices cannot fail to please. Boy's and men's hats and camp of every description, and of the latest styles.
> Our stock of Boots

Shoes

Gaiters

Acc.,

Were never more complete. Ladies, gentlemen, and children can be accommodated with anything in this line, as we are better prepared now to give fits and greater bargains.

Good fits and fashionable goods.

Call at the sign of the Big Boot, in Chambersburg Street.[5]

Cobean & Culp's advertisement shows the type of commerce regularly transacted within the borough. Their shop was just one of many that offered quality goods to a growing population in the county seat.

Along with her sister and brother-in-law, Mary McAllister was the proprietor of a general store on Chambersburg Street. John L. Schick also operated a small store on the west side of Baltimore Street. Farther south, down the street, was the house where James Pierce earned his living as a butcher. Dr. John Runkel also lived on Baltimore Street. Drs. Robert and Charles Horner resided on the north side of Chambersburg Street. Other shops were operated by bakers, several tanners, a brick maker, harness maker, cabinetmakers, marble cutter, an auctioneer, druggist, blacksmiths, and several other merchants. There were several hotels and churches. In addition to the Lutheran seminary and Pennsylvania College buildings, there were schools and other public buildings.

Adams County itself consisted of 618 square miles with a population of 28,000 whites and 474 African Americans. Of this total population, 6,674 were subject to taxes. The county was composed of a network of villages, hamlets, settlements, and thirty boroughs. Nestled among rolling hills, low mountains, and woodlands, the value of all farmland in the county was appraised at nine million dollars. As an inland county, the area's water sources were limited to streams and creeks. The farmers owned around one hundred thousand dollars' worth of livestock: horses, cattle, sheep, and pigs.

Within the county were sixteen lumber mills, forty flour mills, nine lime kilns, twenty-three leather tanneries, and four sheet iron and copper works. Fifteen different companies manufactured horse carts, carriages, and wagons and employed several hundred workers. The county school system consisted of 148 buildings, and 75 churches addressed the spiritual needs of the residents.

Because the Lutheran seminary and Pennsylvania College were situated at Gettysburg, the town was a center of higher education. The faculty and students added a layer of scholarly sophistication to the town's society. These intuitions oozed a learned atmosphere, morphing the town from a rural society to a cultural center thirsting for knowledge and information. The quest for knowledge also supported the town's three newspapers.

The *Compiler*, the *Adams Sentinel*, and the *Star and Banner* published weekly versions of the national and local news. The *Compiler* was a Democratic newspaper, while the *Adams Sentinel* and the *Star and Banner* were supporters and voices of the Republican Party. The papers gathered most of their news from larger newspapers in Baltimore and Washington.

The arrival of the telegraph in late 1862 connected Gettysburg to the rest of the nation. Hugh Scott, the son of John and Martha Scott, operated the telegraph from his parents' property on the north side of Chambersburg Street and within the first block from the Diamond. The population was now in touch with the world and knew what was happening across the country, even though the staunch Democratic and Republican editors often slanted the news to their political vision.

Politics became intertwined with the cosmopolitan culture that developed in Adams County. Just as the nation divided over a bitter dispute, so did these citizens. *Copperheads* was the derogatory label for Southern sympathizers. There was a fairly even number of Democrats and Republicans in Adams County. In the 1860 presidential election, Abraham Lincoln barely carried the county despite the fact that the residents were overwhelmingly against slavery.

YEARS BEFORE the Declaration of Independence, the boundary between Maryland and Pennsylvania was highly contested. In both of the Calvert and Penn charters, the description of the line separating the two colonies was vague. The ambiguity led to a long, protracted disagreement between the proprietors of the two British enterprises. If Maryland had its way, the border between the two states would have been north of Gettysburg. In

1735 the dispute between the Penn and Calvert families was submitted to the English chancery court. A compromise resulted years later, and a survey was commissioned.

Between 1763 and 1767 surveyors Charles Mason and Jeremiah Dixon marked the border between the two colonies. The two surveyors defined a line that ended 244 miles west of the common border with Delaware. Every fifth milestone they positioned bore the Penn and Calvert arms. Before the outbreak of the Civil War, the term Mason-Dixon Line popularly designated the border separating slave states from free states. In the end, Gettysburg was seven miles north of the Mason-Dixon Line.

AFRICAN AMERICANS have a long history in the area of Gettysburg. From the early beginnings of the colony, some Pennsylvanians owned slaves. Some of the earliest settlers of what became Adams County brought their slaves with them. Town founder James Getty owned a slave.

In 1776 Alexander Dobbin, a Presbyterian minister, brought two slaves to construct the stone building that became Dobbin's home and classical school. These two slaves were the first African Americans to live in Cumberland Township.[6] In 1837 John Blake offered a ten-dollar reward for the return of a seventeen-year-old black girl who had run away from his home in Reading Township in Adams County.[7]

While the slave trade flourished, many Pennsylvanians advocated its termination. In 1775 the Quakers and other concerned citizens organized the Pennsylvania Abolition Society. This group's primary purpose was to assist fugitive slaves. In 1780 the state passed the Gradual Abolition Act, mandating that any slave born after March 1, 1780, was to be freed at the end of twenty-eight years of service.

In the years that followed, Pennsylvanians became well known for their resistance in returning runaway slaves. Even George Washington doubted there was much hope of having a slave returned from Pennsylvania when a Virginian's slave had escaped to Philadelphia and was among the "Society of Quakers who has attempted to liberate [him]." Later Washington wrote that one of his own slaves was in southeastern Pennsylvania, "where it is not easy to apprehend them because there are a great number [of people] who would rather facilitate the escape . . . than apprehend the runaway."[8]

For several generations of slaves, getting across the Mason-Dixon Line into Pennsylvania meant freedom. Likewise a journey south of the line into Maryland or Virginia meant a return to the horrific bonds of slavery.

While the vast majority of Adams County residents were against slavery, that did not mean they were abolitionists. Such distinctions led to differing political views. Emotions were deeply rooted and led to some bizarre behavior and accusations during the 1863 battle. Several times citizen turned against citizen, often over such political and social matters.

THE PEOPLE of the growing county held deep-rooted religious convictions. Of the seventy-five churches in Adams County, seven were within the borough of Gettysburg. Clearly their shared belief was a source of strength during the ordeal that befell their area. They were in the right place at the wrong time when two armies maneuvered into the region, ready for battle.

• 2 •

THE REBELS ARE COMING!

The suspense was dreadful.

SALLIE MYERS

ON OCTOBER 10, 1862, Confederate Gen. Jeb Stuart and a cavalry force of eighteen hundred men galloped into Chambersburg, Pennsylvania. Their incursion marked the beginning of a series of Rebel invasions into the North. Chambersburg is about twenty-five miles west of Gettysburg.

Stuart entered the town with explicit orders from his commanding general to treat all citizens, including those who would be taken hostage, "with all the respect and consideration that circumstances will admit." Robert E. Lee's order also defined exactly what his soldiers were permitted to take: "Should it be in your power to supply yourself with horses, or other necessary articles on the list of legal capture, you are authorized to do so."

Lee's orders were supplemented with Stuart's own discretionary orders, which cautioned, "Individual plunder for private use is positively forbidden, and in every instance must be punished in the severest manner, for an army of plunderers consummates its own destruction." The officers made it clear to their men that the town was not to become a battlefield and the citizens were not to be treated as enemy soldiers. Private property and dignity was to be respected. As this first invading raid unfolded, the Confederates followed these "rules of war." They seized hundreds of horses and took five hundred guns, all of which fell within Lee's definition of legal capture. The raiders also destroyed about a quarter of a million dollars' worth of railroad property. Chambersburg's weekly newspaper, the *Valley Spirit*, noted in its October 15, 1862, issue, "The town was surrendered on the terms that private property would be respected and citizens unmolested."

The next day Stuart continued his daring raid into Pennsylvania by turning east toward Gettysburg. By nightfall he was in Cashtown, just eight miles west of the borough. From Cashtown, however, the mounted Confederates turned south to Fairfield. They took horses, provisions, and a small number of hostages. Stuart's scouts were as close as six miles to Gettysburg when they were spotted at Latshaw's Tavern.

After word reached Gettysburg of Stuart's close proximity, panic and alarm spread throughout the community as fast as the shouts, "The Rebels are coming!" Anxiety dissipated the next day when Federal troops arrived. Union cavalry stayed the night.

Stuart skillfully slipped back to Virginia, returning by a route between George B. McClellan's army and Washington, evading numerous Federal expeditions against him. The Confederates' total casualties were one wounded man. The raid, however, had a demoralizing effect on the Federal cavalry.

To the townspeople of Gettysburg, Stuart's venture demonstrated that they were vulnerable. The residents also learned quickly what could happen when the Confederates arrived. Their property and goods would be quickly confiscated. That was something they would not forget.

EITHER BY chance or destiny, in June 1863 the future of the small and prosperous hamlet in southern Pennsylvania changed forever. Still a relatively young nation with a population of about thirty-three million citizens, the United States would see approximately five million men directly engaged in the conflict known as the Civil War. Both sides believed they were fighting for rather simple political ideals: The North wanted to maintain the liberty and the union that the hard-fought Revolutionary War had achieved; the South fought to uphold that liberty as it was defined within the context of the rights of the individual states. A deciding battle was yet to be waged, but it would come soon enough.

For the second time, the Confederate army had invaded the North, daring the Union army to follow, forcing it to protect the Northern states. The Rebels planned to deliver a crushing blow to the Federal army and then offer a peace treaty. It was also believed by the Southern leaders that if they successfully invaded the North, European governments would begin to recognize the sovereignty of the Confederate States.

In June 1863 Lee's army marched northwest from the Rappahannock line toward the Blue Ridge Mountains. On June 13 his army stormed the Federal garrison at Winchester. One of its defenders, Johnston Skelly Jr. of the Eighty-seventh Pennsylvania, a native of Gettysburg, was mortally wounded during the Confederate attack.

This invasion of Pennsylvania was not a well-kept secret. Local newspapers constantly published the details of the Rebels' movements. Gettysburg resident Sarah Broadhead wrote in her diary on June 15, "Today we heard the Rebels are crossing the river in heavy force and advancing on the state." Her information was accurate: The Southerners had crossed the Potomac River and were marching north.

ONLY ONE month had passed since the Confederate victory at Chancellorsville, and now the War Department sent warnings to several Northern states that Lee's army threatened to invade Maryland and Pennsylvania. In early June the Commonwealth of Pennsylvania was divided into two military departments and military commanders were appointed. Gen. Darius N. Couch headed the Department of the Susquehanna (the eastern division), and Gen. William T. H. Brooks commanded the Department of the Monongahela (the western region).

Couch was a combat-hardened commander from the Army of the Potomac who had most recently served as Joseph Hooker's chief of staff at Chancellorsville. After the battle, rather than criticize the commanding general, Couch requested reassignment. When he was appointed to head the Susquehanna department, he found he had little to work with: a handful

of troops and not much equipment. Couch found, however, a highly motivated governor prepared to support him in the defense of the state.

Pennsylvania Gov. Andrew G. Curtin[1] had declared a state of emergency on June 12 and called for militia to help meet the threat: "I now
appeal to all citizens of Pennsylvania who love liberty and are mindful of
the history and traditions of their Revolutionary fathers and who feel that
it is a sacred duty to guard and maintain the free institutions of our country,
who hate treason and its abettors, and who are willing to go defend their
homes and firesides, and do invoke them to rise in their might and rush to
the rescue in the hour of imminent peril. The issue is one of preservation or
destruction." It was a tough time of the year to ask for volunteers. Crops
needed tending, and two years of war had already depleted the number of
able-bodied men.

As the call for volunteers sounded across the state, on June 24 a determined group of sixteen veterans of the War of 1812 responded. A Harrisburg correspondent of the *Philadelphia Press* noted that "the oldest was
seventy-six, and the youngest sixty-eight." They carried a tattered silk
banner, which someone later learned had been borne at Trenton in 1777.
To those who witnessed the sixteen aged veterans march to the capitol to
offer their services, "It was a grand and inspiring sight!" The newsman
noted: "Those old men, scarcely hoping to live through the war, their locks
white with the frosts of many winters, their frames bowed by age, and long
toil in the journey of life, marched as briskly and accurately to the drum
and fife, as any of their grandsons could."[2]

The descendants of these patriots now filled the ranks of the Pennsylvania volunteer troops. Adams County resident Robert Bell, to defend
Gettysburg, raised an independent cavalry from the men of the town and
the outlying areas of Adams County. Soon Bell's men patrolled the roads
west of Gettysburg, warily watching for approaching Confederates. On
June 21 about forty men from the Philadelphia City Troop rode into town
and joined Bell's small force. This combined company was Gettysburg's
sole bulwark against the maneuvering Confederates.

Although they lacked any formal training, Bell's horsemen soon
encountered Southerners in the mountains west of Gettysburg. Some of
Bell's men rode into town to report the news. A group of volunteers decided

to head west to hamper the Confederates' advance by cutting down trees to block the narrow roads. Shortly after marching out of town with axes on their shoulders, a group of fifty men soon stumbled upon some startled Confederates. Already positioned on the eastern side of Southern Mountain, the Rebels fired some warning shots at the woodsmen. The small group—which included Sarah Broadhead's husband, Joseph—quickly returned to town.

Bell's men continued to report their sightings. In response to their information, on Wednesday, June 24, the town received a telegram that the Twenty-sixth Pennsylvania Emergency Volunteers were en route and would arrive in Gettysburg the next afternoon by rail. That did not happen, however. The train carrying the Twenty-sixth Pennsylvania was derailed between Hanover Junction and Gettysburg when it hit a cow on the tracks. None of the soldiers were injured, but they did not arrive until 10 A.M. on Friday.

During the long nights of waiting, the townspeople could see fires burning on South Mountain near Cashtown. It was becoming very clear that the Confederate army was edging ever closer to town. When the Twenty-sixth Pennsylvania marched into Gettysburg, the men paused long enough to receive a rousing welcome from the town.

"We don't feel much safer," Sarah Broadhead recorded in her diary.[3]

REPORTS OF Confederate advances were constant. Travelers brought news from other towns, and the telegraph provided a steady flow information.

"The people did little more than stand along the street and talk," Sallie Myers, a young schoolteacher, recalled. "Whenever someone heard a new report, all flocked to him. The suspense was dreadful."[4]

The June 19 edition of the Adams County *Star and Sentinel* revealed that the previous week "there was a large force of the enemy at Hagerstown, probably 20,000 infantry, 2,000 cavalry, and artillery numbering twenty or more guns." Two thousand Southerners were also reported at South Mountain, and a small force of cavalry had advanced as far as Fairfield, eight miles from Gettysburg.

News of the invasion seemed well disseminated. A Chambersburg merchant sent a letter to his wife in Lancaster. The contents appeared in the

Daily Express. He recounted a thirteen-hour occupation of the town, during which the Southerners seized horses and approximately one hundred blacks, both free and slave. The businessman could only say that "it was a sorrowful sight. . . . The rebels say they will hold the free ones until exchanged for an equal number of their slaves." Meanwhile the merchants were given the choice of opening their stores and selling their wares in exchange for Confederate script or having their goods confiscated. Many store owners had anticipated this and emptied their enterprises before the Southerners arrived. The Chambersburg man noted, "Yesterday we had a gentlemanly class to deal with, but today a few would steal" and "they behaved well in the store, except two or three rowdies." His greatest lament was that "we have not seen a Union Soldier to relieve us from our troubles."

Catharine Hunsecker commented on the futility of selling anything to the Southerners. "They paid for their things with paper 'Greenbacks.' It was absolutely worthless," she commented. "They carried printing outfits with them and made their money as they went. For a while, they had their presses installed in a schoolhouse near [my] home. They would tell us that their money would soon be worth face value as they were going to win the war. They also assured us that our money would soon be worthless."

Hunsecker, the eldest of seven children living on a farm near Chambersburg, recollected the visits of the Confederate army and their methods of procuring goods. "In the beginning of the war everything was pretty quiet so far as we were concerned. Later the Southern soldiers began to make raids thru the north. The Cumberland Valley, being a rich farming section and a continuation of the Shenandoah Valley of Virginia, was one of the favorite sections for raiding parties.

"When word first came that the 'Rebels' were coming, the people became very much scared and hardly knew what to do," Hunsecker reported. "We could hear the noise of the battles in Maryland and Virginia before they came as far north as Pennsylvania. People generally started to hide their goods and valuables as soon as possible in the bottom of the smokehouse, which was kept securely locked. The best of the horse gears were hidden in the bake oven. Some of the older and less valuable harnesses were allowed to remain in the usual place to avert suspicion that things were hidden away."

She added, "Then the horses were taken away since the Confederates were known to be badly in need of horses and took all they could get. The people of the whole community took their horses away. Many of them hid them in the mountains that skirt both sides of the Valley."

Teenager Daniel A. Skelly was employed as a clerk in a dry goods company. He later recalled, "Rumors of the invasion of Pennsylvania by the Confederate army were rife and toward the latter part of the month there was the daily sight of people from along the border of Maryland passing through the town with horses and cattle, to places of safety. Most of the merchants of the town shipped their goods to Philadelphia for safety, as was their habit all through the war upon rumors of the Confederates crossing the Potomac."[5]

Panic and bedlam spread widely through the community on the night of June 16. Twelve miles to the south, a huge fire in Emmitsburg, Maryland, lit up the sky.

Cries that "the Rebels are coming! And they are burning everything as they go!" were heard in the early morning hours. Gettysburg resident Fannie Buehler recalled that the "entire town was in the streets all night long discussing the possibilities." The fire consumed twenty-seven buildings in Emmitsburg, but it was the work of an arsonist, not Confederates. Weary, sleep-deprived Gettysburg residents tried to get a few hours of shut-eye before sunrise.

AS NEWS spread of the approaching Southerners, merchants and farmers began hiding their goods and supplies, and hundreds of African Americans fled. Mag Palm was twenty-four in 1860. She lived with her husband, Alfred, and their son, Joseph, who was not quite a year old.

Mag was known as "Maggie Bluecoat" for the sky-blue uniform coat of an officer of the War of 1812 that she wore while helping runaway slaves. Her reputation for aiding fugitive slaves was so well known that Maryland slave owners attempted to abduct her and sell her into slavery.[6]

David Schick, whose father employed Mag, described one of the attempts to capture her in a letter to Elsie Singmaster: "These men succeeded in tying Mag's hands. . . . She was fighting them as best as she could with her hands tied. She would attempt to slow them and succeeded in one instance in catching [an attacker's] thumb in her mouth and bit the thumb off. John Karseen, who was crippled and ran a novelty shop on Baltimore Street, happened along at just the right time and by using his crutch was able to assist Mag in her fight with these kidnappers and drove them off and freed her from her bonds."

Death itself did not horrify the woman known as "Old Liz" as much as the invading Rebels. She was the haggard scrubwoman of the McCreary household and lived with her husband, Samuel, who was a wagonmaker. They had four grandchildren and owned a modest house worth one hundred dollars.[7]

Southern armies had a policy of rounding up "contraband" and returning them to the South. This policy meant that whenever African Americans were encountered, they were seized and marched back into slavery. One of the first instances occurred in Pennsylvania during Stuart's 1862 Chambersburg raid. Several black men were captured at Mercersburg and taken to Richmond.

When the Confederate army returned to Pennsylvania in June 1863, the Southerners again gathered up African Americans, both runaway slaves and free men. Word of their captures spread rapidly throughout the Cumberland Valley and east.

The Lancaster *Daily Express* published an account of the abduction of all African Americans in the town, although the writer more accurately reported that the Southerners "kidnapped all they could find." The captives ranged in age "from the child in the cradle up to men and women of fifty years of age." They were bound and herded through town, shepherded by soldiers who occasionally fired pistols to encourage the people to move quickly. "It would have made your heart ache to have witnessed this high-handed and brutal outrage," the newspaper commented. Apparently the Confederates marched the captives south in batches, for the story noted that a first group was freed when the lightly guarded Rebel column was captured at Greencastle. Unfortunately, the newly liberated blacks were recaptured by Southerners about ten miles from Greencastle.

Rachel Cormany, a resident of Franklin County whose husband was an officer in the Sixteenth Pennsylvania Cavalry, provided a graphic account of the kidnappings of the black people in her diary. She wrote that the Rebels:

were hunting up the contrabands and driving them off by droves. O! How it grated on our hearts to have to sit quietly and look at such brutal deeds—I saw no men among the contrabands—all women and children. Some of the colored people who were raised here were taken along—I sat on the front step as they were driven by just like we would drive cattle. Some laughed and seemed not to care—but nearly all hung their heads. One woman was pleading wonderfully with her driver for her children—but all the sympathy she received from him was a rough "March along"—at which she would quicken her pace again. It is a query what they want with those little babies—whole families were taken. Of course, when the mother was taken she would take her children. I suppose the men left thinking the women and children would not be disturbed.[8]

In a letter to her husband, Jemima K. Cree reported that she had tried to reason with one of the Confederates rounding up blacks. Two of her employees had been taken, and Cree tried to persuade the soldier that one of them was a free person and should not be taken. She didn't argue for the other, because Cree knew that she was a fugitive slave. Despite her willingness to observe the distinction, her argument was ignored by the soldier, who said he could do nothing but follow orders. In her letter, Cree concluded that she might have been able to persuade the commanding officer had he been there. She then watched the unfortunate women and children march back to slavery. Cree summarized: "They took up all they could find, even little children, whom they had to carry on horseback before them. All who could get there fled to the woods, and many who were wise are hid in the houses of their employers."[9]

Gettysburg resident Albertus McCreary recalled, "A number of colored people lived in the western part of town and when on the first day a great many of them were gathered together and marched out of town. As they passed our house, our old washerwoman called out 'Goodbye, we are going back to slavery.' Most of them were crying and moaning."[10]

Although newspapers reported the plight of free blacks in June 1863, the editors seemed more sympathetic to the loss of personal property than they were to the fate of free Pennsylvanians being sold into Southern slavery. For example, the Gettysburg *Compiler* reported: "About daybreak on

the 18th, a force of about 200 rebel cavalry made a dash into McConnels-
burg and surrounded it in a few seconds. They then commenced their work
of plunder, taking horses [and] Negroes. . . . We are sorry to say that Captain States of Bloody Run had fourteen fine horses taken." Likewise, the
June 23 *Star and Sentinel* noted: "[The Rebels] took possession of Hagerstown on Monday of last week. They remained until Wednesday afternoon.
. . . They carried off with them some horses and quite a number of colored
persons, but otherwise doing very little damage."

Other Northern newspapers reported the flight of "thousands" of free
blacks from the Cumberland Valley escaping to and through Harrisburg.
Many of Gettysburg's African American community fled to the state capital during the last two weeks of June 1863. The *Harrisburg Telegraph*
reported in the June 24 issue: "Contrabands are arriving here constantly,
and it really is a distressing sight to see women and children huddled in
wagons, bringing all their worldly possessions with them."

Maj. Gen. Darius N. Couch was in charge of the capital defenses, and
he promptly ordered all refugee blacks be organized into work crews for the
building of Forts Washington and Couch just outside of the city. They were
paid seventy-five cents per day, twenty-five cents less than white workers
were paid.

Some of Gettysburg's African Americans fled to Yellow Hill, an area
seven miles north of the town and two miles west of Biglerville. Runaway
slaves had founded the community in the late 1700s. According to the
town's tax records, the land to establish a "colored church" in 1856 was
donated by Edward Matthews. This church was the center of the Yellow
Hill community, deep in a heavily wooded area, about two miles off the
main road between Gettysburg and Carlisle. In 1863 eight black families
made up the town. They earned a living by making charcoal for the nearby
Pine Grove furnace. One of the virtues of the village was that it was too
small to attract the notice of any Confederate raiding parties. Lee's army
never came within a mile of the Yellow Hill church.

The exodus of Gettysburg's black population would long be remembered by the area's residents. Tillie Pierce recalled: "Gettysburg had a goodly
number of [African Americans]. They regarded the rebels as having an espe-
cial hatred toward them, and they believed that if they fell into their hands,

annihilation was sure. These folks mostly lived in the southwestern part of town, and their flight was invariably down Breckinridge Street and Baltimore Street, and toward the woods on and around Culp's Hill."[11] The sight of "men and women with bundles as large as old-fashioned feather ticks slung across their backs, almost bearing them to the ground" stayed with Tillie long after the war. Adding to the tragic scene were the children who also bore oversized bundles and tried to keep up with the adults. In addition to the image of the awkward caravan was the palpable fear that gripped the refugees: "The greatest consternation was depicted on all their countenances as they hurried along; crowding and running against each other in their confusion; children stumbling, falling, and crying. Mothers, anxious for their offspring, would stop for a moment to hurry them up."

Fannie Buehler lived east of town. One of her servants, Elizabeth Brine, fled town in early June.[12] By the time the first Confederate troops appeared in Gettysburg on June 26, the African American residents who had remained were in hiding.

Mary Fastnacht remembered that the Reverend Abraham Cole's wife and daughter lived not far from her home. "The daughter's husband was in the Union army," she recollected.[13] Cole's wife and daughter "were alone and did not know what to do. Mother told them to come to our house; that she would dine them in the loft over the kitchen, take the ladder away, and they would be safe. They stayed Friday night, Saturday no Confederates were about and they felt safe to go to their home again. The daughter said she couldn't be paid to put in such another night, that she heard soldiers walking around all night—that they surely knew who was in that loft." The two women fled, and Fastnacht added, "We did not know where our colored friends had gone."

Twelve-year-old Mary Elizabeth Montford described the evacuation in terms of the woman who helped her mother on wash days. She knew her as Aunt Beckie. In addition to the walking bundles described by Tillie Pierce, Mary observed the fearful refugees "pulling wagons or pushing wheel barrows." When Aunt Beckie saw the young girl, she shouted to her, "No rebel is gonna catch me and carry me back to be a slave again."

Charles McCurdy remembered, "Whenever there was a report that the Rebels were coming, [Owen Robinson] would decamp with his family for a place of safety, and not return until the coast was clear."[14] He added, "This time there could be no doubt that the dreaded enemy was at hand, and the Robinson family joined the exodus of colored people. Before going, he asked my father permission to put [his] pigs in our stable until his return. Father consented and promised to have them properly looked after."

Some never returned. Fannie Buehler noted: "I know not whither [she fled], for I never saw [Elizabeth Brine] afterwards. I heard of her from someone who had seen her on the way to Philadelphia." Catherine Foster recorded that the "colored People feared the rebels more than death. They played hiding and peeping all this time."

•3•

THE REBELS ARE HERE

CHEERED AS THEY MARCHED along Chambersburg Street on Friday, June 26, the Twenty-sixth Pennsylvania Emergency Volunteers marched from Gettysburg toward Cashtown. Led by Robert Bell's cavalry, it wasn't long before the militiamen collided with Jubal Early's battle-hardened infantry. They were all of three miles from the town.

Around 2 P.M. riders from Bell galloped into Gettysburg with word of the encounter. The Twenty-sixth Pennsylvania had scattered in retreat, heading northeast. Forty were taken prisoner by the Rebels. Those Confederates not pursuing the volunteers were marching toward Gettysburg. Bell's cavalry, including the Philadelphia City Troop, spurred their horses and dashed down the York road. Gettysburg was defenseless.

Not many in town supposed the news to be true, since they had heard it so often. Sarah Broadhead commented, "No one believed this, for they had so often been reported as coming."[1] But this time the Rebels really were coming.

As this realization set in on the population, schools dismissed early, sending children home.[2] The streets cleared. Merchants closed their stores. Local officials had fled the town the night before.

Teenager Daniel Skelly noted that "about 5 o'clock the last train out of Gettysburg, until after the battle, reached Hanover filled with people getting away from the Confederates. They included revenue officers and clerks, in fact all persons who had any office under the government."[3]

Fifteen-year-old Tillie Pierce's father was a butcher. The family lived above his shop in the center of town. Tillie witnessed the entire battle and published her observations twenty-six years later. She attended the Young Ladies Seminary, which was a finishing school near her home, and was in class when the warning cries echoed through the peaceful streets.

"Rushing to the door, and standing on the front portico we beheld in the direction of the Theological Seminary, a dark, dense mass, moving toward town. Our teacher, Mrs. Eyster, at once said, 'Children, run home as quickly as you can.'"

Soon Confederate cavalry appeared on Seminary Ridge, just one-half mile from town. Citizens fled. Doors locked.

"I am satisfied some of the girls did not reach their homes before the Rebels were in the streets," Tillie recalled. "As for myself, I had scarcely reached the front door, when, on looking up the street, I saw some of the men on horseback. I scrambled in, slammed shut the door, and hastening to the sitting room, peeped out between the shutters."

Near 3 P.M. the Thirty-fifth Virginia Cavalry were the first to arrive in town. They turned onto Chambersburg Street and galloped toward the square, whooping and hollering, screaming and shooting in the air. The intimidation was most successful. "The effect was enough to frighten us to death," Sarah Broadhead noted.[4] Gates Fahnestock, however, commented that he "enjoyed it as if it were a wild west show."[5] The Confederates seemed wild and bloodcurdling.

"What a horrible sight!" Tillie Pierce recalled. "There they were, human beings! Clad almost in rags, covered with dust, riding wildly, pell-mell down the hill toward our home! Shouting, yelling most unearthly, cursing, brandishing their revolvers, and firing right and left. I was fully persuaded that the Rebels had actually come at last. What they would do with us was a fearful question to my young mind."[6]

"Here they come!" shouted Sarah King to her father, who was reading a newspaper. He looked up. "Who?"

"The Rebs! Don't you hear the yell?"

The mounted Southerners galloped down York Street in pursuit of Bell's horsemen. Sarah and her children stood on their porch, watching the thrilling chase.

"Bring the children in and lock the door," her father instructed.

"No, I want them to see all they can of this," she answered.

The King children were indeed spectators to history in the making. Sarah wanted her children to learn about the war. They were about to witness even more history in the weeks ahead. Bell managed to escape.[7]

Officers dispersed their horsemen down the side streets. Thirty minutes later infantry marched into town, filing down Chambersburg Street. At the head of the first brigade was Early. Behind him were Georgia troops whose numbers were estimated at three thousand.

"Then the searching and ransacking began in earnest." Tillie Pierce recorded. "They wanted horses, clothing, anything and almost everything they could conveniently carry away.

Some young boys were trying to lead their horses away from town, but they were soon surrounded by the Southerners. Twelve-year-old Sam Wade, younger brother of Ginnie Wade, was one of the small band quickly taken prisoner by the raiders.

As the Southerners passed the Pierce house on Baltimore Street, Tillie gestured to them. When several rode over to her, she said, "You don't want the boy! He is not our boy, he is only living with us."

One of the men replied, "No, we don't want the boy, you can have him; we are only after the horses."[8]

The Wade family was poor, and Sam was indeed living with the Pierces as a "hired boy." Ginnie Wade, according to Tillie, was holding the Pierce family responsible for Sam's fate. "If the Rebs take our Sam, I don't know what I'll do with you folks!" Ginnie allegedly cautioned the Pierces. It was a mild threat, but nevertheless a threat.

Such matters are an example of how Gettysburg families threatened each other; some did turn others over to the authorities out of a kind of revenge. Tillie's father went to a Confederate colonel to plead for the return of the family's beloved horse, but the colonel denied his request because he had been informed that Pierce was "a black Abolitionist; so black, that he was turning black." Also, the colonel had learned that the Pierces had two sons in the Union army, whom he supposed had taken as much from the South as the Southerners were now taking from him.

Pierce returned to his Baltimore Street home without the horse. According to Tillie, the colonel received his information from Ginnie Wade, who had a "very unkind disposition toward our family." The Pierces watched as the Rebels rode the horse up and down the street until the animal went lame.

The Confederates were on their way east to York, but they wanted supplies from the Gettysburg merchants. Early had sent word that he was going to requisition supplies from the town. Everyone knew that most of what the Confederates would want had been removed already from the town. The merchants and farmers had learned what to expect after the previous year's raid. Shrewd enough not to want to part with their property in exchange for useless Confederate money, most goods and supplies were shipped away or hidden securely.

Instructions also had been received from Harrisburg. The funds on deposit at the Gettysburg bank were sent away. Merchants John Schick and Edward Fahnestock loaded their merchandise and stock into a leased railroad car and shipped everything to Philadelphia.

After he received Early's requisition for supplies, David Kendlehart, the president of the borough council, convened the council in the office of attorney William Duncan, one of the councilmen. Some advocated compliance, others advocated defiance, so Kendlehart informed the general that the town could not meet his demands but the stores would be open for the Confederates to examine and take what they could find.[9]

Early accepted the compromise, and his men eagerly scavenged the stores. Under strict orders, they did not loot the businesses or damage property. Whatever they took was paid for with Confederate currency and script, all of which was worthless to the merchants.

"Nor were they particular about asking. Whatever suited them they took," Tillie Pierce commented. "But our merchants and bankers had . . . already shipped their wealth to places of safety. Thus it was, that a few days after [when the Confederates had moved farther east], the citizens of York were compelled to make up our proportion of the Rebel requisition."

On Chambersburg Street, young Charles McCurdy was standing outside the sweet shop of Petey Winters. He saw a Confederate soldier emerge from the store with a hat filled with candy. "Seeing an expectant looking small boy gazing enviously at his store, [the soldier] gave me a handful," McCurdy recalled.[10]

At the Globe Inn, a lieutenant and three privates demanded to purchase three barrels of whiskey. While the officer wrote out the order, the proprietor, Charles Will, told him, "I want good money." Still, the privates rolled the barrels away, and the lieutenant answered, "In two months, our money will be better than yours as we may remain in your state an indefinite time." Will angrily watched his whiskey being carried away, but he was also worried that the man's words might come true.[11]

To the townspeople, the Rebels looked dirty and ragged. One soldier had a pair of spurs strapped onto his bare feet. As they marched toward York, the requisitioned goods stood out to the onlooking civilians. Sarah King remembered it clearly: "Some of the men had a pile of hats on their heads. Blankets, quilts, and shawls were piled up on their horses."

The local newspapers described the Confederates' arrival in town. The June 27 edition of the *Star and Sentinel,* the Republican newspaper of Adams County, published the headline CONFEDERATES PASS THROUGH GETTYSBURG! The paper noted, "We consider our fortunes to be good as it was a brigade of considerate Georgia soldiers that entered our town and not the dreaded Louisiana cut-throats called 'Tigers' that we hear so much about."

During the night they were in town, the Southerners moved seventeen railroad cars about a mile out of town and burned them as well as a bridge at Rock Creek. Track was torn up, and telegraph wires were cut. Thirty-six prisoners from the Twenty-sixth Pennsylvania Volunteers were first housed at the courthouse and then paroled, but two of their officers were not released. A regimental band set up in the square and serenaded the town with Southern songs, including "Dixie." By 8 A.M. on Saturday, June 27, the Rebels marched toward York.

Elizabeth Masser Thorn was the temporary caretaker of the Evergreen Cemetery, a job normally performed by her husband, Peter, but he was with the 138th Pennsylvania Infantry, which was posted at Harpers Ferry and Washington, D.C., during the Gettysburg campaign. Thorn's parents, Catherine and John Masser, and her three sons—seven-year-old Fred, five-year-old George, and two-year-old John—were all living with her in the cemetery gatehouse at the time of the battle. To round things out, Elizabeth was six months pregnant.

"The battle was on Wednesday, the 1st of July, and it was on the Friday before [June 26] that I first saw the rebels," she recollected. "As the rebels came to Gettysburg, we were all scared and wished for them to go. Six of them came up the Baltimore Pike. Before they came into the Cemetery they fired off their revolvers to scare the people. They chased the people out and the men ran and jumped over fences. . . . I was a piece away from the house. . . . When they rode into the Cemetery I was scared, as I was afraid they had fired after my mother. I fainted from fright, but finally reached the house. . . . They said we should not be afraid of them, they were not going to hurt us like the Yankees did their ladies."[12]

Several riders approached the gatekeeper's house, and Thorn reported, "They rode around the house on the pavement to the window, and asked for bread and butter and buttermilk. . . . My mother went and got them all she had for them and just then a rebel rode up the pike and had another horse beside his. The ones who were eating said to him: 'Oh, you have another one,' and the one who came up the pike said: 'yes, the — shot at me, but he did not hit me, and I shot at him and blowed him down like nothing, and here I got his horse and he lays down the pike.'"[13]

The newcomer then asked Elizabeth about the quality of a nearby horse. "It was our neighbor's horse," she noted, "and I said 'No, it ain't. It is a healthy enough horse, but he is very slow in his motions.' Well, it would not suit. I knew if the horse was gone the people could not do anything, so I helped them."

Thorn recalled that, from the vantage point of her home on Cemetery Ridge, she and her family could see the destruction of the railroad cars and the bridge over Rock Creek. The next morning news came of a small battle near York. "Everywhere they destroyed all they could," she observed.

Little was held back from the scavenging soldiers. "We were trying to feed them all we could," Thorn explained. "I had baked in the morning and had the bread in the oven. They were hungry and smelled the bread. I took a butcher knife and stood before the oven and cut this hot bread for them as fast as I could. When I had six loaves cut up I said I would have to keep one loaf for my family, but as they still begged for more I cut up every loaf for them."

Further accommodating the Southerners in the hot June sun, Thorn added, "We had all the glasses and tins and cups and tubs and everything outside filled with water. All the time our little boys were pumping and carrying water to fill the tubs. They handed water to the soldiers and worked and helped this way until their poor little hands were blistered, and their bread I had given away on Friday."

The first Union soldier killed near Gettysburg happened to be a resident of Adams County. His name was George Sandoe. Just six days after his enlistment, Sandoe was posted on the Baltimore pike near the Nathaniel Lightner home. Early's men were advancing into this area, but Sandoe's unit had not been ordered to withdraw. From his horse he was talking with Lightner's son, Daniel, when Confederate pickets surprised them and called for their surrender. Sandoe's comrades jumped on their horses, leaped over a fence, and escaped.

As Sandoe tried to do the same while firing his weapon, his horse stumbled and fell. The Adams County native spurred the horse, trying to escape, but he was shot in the head by the pickets. Sandoe died on the Baltimore pike just two miles from his home. He was buried in the Mount Joy Church Cemetery. Sandoe's obituary appeared in the June 27 edition of the *Star and Sentinel:*

For those townspeople who experienced the shock of a rebel army in Gettysburg yesterday, it has been truly a day of excitement and despair. George Sandoe was shot and killed by Rebels soon after the arrival of the Confederate forces in the borough's streets. He and several others who had just completed preparations to join their regiment were spotted by an armed group of

Confederates who hailed them and called upon their surrender. George and his comrades sped away with the Confederates in pursuit but to no avail. They did not escape without injury. Poor Sandoe was shot and fell by the roadside a mile south of town. His body has been recovered and will be buried in the family plot of the town cemetery tomorrow.

In addition the newspaper carried news from the state capital at Harrisburg: "The governor has called upon the state to complete the raising of 50,000 troops to gather in Harrisburg to meet the current emergency. General Darius Couch has been ordered to command the Department of the Susquehanna and will concentrate his troops in defense of the capital city. Defenses are being constructed on the west bank of the Susquehanna River above Camp Hill and are expected to be quite formidable. Rebel scouts have been spied as far north as Carlisle."

The paper also carried notices for the county residents, including one from J. Fahnestock regarding the liquidation of merchandise from his store by Confederates in exchange for Virginia banknotes. The Amringe Freight Service announced that it had temporarily suspended service from Gettysburg to York. Interestingly, Schick's Store advertised the arrival of "a wide selection of boots and men's clothing, as well as a good supply of sundries for the ladies."

Before the battle of Gettysburg began, the townspeople had endured much. By the end of June they were frazzled.

• 4 •

THE FEDERALS ARRIVE

It does not seem that people realized the possibility of a battle at their doors.

CHARLES McCURDY

THERE WAS A COLLECTIVE sigh of relief in Gettysburg on Saturday, June 27, when Jubal Early and his army left town and marched east to York. No sooner had the last Confederate departed when four Federal scouts rode into town. When they learned that the Rebels had left, the four men went to the Globe Inn.

A short time later, a wild west scene played out in the streets. A stranger appeared from the west, riding through town. The scouts chased him, and shots were fired. On York Street they captured the man, a Confederate chaplain carrying a message to Early. Not long after this drama, a second messenger wandered into town and was captured. That afternoon the scouts rode off with their prisoners. For a brief time the townspeople were allowed to settle down from all the excitement of the last couple of days.

A relatively peaceful Sabbath passed on Sunday, June 28. Church ser-vices had just ended when a column of Federal cavalry appeared. Horsemen rode up Baltimore Street to the square and reminded everyone how close the Union and Confederate armies were.

The citizens offered water to the cavalrymen and their horses. They also offered the soldiers bread and pies.

"Front doors and windows opened and brought out old and young and feeble alike to hail the Union troops with song and feed them," Catherine Foster remembered.

The rest of the day was peaceful and uneventful. The following morning, the troopers rode out of town toward Littlestown.

Gettysburg was isolated now, cut off from the rest of the world. Since the Confederates' arrival the previous Friday, the town had had no communication with the rest of the country. The Southerners had cut the telegraph lines. There were no trains. No passengers arrived with news of what was happening. Campfires appeared again on South Mountain near Cashtown. Although the armies were known to be nearby, no one really knew for sure.

On Tuesday, June 30, tension rose in and around Gettysburg. During the midmorning, Confederate officers were seen on Seminary Ridge, on the west side of the town. Gettysburg resident Sarah Broadhead spotted them from the back porch of her Chambersburg Street home. Pickets moved closer to the town and were near the Oak Ridge Seminary on the Chambersburg pike.

Word spread of the Rebels' proximity. Suddenly a column of Union cavalry appeared, approaching by way of the Emmitsburg road. To the townspeople, these blue-uniformed troops looked magnificent.

The Confederates also saw the Federal cavalry and quickly disappeared from Seminary Ridge. They rode west, toward Cashtown, along the Chambersburg pike.

THE UNION horsemen were led by Gen. John Buford Jr., and his column was the First Cavalry division of the Army of the Potomac. Part of the force dispatched to find Lee's army, Buford's command was given four days to rest and refit. They guarded the rear of the newly formed Left Wing under Maj. Gen. John Fulton Reynolds. This wing consisted of the First, Third, and Eleventh Corps, all of which were moving north, toward the Cumberland Valley.

Buford's men crossed the Potomac River at Edwards Ferry on June 27. They moved on to Frederick, Maryland, where they captured a spy, Will Talbot, who admitted he was a member of Elijah White's Comanches. Buford ordered Talbot hung. A note was pinned to the body announcing that the corpse was to hang three days and anyone cutting him down before then would hang the remainder of the three days. A large portion of the Army of the Potomac passed by the hanged Talbot as it marched toward Pennsylvania.[1]

On June 29, responding to the call of "Boots and Saddles," Buford's command moved out at 9 A.M., following the base of South Mountain into Pennsylvania. Crossing the Mason-Dixon Line into the Keystone State, all the troopers, especially those of the Seventeenth Pennsylvania, "raised their caps and lustily cheered, again and again" for their home soil. Late that night, Buford saw the Confederate campfires from Monterey Gap on South Mountain. To no one in particular, he said, "Within forty-eight hours the concentration of both armies will take place on a field within view and a great battle will be fought." His men made their camp near Fountaindale.

On Tuesday morning Buford's troopers trekked toward Gettysburg. Near Fairfield they encountered pickets of a Mississippi and North Carolina regiment. The dense morning fog aided the Confederates, but the clash confirmed Buford's belief that the Army of Northern Virginia was in front of him. After the brief skirmish, he turned south toward Emmitsburg then to Gettysburg.

Only eight miles from Gettysburg, Buford's men moved north along the Emmitsburg road, passing Federal infantry along the way. Buford's main body of mounted, worn-out troopers arrived at Gettysburg about noon. His scouts had preceded him by an hour and captured several stragglers from Early's command.

Tired and dusty, the Federals headed toward the center of town and received a rousing welcome. The townspeople waved, shouted, and cheered their arrival. Much like a parade, the mounted men advanced, overwhelmed by their reception. Young women greeted them, waving handkerchiefs and singing patriotic songs. People offered milk, beer, water, and cakes to them. The spontaneous welcome became a joyous jubilee of thanks for the cavalry.

Young boys ran alongside the horses, following them to just beyond the college campus, where the troopers set up camp. The boys stayed with them, admiring the horse flesh, helping with chores, and fetching water. This arrival was almost circuslike; no one had any idea what the next few days held in store.

The day before, Monday, June 29, Gettysburg resident Samuel Herbst mounted a horse that somehow had been overlooked during Early's confiscations. He rode south on the Emmitsburg road to find the Federal army. Herbst returned late that night with word that Union forces were approaching. "The news flew through town like wildfire," Alice Powers remembered.

The appearance of Buford's thirty-five hundred equestrians must have seemed like the arrival of the entire Union army to the townspeople. The mass of men probably seemed bigger than Early's army that had pretty much plundered Gettysburg just days before.

Buford sent a dispatch back to Reynolds about the "terrible state of excitement in the town" and that his men and horses were at their limit. He set up his headquarters at Tate's Blue Eagle Hotel, which was at the corner of Washington and Chambersburg Streets. Buford soon declared martial law and closed the town's saloons to his troopers.

The cavalry's arrival brought much relief and peace of mind to the weary citizens. With the horse soldiers between the Confederates and the town, "[W]e thought the battle was good as begun, fought, and won," Catherine Foster said.

Despite the festive atmosphere surrounding his arrival, Buford had serious work at hand. He too had seen the Confederates on Seminary Ridge as he rode into town. By midafternoon Buford and his officers had closely inspected the terrain around the town. A series of hills and ridges stood to the west, north, and south of the hamlet. They noted the network of roads radiating through town—perfect for infantry. Buford knew that a large concentration of Rebel troops was to his west and north. Reynolds and the rest of the Federal army were to his south. Any confrontation between the two armies would become an obvious race for the high ground.

Climbing up to the cupola of the Lutheran Theological Seminary west of town, Buford was able to see the lay of the land around Gettysburg and far out the Chambersburg pike. He grasped the advantages of waging a battle here. The general determined to stay and fight. He would commit his brigades on this ground.

As Buford planned for the coming battle, the townspeople did not seem to realize the pending danger. Sandwiched between the two armies, they were complacent, having placed all their confidence in the Federal troops now encamped in the area.

"It does not seem that people realized the possibility of a battle at their doors. No restrictions were placed on my goings and comings. I was not wanted to keep near home," Charles McCurdy observed.

As darkness came that last night of June, many families invited the Union troopers into their homes for supper, welcoming them like family and treating them to hearty dinners.

While the residents went to sleep that night, Buford deployed his men into positions to the north and west of town. "The people settled down in their homes with a sense of security," Daniel Skelly recalled. "And with little thought of what tomorrow had in store for them."[2]

Buford's men were hopelessly outnumbered but equipped with Spencer repeating carbines, giving them a five-to-one superiority of firepower. Buford employed a defense in which a few men were positioned in small numbers as far as four miles west of town and as far as six miles to the north. When the Confederates approached, these men would fire on them, forcing the enemy to stop, entrench, and return fire. This method would delay the Southerners' advance and buy time for Reynolds's corps to arrive. Buford's forward-deployed men would then retreat to a fallback position and repeat the challenge before falling back to another position.

For weeks warning cries regarding approaching Rebels had been heard in the streets of Gettysburg. Once again the word spread of oncoming Confederates, but this time Union soldiers stood between the town and the invaders. Within hours, the war came to Gettysburg.

Part 2

THREE DAYS THAT CHANGED EVERYTHING

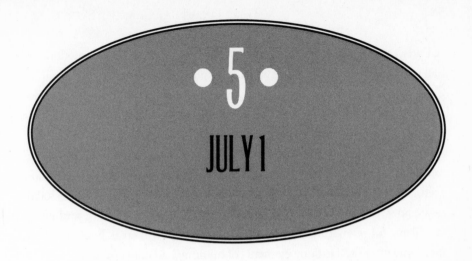

· 5 ·

JULY 1

The ridge was full of men and boys from town, all eager to witness a brush with the Confederates and not dreaming of the terrible conflict that was to occur on that day and not having the slightest conception of the proximity of the two armies.

DANIEL A. SKELLY

HENRY HETH'S BAREFOOT CAROLINIANS desperately needed shoes after their long march into Pennsylvania. For more than a century that was the explanation for the battle of Gettysburg: shoe-hunting Confederates stumbling into the Yankee army. There was no shoe factory in Gettysburg, but there were several tanneries. Confederates knew that from earlier incursions into the town.

Southern armies had been in and out of Gettysburg for a week. Gen. Jubal Early had marched his corps through the town on his way to York and Wrightsville. When he demanded supplies, Early found mostly empty shops. The town's merchants and storekeepers did exactly what their Chambersburg neighbors did: They hid everything of value rather than have it taken or bought with worthless Confederate dollars.

Any valuable supplies, including shoes or boots, would have already been confiscated by the earlier troops. Even if Heth's men had not known of Early's prior passage through Gettysburg on June 26, the Confederates had no reason to believe there was a stockpile of shoes waiting for them in Gettysburg.[1] The Confederate army foraged as it traveled; there were no supply lines connecting the army with depots behind the lines.

In his memoirs after the war, Heth claimed that he had heard of a supply of shoes in Gettysburg. He did not say from where he might have heard this. Some speculated it might have been that the general who graduated last in his class at West Point had seen an advertisement in a local newspaper. It is likely that Heth used the shoe excuse to absolve himself of any blame for prematurely initiating the battle that Robert E. Lee wanted to fight only after the far-flung elements of his army had concentrated.

Confederate scouts had approached Gettysburg on June 30 and noticed Buford's cavalry on the west side of town. The scouts returned promptly to Cashtown and informed Gens. A. P. Hill and Heth. Neither general believed that there was a substantial Federal force in or near Gettysburg. Hill reportedly said that he had hoped that the Federals were there, because that is where he wanted them to be.

The following morning Hill seemed determined to mount a reconnaissance in force to determine the size and strength of the Federals to his front. Supposedly, Heth asked Hill if he had any objections of his going tomorrow "to get those shoes."

The Confederate's search for shoes in Gettysburg seems to be just one of the many legends that developed after the battle of Gettysburg. The reason for the battle was that both armies were in the area. The Federals were pursuing the Confederates, and the Army of the Potomac caught up to the Army of Northern Virginia in Adams County.

Around 5 A.M. on Wednesday, July 1, Heth's troops advanced toward the town along the Chambersburg pike, most likely looking for a fight rather than for shoes that were not there. In his own report, A. P. Hill noted, "I intended to advance the next morning and discover what was in my front."[2] Heth's Confederates soon clashed with Buford's dismounted troops west of the town.

At 7:30 A.M. men from Company E, Eighth Illinois Cavalry, were on picket duty on Knoxlyn Ridge at the Whisler Blacksmith Shop, nearly four miles west of Gettysburg on the Chambersburg pike (Route 30 today).

They were from Col. William Gamble's brigade. These forward-positioned men saw a cloud of dust, indicating the movement of a large number of men. Sgt. Levi Shafer summoned Lt. Marcellus E. Jones. The troopers first spotted horsemen, followed by infantry, crossing Marsh Creek not too many yards to their front. It was the vanguard of Heth's division. Jones borrowed a carbine from one of his troopers, rested it on a fence post, and fired a round into the oncoming force. It was the first shot of the battle of Gettysburg. Jones's shot apparently hit nothing.[3]

The Confederates began to form a line, a process that took some time to set up—time that Buford needed as he awaited Reynolds's arrival. Company E pulled back to Herr's Ridge, about two miles from Gettysburg. They waited for the Confederates to push toward them.

WORD FINALLY reached Reynolds of the Confederates' proximity to Gettysburg. Reynolds sent messages to Meade, advising him of the enemy buildup at Gettysburg, and to Buford, advising Buford that he would be joining him. Then he ordered his corps to march to Gettysburg.

Six cannons—the only artillery at Buford's disposal—were positioned on McPherson's Ridge. While the Confederates continued pushing east, the rest of Buford's cavalry repositioned closer to the town. They made a stand at Herr's Ridge then fell back to McPherson's Ridge.

Buford worried about the battle and Reynolds's arrival. He had the reputation of a fine commander and was later described by Col. Theodore Lyman of Meade's staff as a "compactly built man of middle height with a tawny mustache and a little triangular gray eye, whose expression is determined, not to say sinister." His greatest fear that morning was that the Confederates would soon outflank his line and overrun his men or that his men would run out of ammunition. To watch for Reynolds and gauge the Southern advance, he went to the cupola of the Lutheran seminary.

From his high perch, the general watched his artillery and his men inflict significant casualties on the Confederates. The first field hospital was established haphazardly at Herr's Tavern, but the Southerners also set up their artillery in the yards and among the buildings near the tavern. As they fired on the Federal positions, return fire was targeted back to their position. A Union shell crashed into the second floor of the tavern building, destroying most of the outside wall. Soon the barn and outbuilding filled with wounded Confederates.

Buford knew that his men had been lucky up to this point. Heth had only advanced his skirmishers and had not pushed his infantry forward in solid battle lines. Buford, however, grasped that the Southern force was steadily growing as he glimpsed dust clouds announcing the arrival of more Confederate troops and artillery.

Heth finally realized how slender the Union line was and sent forward his two leading brigades under Brig. Gens. James Archer and Joseph Davis. With their battle flags unfurled, the Confederates charged toward the Union troopers whose time was fast running out.

"How goes it, John?" someone called up to Buford from the ground.

The familiar voice of John Reynolds startled him. "The devil's to pay!" Buford replied and descended from the cupola.

"I hope you can hold out until my corps come up," Reynolds commented.

"I reckon I can," Buford answered.

The generals mounted their horses[4] and rode to the front lines, surveying positions and determining where to place oncoming troops. A short time later, Reynolds was on the front line as the First Corps rushed up.

"Forward, forward, men! Drive those rebels out of those woods! Forward! For God's sake, forward!" he ordered. Reynolds was at the western edge of Herbst's Woods on McPherson's Ridge, urging the men of the Iron Brigade into the woods. High on his horse, Reynolds presented himself as a perfect target. He turned to look back, and a bullet struck the Pennsylvania native in the back of the head at his neck. He fell dead to the ground. Three aides, under enemy fire, picked up the dead general and carried him to the rear. Reynolds was the first and highest-ranking general killed at Gettysburg. Soldiers placed his body in an ambulance and took it back to town.[5]

"Up and down the line men reeling and falling . . . horses tearing and plunging, mad with wounds or terror, drivers yelling, shells bursting, shot shrieking overhead, howling above our ears or throwing up great clouds of dust where they struck the musketry crashing on three sides of us bullets hissing, humming and whistling everywhere," wrote one of the artillerists who survived the onslaught on Seminary Ridge on July 1. "Smoke, dust, splinters, blood, wreck and carnage indescribable."[6]

DURING THE morning, as the fighting started and became intense, some of Gettysburg's residents—not doing the smartest thing—climbed to their rooftops to watch the fighting. The sounds of battle grew closer. Others in the town gathered foolishly along Seminary Ridge. One of these was Daniel Skelly.

"The ridge was full of men and boys from town, all eager to witness a brush with the Confederates and not dreaming of the terrible conflict that was to occur on that day and not having the slightest conception of the proximity of the two armies," Skelly said. "I climbed up a good-sized oak tree so as to have a good view of the ridge west and northwest of us, where the two brigades of cavalry were then being placed. We could then hear distinctly the skirmish fire in the vicinity of Marsh Creek, about three miles from our position and could tell that it was approaching nearer and nearer as our skirmishers fell back slowly toward the town contesting every inch of ground."

Skelly watched the formation of Buford's line and the gradual fallback. Soon Confederate artillery opened fire, and the civilians began to reconsider where they should be.

"Shot and shell began to fly over our heads, one of them passing dangerously near the top of the tree I was on. There was a general stampede toward town and I quickly slipped down from my perch and joined the retreat to the rear of our gallant men and boys," Skelly recalled.

As Daniel Skelly headed for town, he crossed over a field to the Chambersburg pike on the east side of Carrie Sheads's school. When he was about in the middle of the field, a cannonball fell about fifteen or twenty feet away from him. Skelly noted that the explosion quickened his pace considerably.

Just as he reached the Chambersburg pike, he saw a general and his staff gallop past him toward Seminary Ridge. He always assumed the general was Reynolds. Skelly was back in town around 9 A.M.

From his home on Chambersburg Street, John L. Burns—a stubborn, craggy, seventy-year-old veteran of the War of 1812—readied his old musket for battle. His rugged, worn face and disheveled frosty-white hair made the eccentric old man look like an ancient fanatic. He watched with dim eyes from his window until he saw the Stars and Stripes—and it was more than he could stand.

"Burns, where are you going?" his wife asked. The peculiar husband and wife had a reputation on Chambersburg Street. To many they looked like a pair of weathered relics.

"Oh, I am going to see what is going on," he replied, grabbing his old musket and slipping out the door. John Burns was not one to sit and watch.

Burns walked west on Chambersburg Street and approached an officer of the Pennsylvania Bucktails (the 150th Pennsylvania). He asked to be allowed to fall in with the regiment. Not believing what he was seeing or hearing, the officer was too busy to argue and allowed the elderly man to take a position in the woods next to the McPherson farm. As Burns took a place in line, the soldiers gave him three rousing cheers and handed him a more up-to-date rifle and twenty-five rounds.

The old veteran fired eighteen cartridges. Later he claimed that he "killed three Rebels for certain." Then Burns was wounded. When the Federals had to pull back, the dead and wounded remained on the battlefield. Having fought for hours, the old man was exhausted as well as hurt. Burns was unable to get away. Surprisingly, after questioning him, the Southerners who found him carried him off the field.[7]

"I was not long in reaching town and found the streets full of men, women and children, all under great excitement," Daniel Skelly remembered. "Being anxious to see more of the battle, I concluded I would go up upon the observatory [likely an observation deck] on the store building of the Fahnestock Brothers, situated on the northwest corner of Baltimore and West Middle Streets, and just across the street from the court house. The observatory was on the back of the building fronting on West Middle Street and . . . had a good view of the field where the battle was then being fought."

Along with Isaac L. Johns, Augustus Bentley, and Maria Fahnestock, he watched the growing battle. When he saw Union Gen. Oliver O. Howard trying to get into the Adams County Courthouse's belfry to observe the battlefield, Skelly went to the street and offered him a position on the store roof. The general accepted. From there, using his field glasses, Howard observed the fighting. While he was there, a scout rode up and delivered the news that Reynolds had been killed. Howard left to go to the battlefield.

Skelly and the others stayed on the roof until noon. By then it was getting too dangerous to remain, so the four civilians went into the building. Skelly had seen the Iron Brigade march a column of Confederate captives up Middle Street. Among their prisoners was Gen. James J. Archer.

The Eleventh Corps advanced up Washington Street to engage the Confederates entrenched north of the college. Union officers rode through the town and warned all noncombatants to take cover in their cellars. Few did not heed the advice. From the safety of their subterranean shelters, the civilians could only hear the sounds of the rifle and cannon fire getting closer. Later that afternoon, the ravaged elements of the Eleventh Corps retreated through town and were repositioned on Cemetery Hill.

THE ADAMS County Courthouse had been built in 1859 at 111 Baltimore Street. Four years later the building provided asylum for wounded men while regimental surgeons tended their injuries. The horrific task of the army doctors began on July 1 and continued long after the armies marched away from Gettysburg.

Fannie Buehler's home at 112 Baltimore Street was opposite the courthouse, and she vividly described the scene of the makeshift hospital: "The sights and sounds at the Court house for a week after the battle are too horrible to describe. . . . Limbs were amputated amid the cries and groans of suffering humanity. . . . Loads of arms and legs . . . were carted outside of town to be burned or buried." Buehler noted the regular afternoon performances of regimental bands for several days after the battle. They performed patriotic pieces to mute the moaning of the many injured.

During the first day of fighting at Gettysburg, almost immediately, some of the townspeople sacrificed their own safety to tend the wounded. Agnes Barr prepared food in her Baltimore Street home for the makeshift hospitals. Her kitchen was in use nearly around the clock for the next several days as she did all she could for both the wounded and the caregivers occupying the nearby Presbyterian church.[8] Many others did likewise for the casualties in the courthouse.

The fighting had begun about four miles west of town, but the Confederates quickly pressed against Buford's vedettes, and the battle came closer to the edge of town. The thunderous, pounding echoes of the Rebel artillery became clearer—and closer.

One of the last black civilians of Gettysburg to leave was Basil Biggs. When he heard the news of the impending Confederate invasion, he promptly sent his family away but decided to remain. Biggs finally fled during the afternoon of July 1. While Rebels swarmed into the town's square via the Chambersburg and Carlisle roads, Biggs borrowed a horse and escaped a most probable return to slavery by going east on the York road.[9]

Other African Americans stayed in Gettysburg not by choice but because they were physically incapable of leaving. One of the townspeople knew a farmhand known as Jack. Like all blacks who lived and worked so close to the Mason-Dixon Line, the man was aware of the threat to his freedom and the likeliness of being captured by Confederate raiders. Jack was also bowlegged and a poor runner. When the others fled, he hid under a haystack and stayed there without food or water for three or four days.

Daniel Skelly left the observation deck of the Fahnestock building to stand at a Chambersburg Street corner while Gen. Alexander S. Schimmelfennig's Eleventh Corps division marched through town toward the fighting. "The day was hot and sultry and they were marching 'quick time,' all seeming eager to get to the front. All along Washington Street the people of the town were out with buckets of water and the soldiers would stop for a moment for a drink and then hurriedly catch up to their place in the line," Skelly remembered. "They appeared to be straining every effort to reach the scene of conflict, and yet not an hour elapsed before the slightly wounded were limping back and those badly wounded were being brought back in ambulances to the improvised hospitals in the town. The hospitals were located in warehouses, churches, the courthouse and in various private homes. Many others were left dead on the field they were so heroically eager to reach such a short time before."

Skelly's first glimpse of the wounded came shortly after he saw his mother on Center Street. She was carrying two buckets of water into one of the makeshift hospitals. Skelly commented, "It was a striking irony of war that at that time two of my brothers, members of Company F, Eighty-seventh

Pennsylvania regiment, should be prisoners of war, having been captured at Winchester, Va., in an engagement while the Confederate army was on its way to Gettysburg." One of his brothers, Jack, had been mortally wounded there and taken to a Confederate hospital. No one in Gettysburg, however, knew of Jack Skelly's injuries at the time of the battle.

On the morning of July 1, Daniel helped his mother haul the buckets of water "down Carlisle Street to the McCurdy warehouse, just below the railroad, where the wounded were being brought in. . . . No provision had yet been made for their care in the town and they were laid on the floor. We remained there quite a while giving them water and doing what we could for their relief."

Skelly's recollection of the battle includes a description of care given the wounded. He noted that the churches and warehouses on Chambersburg, Carlisle, and York Streets were the first to be filled with the wounded since these structures were the closest to the fighting. Next came the courthouse and the churches and school on High Street. Finally private homes were opened to the medical corps, and the civilians volunteered to do what they could rather than hide in their cellars. Skelly noted "quite a number of our townspeople were . . . doing everything they could in the relief work as the wounded were carried in."

For his part, Skelly hauled buckets of water. Accompanying him was Julia Culp, a neighbor with one brother in the Union army and another in the Army of Northern Virginia. The teenagers entered the courthouse, and Skelly noted that some of the injured "were so frightfully wounded that a lady could not go near them. These I gave water to, while [Julia] cared for those who were not so severely wounded."

During the afternoon on July 1, the Confederates controlled the town of Gettysburg. Around 4 P.M. one of the regiments of the Iron Brigade passed Daniel Skelly's home on West Middle Street. As they turned onto Middle Street from Washington Street, one of the brigade's lieutenants was wounded in the foot. He tried to keep up with his men but when he reached the Skelly house, he was unable to go any farther. He came into the yard and hid his sword, pistol, and sword belt. He was soon discovered by the pursuing Confederates, and they took him prisoner. Skelly's mother asked the Confederates to allow the wounded lieutenant to come into her house and she would care for him. They agreed and continued their pursuit of the retreating Union troops. She took the wounded soldier into one of the inner rooms and kept him there without the Confederates finding him again. Several days later, and after the battle, the Skelly family took the wounded Federal officer to one of the hospitals.[10]

THE MORNING of July 1 was a busy time for the Federal surgeons. When the fighting broke out about a mile west of town along the Chambersburg pike and the old, unfinished "Tapeworm" railroad-track bed, Union surgeons rode into town to search for buildings to use as hospitals. There was little time to negotiate the much-needed accommodations, and the custom of the armies during the war was to commandeer any building near the fighting as a field hospital. These were hospitals in name only, since they offered little more than water and shelter from the fighting and the elements. In addition to the courthouse, Gettysburg's churches were the first to open their doors to wounded combatants.

Trickles of wounded men appeared in town almost as soon as the army surgeons procured the buildings. Commercial warehouses along the railroad tracks in the center of town provided the largest sheltered area in which the surgeons could address the needs of the injured. Surgeons also conscripted the train station ticket office and the passenger platform. Wounded from the Sixth Wisconsin, a unit in the Iron Brigade, were among the first to be brought to the station hospital for care.[11]

Nancy Weikert was one of the first civilians to try to help when she told neighbor Mary McAllister: "Let's go to the church. We can be of use there."[12] Forty-one-year-old Mary McAllister was the proprietor of a small shop on Chambersburg Street. She lived with the John and Martha Scott family and operated the store from the house, which was directly across the street from Christ Lutheran Church. Mary was Martha's sister.

"Martha had torn up sheets for bandages and I gathered up sheets and water and Mrs. Weikert and I went to the church and we went to work," McAllister recalled.

The wounded soldiers poured into the church. Soon the pews were filled, and the wounded men were laid in the aisles. The women did whatever they could.

"After a while they carried in an awfully wounded one. He was a fine officer. They did not know who he was," McAllister said. "A doctor said to me 'Go and bring some wine or whiskey or some stimulant!' When I got outside, I thought of Mr. Guyer near the church."

When she asked him, Guyer replied, "The rebels will be in here if you begin to carry that out." She implored until he agreed, then she hid the wine under her apron and went back to the church with it.

"They poured some of it into the officer's mouth. I never knew who he was, but he died," McAllister recorded.

McAllister ministered to the wounded as she was told to do—wetting cloths and putting them on open wounds. "Every pew was full; some sitting, some lying, some leaning on others. They cut off legs and arms and threw them out of the windows."

She recalled "a boy with seven of his fingers near off. He said, 'Lady, would you do something for me?'"

The surgeon came along and said, "'What is the use [of] doing anything for them?' and he just took his knife and cut off the fingers and they dropped down. Well, I was so-sorry."

The church was full when a shell struck the roof. More than one hundred men had crowded into the central portion of the building, stretched upon boards placed across the tops of the pews. There were an additional forty or more packed into the lecture room in the basement of the church.

"They got scared, and I was scared," McAllister said. "I wanted to go home. I looked around for Mrs. Weikert."

Others claimed that the church was about to be fired upon. According to McAllister, "[T]hey begged me not to go, but I went out and there the high church steps were full of wounded men and they begged me not to try to cross the street. Our men were retreating up the street. Many wounded ones who could walk carried the worst wounded ones on their backs. I said, 'Oh, I want to go home.' So they let me go at last. I struggled through the wounded and the dead and forgot the horror in the fright."

McAllister was finally able to cross the street and get back to her house. The sight was not a warm one. "When I got to the door," she reported, "it was standing open and the step was covered with blood. 'Oh,' I thought, 'all are dead!' and I ran through. I could hardly get through, for the dining room was full of soldiers, some lying, some standing. Some ran in to get out of the shooting. The Rebels were sending grapeshot down the street and everyone who was on the street had to get into the houses or be killed and that is the way some of these Union men got into our house."

She found Col. Henry Morrow of the Twenty-fourth Michigan bleeding in the house. She saw blood on his face, a wound from a saber. "Can I do anything for you?" she asked.

"Yes, if you would just wash this handkerchief out," Morrow answered. McAllister rushed out to get water, washed the handkerchief, and placed it on his head.

McAllister observed: "There was a young Irishman in there, too. His name was Dennis Burke Dailey, 2nd Wisconsin. He was so mad when he found what a trap they were in. He leaned out of the kitchen window and saw the bayonets of the Rebels bristling in the alley and in the garden. I said, 'There is no escape there.' I opened the kitchen door and they were tearing the fence down with their bayonets."

Dailey called out, "I am not going to be taken prisoner, Colonel!" Then he asked McAllister where he could hide. She pointed him upstairs. He decided to hide in the chimney, but the colonel ordered him not to try, saying, "You must not endanger this family."

Dailey turned to McAllister, who recalled, "He was so mad he gritted his teeth. Then he says to me, 'Take this sword and keep it at all hazards. This is General Archer's sword. He surrendered it to me. I will come back for it.'"

Mary looked at the weapon, a Confederate general's sword, then "ran to the kitchen, got some wood and threw some sticks on top of it. The Iron Brigade was the one that captured General Archer and made him give up his sword. This Dailey was the only officer and General Archer would not give it to a private. So Dailey stepped up and said, 'I am next in command!' and he took the sword."

Morrow gave her his diary, explaining, "I do not want them to get it." She did not know where to hide it, so she opened her dress and put it there.

Other wounded Union soldiers crowded around and gave McAllister their addresses. "Then this Irishman," she recalled, "he belonged to the 2nd Wisconsin, said, 'Here is my pocketbook, I wish you would keep it.'

Afterward, I did not remember what I did with it, but what I did was to pull the little red cupboard away and put it back of that."

Martha Scott came downstairs with a coat for the colonel to wear, but he would not take it. Morrow explained that he "would not stoop to disguise himself and he gave the others orders that they were to give their right names when they were taken prisoner. He kept his officer's coat and epaulettes. Then, there came a pounding on the door. Colonel Morrow said, 'You must open the door. They know we are in here and they will break it.' By this time, the Rebels came in and they said, 'Oh, here is a bird!' He was such a fine looking man. But they just demanded his sword. He had a beautiful sword."

Mary knew that some of the Union soldiers captured in her home were later paroled. She recalled, "There was a young man there from Michigan, the same as Colonel Morrow. He said, 'Do write to my mother. I am slightly wounded, but I guess they will take me prisoner.'"

The man known as Dailey was "so stubborn," according to McAllister. "He was a Major then. He stood back so very solemn. Then they took him prisoner. He asked them to let him come back into the house. Then he said to us, 'Give me a piece of bread.'"

Martha told him that she had only "one piece and that is not good."

Dailey answered, "It don't make any difference, I must have it. I have not had anything to eat for 24 hours."

Then the Rebels took him, but they did not seize all the men in the house. "Those that are not able to walk, we will not take," they told the sisters. "We will parole them. But they said to these wounded men, 'Now if you ever get to fight you know what we will do.' But the wounded ones did not pay much attention to that. Then they took away as prisoners all that could walk. The next thing then was to get these wounded fixed."

Five surgeons came to the McAllister house. While they looked the home over, one said, "Now if you had anything like a red flag, it would be a great protection to your house, because it would be considered a hospital, and they would have respect."

Martha fetched a red shawl while Mary retrieved a broom, and they went to place the banner out the front window. Suddenly a handful of Rebels appeared in the street and fired their weapons. The Confederates stopped at the church and exchanged words with some of the wounded who had sought safety on the high steps leading into the building. A few minutes later the sisters heard a shot and witnessed one of the wounded men fall to the street, "lying with his head toward us on the pavement," Mary reported.

The men on the steps reproved the Confederates, saying, "Shame! Shame! That was a Chaplain!"

The dead man was Horatio Stockton Howell,[13] a Presbyterian minister from Philadelphia. He ran a private school for boys at Delaware Water Gap before the war. The forty-two-year-old chaplain of the Ninetieth Pennsylvania Volunteers was known as the "chaplain militant" because of a fondness for wearing military attire as a substitute for the regulation black chaplain's uniform. Howell wore a captain's uniform complete with shoulder straps, a sash, and sidearms.

Sgt. Archibald B. Snow of the Ninety-seventh New York had just had his wounds treated and was directly behind Howell at the door of the church. According to him, one of the Confederate skirmishers had demanded Howell's surrender, and the chaplain tried to explain that he was a noncombatant. Despite the fact that he was armed, Howell did not surrender his sword or raise his hands. The Confederate shot him, killing him instantly.[14] Southern witnesses on horseback claimed that Howell was about to fire on them, but the wounded Northerners on the steps insisted that Howell was not armed.

The sisters noted only that the two groups of men exchanged "a good many words" before the Confederates abruptly "rode off again, shooting as they had come."

On July 1 twenty-one-year-old Salome "Sallie" Myers sat on her doorstep and listened to the sounds of battle echoing from the west. The schoolteacher was startled when "[a]t 10 o'clock that morning I saw the first blood. A horse was led past our house covered with blood. The sight sickened me."[15] In the next few moments, "three men came up the street. The middle one could barely walk. His head had been hastily bandaged and blood was visible. I grew faint with horror. I had never been able to stand the sight of blood, but I was destined to become used to it."

Sallie Myers was born on June 24, 1842, to Peter Appel Myers and Hannah Margaret Sheads in Gettysburg. Her father was a cabinetmaker, the justice of the peace, and the judge of elections for the borough. The family was related to the Sheads and Culp families, both prominent names in the story of the battle. Sallie was one of seven children. She attended school until 1859, when she became a teacher at the High Street School and worked there as the fifth assistant to the principal.

As the fighting became louder and closer, Sallie and her family sought safety in the cellar of their West High Street house, which was near Washington Street. Enscounced there, they could only hear the sounds of the battle. In her account of the experience, Sallie noted: "From 4 to 6 we were in the cellar and those two hours I can never forget. Our cellar was a very good one and furnished a refuge for many besides our own family. The noise above our heads, the rattling of musketry, the screeching of shells and the unearthly yells, added to the cries of the children, were enough to shake the stoutest heart. . . . I am sure that never were more fervent prayers borne heavenward." Captive Federals were collected outside the house, and several gave their names and addresses to the Myers family through a cellar window. Three soldiers crept down into the cellar, and the family concealed and fed them.

Around 6 P.M. most of the firing ceased, and the Myers family emerged from the safety of the cellar. By now droves of wounded soldiers were being carried into town. Just a few doors east of the Myers' residence, the Catholic and Presbyterian churches were opened to house and treat the casualties.

Sallie recalled the work of one of the surgeons who appealed to the townspeople for help: "Dr. James Fulton [143d Pennsylvania] did splendid work getting things in shape. From that time on we had no rest for weeks."

First she went to the Catholic church and observed that "the men were scattered all over it, some lying in the pews and some on the bare floor." Sallie was not put off by the sight or the sounds of the wounded and dying. She knelt beside the first man she encountered and asked what she could do to help him.

"He looked up at me with mournful, fearless eyes," she recalled, "and said, 'Nothing, I am going to die.'"

Such fatalism was unnerving to the young schoolteacher. In her diary she wrote, "To be met thus by the first one I addressed was more than my overwrought nerves could bear and I went hastily out, sat down on the church step and cried."

Regaining her composure, she went back into the church and again knelt beside the dying man. He was wounded in both the lungs and spine, so there was little doubt that he was going to die soon. The dying man was Sgt. Alexander Stewart of the 149th Pennsylvania. He asked her to read a chapter of the Bible to him. It was the same passage his father had read to the family before the son had left home to enlist. Stewart died on Monday, July 6.[16]

Chest wounds were another matter. One such story is that of Walter S. Niles. He was twenty years old when he joined the Twenty-fourth Michigan, one of the regiments of the Iron Brigade. When his regiment went into action at Gettysburg, the fifes and drums were playing "The Campbells Are Coming." His unit held its ground with such valor that they left seven distinct rows of dead and wounded. Three-fourths of the Twenty-fourth Michigan were struck down at Gettysburg.

Niles was wounded on July 1. A bullet hit him just below the heart and lodged under the skin of his back. He was carried to the porch of a nearby house where a Confederate surgeon removed the bullet. The Southerner gave him the slug as a souvenir. Niles thought it was a poor keepsake, but he managed to hold on to it through the three days that he lay at the field hospital while the battle raged. The poorly supplied Confederates took his hat, shoes, and musket, but they allowed him to keep his canteen. Niles regretted most the loss of his black hat with the black plumes that was the distinguishing mark of the Iron Brigade, which was also known as the Black Hats.

The young man took some time to recover. Still holding on to his souvenir bullet, he was sent to hospitals at Washington and Philadelphia. Somewhere during his recovery, he decided the bullet was a worthy memento and sent it to his parents. When he finally recovered from his wound, he served out his enlistment as a guard at the prison camp at Elmira, New York. After the war he turned to farming. Niles died at the age of eighty-one.[17]

When the sun set on July 1, the town of Gettysburg was transformed into a large hospital for thousands of wounded soldiers. Stoops were crowded with injured men awaiting medical attention, and churches, warehouses, and homes acted as operating rooms for the gruesome work that fell to the surgeons. Blood stained the floors and furniture of the finest houses and the humblest abodes as well as the barest storage buildings and the grandest houses of worship. Amputated limbs—legs, arms, feet, and hands—stood in piles outside nearly every building in town. Moans, groans, and shrieks filled the air. Years later someone commented, "The churches looked much as though they had been converted into butchers' stalls."[18]

Charles McCurdy lived near Sallie Myers. He was shocked at what he saw when he entered one of the neighborhood churches packed with wounded men. He noted: "Surgeons were at work under very crude conditions. The Church yard was strewn with arms and legs that had been amputated and thrown out of the windows."

The victorious Confederates did not interrupt the surgeons' work, but they did place guards at the door. McCurdy also observed the Southerners searching homes for Union soldiers.

Shortly after the fighting commenced on July 1, the Martin Stoever family quarters in the Stoever-Schick Building, at 1 Baltimore Street, became a spur-of-the-moment hospital for about twenty wounded Union soldiers. This 1817 Federal style building housed both Stoever's family and John L. Schick's general store. Surgeons quickly took over the professor's "recitation room." In addition to the wounded soldiers in his living quarters, the professor hid three Federals in the cellar. Confederates found them on July 3.

One of the eyewitnesses to the beginning of the battle was Isaac Smith, a thirty-two-year-old black farm laborer. On the morning of July 1 Smith was caught up in his work in the fields west of town. He vividly recalled:

A great many people had skedaddled, but . . . we were right there when the battle begun, and then we loaded up a wagon with provisions and grain, and [we] got away with seven or eight of our horses down an old road into the woods. After we'd gone far enough to be well out of sight and hearing, we unhitched the horses that drew the wagon. . . . There I stayed fearin' and tremblin' and looked after the horses. If the Rebels had happened to come through they'd have took 'em and me too, but they didn't get there. . . . The man's sons come back'ards and for'ards to bring me something to eat and make sure everything was all right.[19]

Smith's wife was stranded in a farmhouse behind Confederate lines throughout the entire battle. Soon the Southerners occupied the house as a field hospital. She recalled that she "got down into the cellar, and I crawled way back in the darkest corner and piled everything in front of me. I was the only colored person there, and I didn't know what might happen to me."

She realized a wounded officer was brought in upstairs, and he "wanted the women to come up out of the cellar to take care of him and do some cooking and he promised they should be well treated." The farm owner asked the officer, "Would you see a colored person protected if she was to help with the work here?" The officer agreed, and "he sent out a written somethin' or 'nother orderin' the men to keep out of the kitchen, and he had the door boarded up halfway so they could hand in things to be cooked and we could hand 'em out afterward."

During the night reinforcements for both armies arrived. Federal losses were about nine thousand soldiers—three thousand of whom were captured as prisoners. The Army of Northern Virginia had suffered about sixty-five hundred casualties.[20]

To avoid capture, Lt. R. B. Beath of the Eighty-eighth Pennsylvania impersonated a surgeon's assistant by placing a band of white cloth around his arm, which marked him as one of the hospital corps. The Confederates allowed him to pass to the rear of their lines to help the wounded. According to an 1886 account of the incident: "[U]pon reaching McPherson's barn [Beath] found it full of bleeding and mangled soldiers in a most distressed and sickening condition, without a surgeon to dress their festering wounds and bind up their splintered bones. Many of the unfortunate were so shockingly lacerated that they were unable to move, glued to the floor by the blood flowing from their gaping wounds congealing in pools under them, and all were in torment, suffering from thirst and hunger."[21] At the sight of this, Beath dropped all pretense and did all he could to treat the wounds of these men.

When the battle began, Tillie Pierce escaped the immediate fighting to find refuge behind the Union lines. The fifteen-year-old joined up with

Henrietta Schriver and her children as they fled to the home of Schriver's father, Jacob Weikert, which was three miles south of town on the Taney-town road near Round Top. Tillie's parents chose to stay in town.

"It was not long after our arrival," Tillie recalled, "until Union artillery came hurrying by. It was indeed a thrilling sight. How the men impelled their horses! How the officers urged the men as they all flew past toward the sound of the battle! Now the road is getting all cut up; they take to the fields, and all is in anxious, eager, hurry! Shouting, lashing the horses, cheering the men, they all rush madly on."

The bustling scene turned tragic in a single moment. "Suddenly we behold an explosion; it is that of a caisson," Tillie reported. "We see a man thrown high in the air and come down in a wheat field close by. He is picked up and carried into the house. As they pass by I see his eyes are blown out and his whole person seems to be one black mass. The first words I hear him say are: 'Oh dear! I forgot to read my Bible to-day! What will my poor wife and children say?'"

The fifteen-year-old did not flee the scene. "I saw the soldiers carry him up stairs; they laid him upon a bed and wrapped him in cotton. How I pitied that poor man! How terribly the scenes of war were being irresistibly portrayed before my vision."

By the evening of July 1, Lee's army occupied the entire town; Meade's army entrenched south of the town on Cemetery Ridge—the same ground that Buford had appraised earlier as the best place to position the army for the engagement. In Tillie's memoir of the battle, she recalled that night after the fighting had died down: "Beckie Weikert and I went out to the barn to see what was transpiring there. Nothing before in my experience had ever paralleled the sight we then and there behold. There were the groaning and crying, the struggling and dying, crowded side by side, while attendants sought to aid and relieve them as best they could. We were so overcome by the sad and awful spectacle that we hastened back to the house weeping bitterly."

In town as evening fell, Daniel Skelly observed: "When I went out in front of the house about 7 o'clock in the evening, the Confederate line of battle had been formed on East and West Middle Streets, Rodes's Division of Ewell's Corps lying right in front of our house. We settled down quietly

this night. There was no noise or confusion among the Confederate soldiers sleeping on the pavement below our windows and we all enjoyed a
good night's rest after the feverish anxiety of the first day's battle."

As WAS noted earlier, Elizabeth Masser Thorn was serving as the caretaker
of the Evergreen Cemetery while her husband was in the army and she was
six months pregnant at the time of the battle. Whereas some Confederates
had visited the area prior to the battle, requisitioning horses and supplies,
once the fighting had begun, most of the soldiers Thorn saw wore blue.

She described the approaching Federals: "I saw them come in on the
ridge near McMillan's house, near where the Springs Hotel now is they
came and got more help. While they were fighting on the ridge the Union
soldiers came from all directions." After the Rebels had driven the Federals
back through Gettysburg, she noted that the Union artillery assembled on
Cemetery Hill and fired on anything that moved, including comrades:
"And as they fired towards the direction of the Poor House they were firing
at our own men, but they did not know it, and I heard them say this
amongst themselves, that they did not know it."

Within a short time, the battle was brought to Elizabeth Thorn's doorstep at the cemetery gatehouse: "So at last they came to the Cemetery
House and wanted a man to go along out with them (a young boy was there
about thirteen years, and I thought he was too young, and my father was
too old) I offered myself to go along. He refused at first, but I thought there
was danger all around, and said I wasn't afraid so he said 'Come on.'"

She guided a party from Oliver O. Howard's corps through fields of flax
and oats until they came to a wheat field: "They all held against me coming
through the field, but as he said I was all right, and it did not matter, why
they gave three cheers and the band played a little piece, and then I walked
a little past a tree to where I could see the two roads. I showed him the
Harrisburg Road, the York Pike, and the Hunterstown Road. . . . Then he
took me back home."

Anxious to see what might happen, Elizabeth explained, "I wanted to
go upstairs once more to see if our men gained, but when I came on the
stairway a shell had cut in the window frame, then jumped a little, then
went through the ceiling, so I would not go up any more."

Blocked from watching the fighting, she soon was greeted by another soldier from Howard's corps, although he ordered her to prepare a supper for the general. She noted that she had no bread, for she had given it away that morning, but would have cake instead, which the officer said was "good enough for war times."

Despite her preparations, the general did not appear until close to midnight. Accompanying Howard were Daniel E. Sickles and Henry W. Slocum. Due to the lateness of the hour and the fact that the house had been taken over by the army, Elizabeth's three sons had to sleep on the kitchen floor—a fact that the generals could not miss but only commented on how "very sad" the situation was for children.

After the generals had eaten and gathered their things to leave, Elizabeth asked if the lateness of the hour meant that it might be safe for her to move her family and parents out of the house. Howard advised her to stay and move whatever she valued to the cellar, along with her children and parents. The general said that he would send some men to help her, but he knew the fighting would begin anew in the morning, probably by 4 A.M. By then she had best be in the cellar. Howard added that if he gave orders for her to evacuate the house, she should do so immediately.

At the appointed hour she had accomplished all that the general had recommended:

There were seventeen of us [neighbors as well as family]. . . . We were in the cellar about two or three hours. The noise of the cannonading was terrible. At last the door flew open and someone said: "This family is commanded by Gen. Howard to leave this house and get as far in ten minutes as possible. Take nothing up but the children and go." They said we should keep [to] the pike, where the soldiers could see us, and that would save us. When we were a little way down the pike a shell bursted back of us, and none of us were killed, but we commenced to walk faster. We went down the pike one and one half miles when we began to feel weak and sick, we were so hungry, for we had eaten nothing that day before we were so scared when the battle commenced. So we went into a farm house to buy bread . . . but the bread was doughy and we could not eat it. Later we stopped at a farm house,—Musser's. We did not feel like going farther as it was full of soldiers and army wagons and provision wagons.

That evening, after things had quieted down, Elizabeth and her father ventured back to their house to take care of whatever livestock might still be there and to note anything that had happened that day:

We had to pass through a room where the Union soldiers were sleeping, lying in two rows, with only one candle to light the whole room. About the middle of one row a man raised himself on his elbow and motioned me to come to him, my father signaled I should go to him, and he took a picture out of his pocket and on it was three little boys, and he said they were his, and they were just little boys like mine, and would I please let him have my little boys sleep near him, and could he have the little one close to him, and the others near him? And so, he took them and had them lying by him.

Once off the Musser property, Elizabeth and her father found that they could not easily return to the gatehouse:

When we got on the pike we had an awful lot of trouble to get up, because the guard was not going to let us through. But as they listened to what I had to say—that we wanted to look after our things in the cemetery house—they let us pass. We had fat hogs and we wanted to look after them. When we got to the stable we could hear the wounded men holler and go on, laying around the house,—in the cellar too, and there is where we had carried our good things, that Gen. Howard had told us to leave there. We could not get near the house for [the] wounded and dead. They had been brought there from the first day's fight.

John Masser, Elizabeth's father, checked on the pig pen and found that the animals were gone. Then he found someone to help them look over the house:

My father got a man to take us into the cellar where six wounded men were, and they had our bed clothes all around. We went to the cellar thinking we could get a pillow and quilt, but all I could find was my mother's shawl and no pillow. The poor wounded men were crying and goin' on so that we did not want anything then. They called their wives and children to come and wet their tongues. Then we went down the pike again. We had no trouble with the guards going back. And when we came again to the farmhouse we picked up our little boys out of the soldier's arms, and got ourselves ready, and about three o'clock in the morning we started on another journey, and went down the pike to the White church, and then it was daylight, and we stopped a little bit there and saw some of our neighbors; then we went into a big farmhouse. We wanted water but there was none to be got, the pumps were all broken, and we were tired and hungry again and still had nothing to eat.

Elizabeth noted that the surgeons were busy here: "They had there a big wagon shed where they brought the wounded and took off their limbs, and threw them into the corn crib, and when they had a two horse load they hauled them away."

Another woman and Elizabeth went into the house and appealed for food from the officers there. "I told him I lived in the Cemetery House," she recalled, "and we were driven away from home and had nothing to eat or drink, and we thought we would lay in complaint."

He laughed and said, "You want to live on the army then?"[22]

FARTHER NORTH, in town, Agnes Barr continued to cook for the Union surgeons and their patients. While the assault on Cemetery Hill was going on, several ate at her table. This did not go unnoticed by nearby Confederates.

They asked why she was feeding Federal soldiers, and she told them they were doctors, taking care of the wounded at the nearby church. The Southerners gallantly declined her offer to feed them, telling her to give it to the wounded.

Under orders from the occupying Confederates, the town's bakeries worked into the night. Kitchens in various homes were active, too, as the women prepared food for their families, the wounded, and the soldiers.

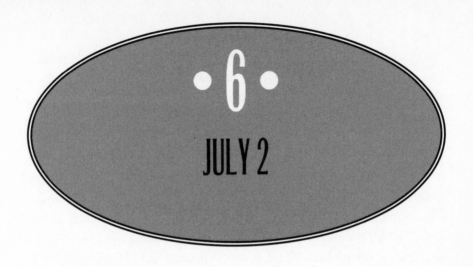

•6•
JULY 2

I took Bessie and tied her in the parlor. She's been there since. Now we have milk to share with our neighbors.

LEM SNYDER

THE SECOND DAY OF battle brought fiercer fighting outside the town, more deaths, more wounded. Many residents stayed in their basements. Others ventured up from their cellars and peered outside to try to see what was happening.

During the night of July 1 and throughout the next day, the towns-people had to dodge stray bullets. Confederate soldiers vandalized homes and businesses while searching for Union stragglers. During these searches, the Southerners also sought precious items such as medicines and surgical instruments, telegraph equipment, and tools. Whenever they encountered civilians, they demanded food.

Just before midnight after the first day of fighting, Sarah Broadhead was still awake. Restless, she peered out the front window of her Chambersburg Street home and watched Confederates loot a house across the street. The homeowner's family had fled prior to the town's occupation. The plunderers loaded a wagon with their loot. She feared that they might turn their attention to her home and break down her door.[1]

Just before dawn on July 2, the Foster family was awakened by a pounding at their back door. Two Confederates demanded to search the premises for Yankees. The family tried to dissuade the Southerners, but the soldiers insisted. Catherine Foster finally let them into the house, and they immediately pointed their weapons at her father, James. The Rebels demanded fifty dollars. He said that he had nothing more than what was in his wallet, so they took his wallet and left the house. In the Foster cellar, just beneath the scene of the robbery, Cpl. Leander Wilcox of the 151st Pennsylvania was hiding. He stayed there until July 4.[2]

On Baltimore Street, just south of the Diamond, Moses McClean, a prominent attorney, lived with his family. Early Thursday morning there was loud and persistent knocking at his front door. He looked out a second-floor window and saw Confederates. When he asked what they wanted, the soldiers responded that Gen. Stephen Dodson Ramseur ordered them to confiscate a supply of bacon.

McClean protested that his house was private property, but the Southerners threatened to break down the door. With his family in the house, McClean decided it was best to cooperate. He led the soldiers through his back yard to a smokehouse. The hams were gathered, and the small party returned to the house to complete the transaction.

Using the light from McClean's oil lamp, the officer wrote out a receipt for the confiscated hams. As he handed the paper to McClean, the officer said, "Your government ought to pay you for that."

Lizzie, an outspoken domestic residing with the McClean family, quickly snapped back, "Our government would have a great deal to pay with all you steal."[3] The officer and his men left without comment or further confrontation.

Mary McAllister tried to sleep while sitting in a chair in front of an open second-story window in her bedroom. She rested her head on her crossed arms on the windowsill, only catching short naps during the night. Her "post" was an attempt to protect her property. Behind her, four nieces and nephews, along with her sister, slept crisscrossed on a bed. There was not much space available for family members in a house filled with wounded soldiers.[4]

At sunrise the people of Gettysburg awoke in an occupied town. The Confederates started cook fires along the streets. They looked for places to serve as latrines. The Southerners did not restrict the people from moving about. Some of the civilians did venture out of doors, but cautiously and ready to duck quickly into a doorway for cover. Others decided it was best to remain in their homes. With the exception of visits to nearby hospitals or to fetch milk or some other commodity, the people stayed off the streets.

While they controlled the town, the Confederates built barricades in the dirt streets. They placed these to hinder any Federal advance through the town. On West Middle Street they dissembled a log cabin, using the timbers to block the street. The Southerners ripped down wooden fences, using the material to block alleys and streets. Removing the fences also made it easier for Lee's troops to move through town.

A leery calm pervaded. Except for the occasional crack of rifle fire, the morning was quiet. Yet the busy activities of the Confederates signaled a warning to the town's residents. As the Southerners prepared for an attack, the civilians feared their town would be shelled. This was a quandary for them—leave, knowing their homes would likely be ransacked by the occupiers, or stay and risk being injured during a shelling. Most opted to stay in their homes. One person managed to move a railroad car in front of his house on Railroad Street, hoping that stray bullets or shells would hit it rather than his home.

The Confederates also commandeered the houses with windows that promised the best position for snipers. There they placed sharpshooters who would fire at anything that moved suspiciously. By taking positions in private homes, the Rebels attracted fire from Union posts. Nevertheless Southerner sharpshooters used several houses on Baltimore Street.

Confederate officers entered the Globe Inn and inquired if they could order breakfast. The proprietors, ready to make a profit, increased their prices by 50 percent. The Confederates were willing to pay the higher prices, so Charles Will and his son, John, prepared the meal in their York Street Inn. When the meal was done, the Confederates paid their tab with gold and greenbacks. What could have been an explosive situation was instead a pleasant business transaction. Will kept his dining room open throughout the day, and the Southerners ate at a large table, capable of seating forty-six people at a time.[5]

In front of the Globe Inn was a dead horse. John Will implored an officer to have it removed. "You people up here are very nice," the man responded. "Why didn't your men help us take away the dead from our doors in Fredericksburg?" Without saying another word, the soldier rode off. The dead horse remained in front of the inn.

During the morning of July 2 some Confederates looted the Washington Hotel on the corner of Railroad and Carlisle Streets. They broke into the basement and stole whiskey. A short time later their crime was discovered when the drunken soldiers became loud and boisterous.

Throughout the day the Confederate army occupied Gettysburg, using buildings and other facilities as lookouts and hospitals while the main fighting droned on south of town. Yet there were several skirmishes within the town limits.

Before sunrise, Catherine Garlach and her twelve-year-old son, Will, began the task of making their basement more comfortable. A foot of stale rainwater had collected in the cellar, so the Garlachs brought in logs for a makeshift platform. Henry Garlach was a cabinetmaker by trade, so there was extra lumber at their Baltimore Street house.

The Garlachs' house was in the line of fire for a Union sharpshooter, so residents worked to make the damp cellar inhabitable. After erecting the platform floor in the basement, other neighbors were invited into the relative safety of the shelter. These include the Sullivan and McIllroy families and Sarah Bream and her daughter. From there they heard the cracking of gunshots on the street and noted sporadic lulls in the fighting.[6]

Garlach occasionally left the safety of the underground room to peek outside to see what was happening. She watched Confederates build and hide behind a barricade. Putting one of their hats on a stick, the Southerners drew fire from Union sharpshooters. They noted where the powder smoke appeared and returned fire.

Several times Confederates tried to commandeer the Garlach home for a sharpshooter. Each time they encountered the wrath of Catherine Garlach. One soldier finally entered the house and started up the stairs.

Catherine stopped him and said that if he fired his weapon he would attract fire on her house, which was "full of defenseless women and children."

The man said that he would be killed if he tried to leave the house. She offered to let him stay. Apparently he feared her more than Yankee bullets, because he decided to leave.

Foolishly, Catherine and her son went to the top floor of their home to look out the garret. During a lull in the gunfire, they removed a window board and peered south toward Cemetery Hill.

Mother and son were nervous, so they kept their observation brief then replaced the window cover. No sooner had they started toward the stairs when a bullet crashed through the window jamb. Seeing activity at the garret window was enough to draw the attention and fire of a Federal sharpshooter. Catherine and Will scurried back to the safety of their basement. The Garlach house, as well as the Sweeney and Schriver houses, was pelted with bullets throughout the day.

Confederate soldiers in private homes created problems throughout the day. Cpl. William H. Poole, Ninth Louisiana, took position on the second floor of the Samuel McCreary house on the east side of Baltimore Street. Poole kneeled behind a table that was lying on its side and fired on the Union position. Federals returned fire, and one of their bullets smashed through the tabletop, striking Poole in the chest and killing him instantly. The McCrearys later had the task of burying him. They also had to clean up blood and splattered flesh from the sniper's nest.[7]

Several Baltimore Street homes were occupied by Confederate troops. At 401 Baltimore Street, a two-and-a-half-story brick house was used by sharpshooters. Catherine Sweeney and daughter, Lizzie, fled to safety. The attic made a perfect sniper's nest for the sharpshooters. They were a tough target for Union sharpshooters as they hid in the attic, using only the small window to do their dirty work. More than 150 bullet marks are still visible in the brick near the home's garret window.

Just across the street at 404 Baltimore, the John Winebrenner home was strategically situated close to the Union lines on Cemetery Hill. This made the house very desirable, so Confederate sharpshooters commandeered the home. They also ate everything they found, except for a small amount of coffee and a tiny piece of dried beef. During the daylight hours of July 2 and 3, the Southerners forced the Winebrenners to stay in their cellar. M. L. Culler, a student at the Lutheran seminary, stayed in the cellar with the Winebrenners. The Rebels attracted a great deal more Union fire.[8] Miniés repeatedly struck the front of the house, creating permanent scars in both the walls and shutters.

In a letter to his sister, John Rupp commented later, "Our men occupied my porch, and the Rebel men the rear of the house, and I in the cellar. . . . Our house is pretty well riddled." His home was a brick two story that was replaced with a Gothic Revival two-and-a-half story. The home reflected his prosperity and the success of his steam tannery, which was north of the house. The Rupp tannery consisted of several bark sheds, a two-story tan shop, a finishing and drying shop, and a bark mill able to produce five thousand finished hides a year.

Baltimore Street was not the only street whose homeowners stayed in their basements. At 127 Washington Street, the Lashell family remained in their cellar throughout the battle. Both Federals and Confederates occupied the house while the Lashells hid in the darkness.

The close proximity of the soldiers forced many other Gettysburg families into their basements. Being below ground was the safest place. Union sharpshooters, one thousand yards away on Cemetery Hill, fired at Confederates when they saw them moving in the town's streets. From that perch, they could see into the Diamond at the center of town, but at that distance, they could not differentiate between soldier and civilian. They fired at anything that moved. People moved quickly if they ventured outside.

The primary focus of the fighting moved from the town to the surrounding countryside. Lee decided to strike the left and right flanks of the Union line on Cemetery Hill, but it took hours for his men to get into position.

Around 4 P.M. the reality of war returned forcefully. Heavy artillery opened, sending shells over portions of the town. As the bombardment grew in intensity, civilians rushed to the safety of their basements. Several narrowly escaped stray bullets. In her home, Sallie Myers was at the bedside of mortally wounded Sgt. Alexander Stewart. She was fanning him, trying to make him as comfortable as possible for his last hours. She stood up from her stool to stretch a moment, and "a minié ball came through two walls and struck the floor where I had been sitting a minute before. I would have been struck in the neck."[9] Myers watched over Stewart for the next four days, until he succumbed to his wound.

Attorney William McClean barely escaped injury when he looked out a window of his East Middle Street house. It was enough to catch the eye of a Federal sharpshooter. A minié crashed through the shutter and sash. The bullet continued "on a line of where my breast had been a few seconds before, entered the foot board of the bed in which my sick wife had been and passed into the mattress."[10] McClean scurried to the safety of his cellar. (The bed with the bullet hole and the bullet recovered from McClean's mattress are on display at the Gettysburg National Military Park Visitors Center Museum.)

Despite repeated attempts, Lee's forces were unable to break through the Union line. At the end of the second day's fighting, each army had suffered some nine thousand casualties. The Confederates had again gained ground but failed to dislodge the Federals.

Confederate Gen. William Barksdale did not live to see the brilliant charge of his Mississippi Brigade from Pitzer's Woods glorified in Southern newspapers. The fiery general collapsed on the field, wounded at the conclusion of his charge toward the Peach Orchard. With his long, flowing gray hair quite visible, Barksdale lay helpless on the battlefield until night. When soldiers from the Fourteenth Vermont discovered him, they took him to a hospital at the nearby Jacob Hummelbaugh farm. A surgeon examined the general and pronounced his wounds mortal. Barksdale was moved into the yard. Out of respect for his rank, he was attended by a steward for several hours, "defiant and obstinate" until death finally came. His body remained in the yard where inquisitive Union soldiers could pause to view this famous dead Southern officer. Buttons and his collar insignia were stripped from his dazzling uniform as souvenirs. The colorful general was later buried in a common grave on the Gettysburg farm where he had died. After the war, his remains were disinterred and moved to Jackson, Mississippi.

One of the hot spots of the day's combat had been Little Round Top. At the nearby Weikert home, Tillie Pierce carried water to the roadside for the passing Union troops while others in the house baked for the soldiers. Around noon, Tillie "noticed a poor, worn-out soldier crawling along on his hands and knees." An officer accosted the man, shouting at him to get up and march with language seldom heard by a fifteen-year-old girl. The man said that he couldn't get up, so the officer struck him three or four times with the flat of his sword and returned to the march. Other men fell out of line to help their collapsed comrade and carry him into the Weikert house. The man was suffering from sunstroke and didn't regain consciousness until sometime later. As they left the house, his friends commented, "We will mark that officer for this." Many years later, when Tillie reflected on the matter, she commented, "It is a pretty well established fact that many a brutal officer fell in the battle, from being shot other than by the enemy."

Food became a source of contention between the Confederates and the civilians. Soldiers relentlessly searched for food. They procured hams from smokehouses with worthless receipts. They ransacked stores. Hungry Southerners smashed the tops from kegs of salted mackerel, snatched the fish from the brine, and ate them—heads, tails, and all. Nellie Aughinbaugh recalled that whatever the soldiers could scavenge they ate.[11]

Two hungry Confederates begged for food from Martha Scott at her Chambersburg Street house. She gave them a freshly baked pie. Her willingness to feed them provoked suspicion. "You eat a piece," one demanded, fearing that the pie was poisoned. Mary McAllister witnessed the scene and told the men, "Do you think it is poisoned? The women here don't poison food." The hungry Confederates left without eating or taking the pie.[12]

After a month's anticipation of Confederate raids—but not necessarily a three-day pitched battle in their town—Gettysburg's people had taken the steps deemed appropriate so as to limit the supplies Southerners might collect from the stores, homes, and farms. Jubal Early had noted as much in his account of the situation: "The authorities of Gettysburg declared their inability to furnish any supplies, and a search of the stores resulted in securing only a very small quantity of commissary supplies, and about two thousand rations were found in a train of cars, and issued to Gordon's brigade." He added, "I had no opportunity of compelling a compliance with my demands in this town, or ascertaining its resources, which I think, however, were very limited."

One of the townspeople, Lem Snyder, had outsmarted the Confederates. He provided milk to his neighbors so they could make pancakes and biscuits. When Mary Montford asked him how he kept the Rebels from taking his cow, he explained, "I took Bessie and tied her in the parlor. She's been there since."[13]

Physical disability proved advantageous to those African Americans who couldn't evacuate prior to the appearance of Lee's army. Only the able-bodied were taken back to the South. Sallie Myers noted, "Those who were obliged to stay at home were, at the shortest notice, suddenly transformed into limping, halting, and apparently worthless specimens of humanity."

Some of the few blacks who remained were able to escape capture with assistance from their white employers. Jacob Taughinbaugh later remembered: "My mother had two Negro servants. We were sure if the Confederates found them they would be taken away. Our front porch was a few feet above the ground, and at one end there was an excavation below ground where you could get to the cellar from the outside. This entranceway was separated from the rest of the space under the porch by a wall made of stones without mortar. My mother took away stones enough to let the servants crawl through, then put the stones back."[14]

Taughinbaugh added, "She had to take out a good many stones, too, because one of the Negroes was a great big woman. Someone had to keep a sharp lookout all the time, and as soon as a soldier was seen coming, Mother would take the servants down and stow them away. Sometimes there would be men hanging around the house all day. The best she could do then was to take down some food and slip it to them."

Several homes stopped bullets and shells from the army's guns. One of these was at 155 South Washington Street. The brick house had been built in 1859 and was owned by James and Catherine Foster. For two days two Union doctors used the house as an operating room. They left in the early morning of July 3 shortly after breakfast. Five minutes later a shell crashed into the bedroom where the doctors had been sleeping. The damage was extensive. A second shell struck over the table where the two had just finished breakfast. The explosion drove the weights of a clock through the opposite wall. A third shell struck the fireplace, hurling the mantel across the room.

Missing from the town during the battle were several prominent citizens. This was a common occurrence when a town was threatened with a raid or other incursion. With sufficient warning, they would take with them livestock, money, and other prized possessions.

Some left because, in some way, they represented the government. David Buehler was the town postmaster; he left with the town's mail. His wife, Fannie, remained behind with their six children. She closed the shutters, took down the post office sign, and locked the doors.

In general, businesses closed, and the dirt streets were not likely to see many citizens. There was no train service. The telegraph was out of service. People hid in their basements whenever fighting erupted. John Schick smoked twenty-one cigars a day while the battle droned on around the town. When the shooting stopped, people ventured into the streets, confirming who might not be there, always leery and ready to duck into the closest haven of safety.

Adding to everyone's discomfort—both soldier and civilian—was the summer heat. This made water one of the most prized commodities in the area. Soldiers searched the buildings for the enemy and pilfered whatever food they could forage. Many structures, however, held mostly wounded men and exhausted caregivers.

As THE battle intensified, most people remained in the safety of their homes or basements. Some did not and were just stupid. John Will climbed to the roof of the Globe Inn to watch the cannonading and the progression of the battle. Several times Confederates ordered him off the roof, but he ignored them and moved to another position. One soldier even aimed a rifle at him. What eventually got his attention was a mounted officer, revolver in hand, ordering him off the roof to report to Jubal Early. Will followed the officer and received a stern lecture. After the general was satisfied that Will was not spying, just curious, he released him.[15]

Henry Jacobs and his father were sitting on top of their cellar door, listening to the sounds of the battle. Miniés pelted the Jacobs house on Middle Street. They quickly slipped below ground. A Rebel took their place on the cellar door, and a short time afterward the Jacobs heard him moan as he was hit. He slumped over onto the cellar door and died.[16]

Although the townspeople feared being caught on the receiving end of artillery, neither army trained its guns on the town. Still, shells did fall within the borough. The misguided ordnance did some damage and scared the civilians. Three shells smashed into the yard of George Little on Middle Street. Laura Bergstresser was in the second-floor bedroom of her Baltimore Street home when a shell crashed through the wall, rolled on the floor, and bounced out a window without exploding. Bergstresser, the daughter of a Methodist minister, was never harmed.

An artillery shell struck David Troxel's house on Chambersburg Street, but the ordnance did not explode. Meanwhile, twenty-two people huddled in the basement below. They were scared but managed to keep each other's spirits up.

Just before dark the sounds of battle quelled. Some people emerged from their underground rooms to see what was happening. Then Jubal Early ordered two brigades to attack Cemetery Hill. The lull ended with an explosion of gunfire, and the townspeople scurried back to their basements.

As darkness overtook the battlefield on July 2 and the last shots of the day faded away, weary Federal officers rode into the yard of Lydia Leister's home. Situated on the Taneytown road just behind Cemetery Ridge, Leister's humble two-room house served as George Gordon Meade's head-quarters. Owning a modest, wood-frame, single-story structure with a single fireplace, the widow made her living by working a small farm that included a log barn, a small orchard, and a vegetable garden. Now the widow's fences had been knocked down and her garden trampled. Her food stores had been raided by Meade's staff and headquarters guards. Some of her furniture was hauled into the yard and used as writing desks. Now her small home was the site of one of the most important meetings that would occur during the battle of Gettysburg.

The generals convened in the main room of the Leister house to decide whether to stay in their positions or fall back. They determined it was better to strengthen their lines and wait for Lee to attack rather than attack him. Meade predicted that the next day Lee would attack the center of the Federal line.

During the night the regimental bands played for hours in a crude attempt to drown out the moans and screams of the wounded who lay in the battlefields. The number of men needing medical attention was staggering.

JULY 3

The vibrations could be felt and the atmosphere was so full of smoke that we could taste the saltpeter.

ALBERTUS McCREARY

ON JULY 3, THE third day and the final day of the battle, the fighting began at 4 A.M., when Gen. Henry W. Slocum attacked Gen. Edward Johnson's division at the base of Culp's Hill. After six hours of fighting, the Confederates retreated to Rock Creek, and Slocum regained control of Culp's Hill.

During that same time, James Longstreet protested Lee's plan to attack the center of the Union line. Lee, however, ignored Longstreet's warnings and proceeded. The result was Pickett's Charge.

In the meantime, the action had not ended at Culp's Hill. At 4 A.M. cannonading jolted both soldier and civilian awake. It was the beginning of a seven-hour struggle to wrest the position from the Federals. People scrambled to their cellars, and skirmishes occupied the troops in town.

Mary Virginia "Ginnie" Wade was the only citizen of Gettysburg to be killed during the three days of fighting in her town. Over the decades since the battle, her story has become folklore through the telling of stories that combined fact and myth.

She was born on Baltimore Street in Gettysburg on May 21, 1843, the daughter of James Wade and Mary Ann Filby. During her early childhood, Mary worked for her father's tailoring business. She was known to her peers as "Gin" or "Ginnie" because of her middle name, Virginia. After the battle of Gettysburg, a newspaper inaccurately referred to her as "Jennie," and this is the name that has stuck with her since.

In the spring of 1863, twenty-year-old Ginnie became engaged to Cpl. Johnston H. "Jack" Skelly Jr. of the Eighty-seventh Pennsylvania Infantry. In late June, however, Skelly was nowhere near Adams County when the Confederates first entered his hometown. For Ginnie Wade, June 26 became an extremely busy day when her brother, Samuel, was arrested by Rebel troops for refusing to surrender the family horse.[1] Ginnie also helped to care for six-year-old Isaac Brinkerhoff, a disabled child.

When the fighting began on July 1, Ginnie decided to leave her house on Breckinridge Street and stay in her sister's house on Baltimore Street, because many believed this area would be out of the line of fire. She could also help to care for her sister, Georgia McClellan, who was homebound with a newborn. As the fighting escalated, the McClellan residence was not as safe as the women had reasoned; it was directly between groups of Union and Confederate sharpshooters throughout the three-day battle.

As the Federals fell back from Seminary Ridge to Cemetery Ridge, many stopped by the McClellan residence in search of food and water. Ginnie spent a great deal of time filling their canteens and baking bread for them. She continued doing this throughout the three days.

Ginnie awoke on July 3 at roughly 4:30 A.M. to prepare more bread for the Union soldiers. Her sister noted that Ginnie's last words were, "If there is anyone in this house that is to be killed today, I hope it is me, as George [Ginnie's nickname for her sister] has a little baby." Shortly after that the McClellan house was pelted by Rebel fire.

At approximately 8 A.M., while she was at work with her bread-making, a Confederate bullet smashed through the kitchen door, struck Ginnie in the back below the shoulder blade, and pierced her heart. She died instantly. Union soldiers heard the screams from Ginnie's sister. They carried the body to the basement and wrapped it in a quilt, where it remained until July 4. That afternoon Ginnie was buried behind the McClellan residence, reportedly with bread dough still on her hands.[2]

Ginnie did not know that her fiancée, Jack Skelly, had been wounded on June 15 near Winchester, Virginia, during the battle of Carter's Woods. News of Skelly's condition was being brought to her by John Wesley Culp, a former Gettysburg resident and childhood friend of Jack and Ginnie. Long before the war, Culp's family had moved to western Virginia, and he had since enlisted in the Confederate army and served in the renowned Stonewall Brigade. He met up with Jack Skelly after Skelly was wounded, and Jack gave him a message for Ginnie.

Wesley's brigade marched to Gettysburg, and at some point he had an opportunity to visit a cousin who still worked the family farm on Culp's Hill. Wesley mentioned Skelly's message to his cousin but said that he had promised to deliver it in person. He never had the opportunity to follow through with his promise. On July 3, the same day on which Ginnie Wade died, Wesley's brigade engaged the enemy in a fight for Culp's Hill. He was killed in action, the only member of the Second Virginia to die that day.

Jack Skelly died of his wounds on July 12. He never knew what had happened to Ginnie.

After the war Ginnie and Jack were reinterred in Gettysburg's Evergreen Cemetery, less than one hundred yards apart. Wesley Culp's body was never found by his family.

THE TOWNSPEOPLE mostly stayed inside on July 3, but Agnes Barr left her Baltimore Street house to get supplies. When she returned, she had to dart between the buildings to avoid sharpshooters.[3]

Sitting in his Chambersburg Street house, John Burns was recovering from multiple gunshot wounds. He had been shot three times on July 1 during his brief stint with elements of the Iron Brigade. A Confederate surgeon had treated him on Thursday, and Burns admitted that he had received "decent treatment" from the Southerners.

Confederate officers arrived at Burns's house on Friday morning to question him. Up to this point, the Southerners had not suspected that old John Burns had been firing at them. According to Burns, "A 'Copperhead' woman living opposite, told on him." The Rebels questioned him, and he lied about his reasons for being in the area of the battle. His responses gave them "little satisfaction," but the officers left.

A short time later two bullets crashed into Burns's home, and the old patriot forever after maintained that the Southerners had attempted to "assassinate" him. One of the bullets was high, passing over Burns's head, and "struck the wall behind the lounge on which he was lying." The second was "low, passing through a door."

At Moses McClean's house, on Baltimore Street, an artillery shell crashed through a fifteen-inch brick wall. Hannah McClean was working in the garret, attempting to move a mattress. She decided to have one of her sons do the heavy lifting and waited for him at the bottom of the steps. All of a sudden the shell struck, crashed through the wall, and rolled down the stairs to the first landing. Dust in the McClean garret was so thick that, at first, it was thought to be smoke. The shell did not explode.[4]

For the residents in town, the morning remained relatively quiet and uneventful. From the previous day they had learned what to expect from the Confederates as the borough remained occupied. Hungry Rebel soldiers scavenged for food, often raiding the residents' gardens. Whenever the soldiers found a vacated house, they plundered it. They took what food they could find and quickly devoured it. Southerners ransacked Joseph Gillespie's grocery store next to the Globe Inn. They killed Harriet Bayly's chickens then brought them to her to clean and cook.

The day was a busy, adventurous morning for Albertus McCreary. First, the daring youth nearly lost his life. He was looking at the surrounding rooftops from a door to the roof of the McCreary house on the southwest corner of Baltimore and High Streets. He saw sharpshooters on almost every roof, and he also saw a neighbor hiding behind a chimney. The man was nearly killed when a bullet hit the chimney. McCreary laughed at how fast the neighbor fled the roof. Then two bullets hit the McCreary roof, and young McCreary disappeared just as fast as his neighbor.

So the young McCreary moved to the front porch and watched a Confederate unit march past. The Southerners saw that McCreary wore a Federal kepi. At the sight of the Union headgear, an officer halted his men and ordered the boy arrested.

Some of the first images of the battlefield were taken by the three-man photographic crew led by Alexander Gardner and including Timothy O'Sullivan and James F. Gibson. While focusing on the bodies still on the field, the photographers encountered these scenes near the Rose Woods, an area heavily contested on July 2 when the Union Third Corps advanced into a Confederate thrust. At one time these bodies were believed to be Union soldiers, but recent research suggests that they are either Georgians or South Carolinians. Gardner's portable darkroom can be seen in the left background of the two images below.

These photographs, taken as soon as Gardner's crew arrived on July 5, afford rare views of Federal corpses in the field. Encountered near the Peach Orchard, they reveal another side to leaving men on the field after combat, namely, unintentionally resupplying the enemy. In these instances the bodies are shoeless, and some belongings litter the ground. Burial details waited while the cameramen worked.

Left: Recent research suggests that this is one of three images the Gardner crew made on July 6 of six Rebel corpses near the base of Big Round Top. *Below:* The Gardner team likely posed this Confederate body in Devil's Den. The rifle is probably a prop the photographers added to create a dramatic scene.

Right: These two soldiers killed in the Slaughter Pen near the Little Round Top were photographed by Gardner. The two were likely from the Forty-fourth or Forty-eighth Alabama and were killed on July 2.

Above: Grotesque wounds were everywhere on the field of Gettysburg. Gardner's crew posed this image after surmising that the man had been disemboweled by artillery. Recent research, however, suggests that the corpse attracted wild hogs.

Below: Gardner titled this image of a Confederate corpse in Devil's Den "A Sharpshooter's Last Sleep."

Facing page (bottom): Near the Rose farm, O'Sullivan photographed a shallow mass grave of Confederates. The men in the background may be part of a detail charged with clearing the field of discarded weapons.

Above: Alfred R. Waud, an artist for *Harper's Weekly,* was photographed by O'Sullivan while he sketched Devil's Den. *Right:* Three Confederate captives await transport to a Federal prisoner-of-war camp. These men were likely apprehended during Lee's retreat.

More than five thousand horses and mules were killed during the battle. Pictured to the right is the wrecked ammunition chest for a 12-pounder gun and one of the animals killed in action.

Numerous horse carcasses litter the ground of the Abraham Trostle farm, which was south of the town along the Emmitsburg road and was briefly used by Daniel E. Sickles as his headquarters. The animals formerly served Capt. John Bigelow's Ninth Massachusetts Battery but were killed in action on July 2. Without the animals, Bigelow's men had to haul their guns from the field themselves or abandon them under fire. Forty-five horses were killed here.

Lydia Leister's farm was appropriated as Meade's headquarters. As soon as the armies marched south, her property was taken over by the medical corps. Even in this image one can still see several dead horses on the ground.

The Mary Thompson home on the Chambersburg pike served as Lee's headquarters. The general's tent was near the house, which was also in close proximity to the seminary cupola from which Lee observed the battle from time to time.

Abram Bryan, a free black, abandoned his house on the crest of Cemetery Ridge when he learned of the Confederate invasion. In Bryan's absence, his property was appropriated to serve as headquarters for Union Gen. Alexander Hays.

Evergreen Cemetery's distinctive gatehouse was a prominent landmark during the battle around Culp's Hill. Elizabeth Thorn and her extended family lived here prior to the action. Battle damage is apparent in this image taken during Mathew Brady's photographic mission. One of Brady's assistants posed in the picture.

Right: This 1866 view of Spangler's Meadow was taken by the Tyson brothers and faces a Rebel line that was attacked on the morning of July 3. Two Union regiments suffered 40 percent casualties in a matter of minutes.

Gardner photographed this section of breastworks on the southern crest of Little Round Top. This image likely is of a portion of the Union line held by the 140th New York.

Below: In this image of the western slope, the summit of Little Round Top is slightly obscured by mists much as the area was during the time of the fighting on July 2.

Gettysburg's two institutions of higher learning: Pennsylvania College (*above*) and the Lutheran Theological Seminary (*right*). Both served as hospitals for several weeks after the battle.

Below: Gardner's crew captured this panoramic view of the town from Cemetery Hill, possibly from the top of the Evergreen Cemetery gateway. The roadway is the Baltimore pike, and the tents belong to militia troops that arrived on July 7.

Above: Camp Letterman was situated on the George Wolf property and began receiving patients from various field hospitals and homes on July 22. The image above may have been taken by P. S. Weaver.

Below: This amputation scene was staged in October or November for the camera. The evergreen wreath and garland are part of some decorations put up for a gala on September 23 and left up until the camp was deactivated in November. Evergreens were particularly helpful in warding off unpleasant odors and insects.

Camp Letterman offered cots to men who had mostly slept on the ground prior to their wounding. The medical corps oversaw the camp, noting that the requisite drainage ditches were dug and providing cooking supplies and other sanitary facilities. Supplementing these measures were private organizations such as the U.S. Sanitary Commission and the Christian Commission. These groups offered personal items to the men as well as food and supplies over and above the rations provided by the army. The Tyson brothers, local Gettysburg photographers, captured this image of the Sanitary Commission headquarters tent at Letterman.

Sixty-nine-year-old John Burns, a veteran of the War of 1812, recovers from three wounds he received after pitching in with the 150th Pennsylvania on July 1. Two weeks later Mathew Brady's crew photographed him and published his story. Almost overnight, Burns became a national hero.

Above: Embalming was a new science, and several specialists traveled to Adams County to offer their services to families who wanted to bring their fathers and sons home for burial. *Below:* Frederick Gutekunst, a Philadelphia photographer, took this image of some tents of the Christian Commission near the Peach Orchard.

Facing page

Above: George Weikert's house was a prominent landmark on the field around the Peach Orchard and the Wheatfield on July 2. At the time of the battle, however, the structure was only one-story. Situated to the front of the main Union line, it offered limited usefulness as a field hospital but saw plenty of skirmishing.

Below: This farmhouse belonged to Basil Biggs, one of the last African Americans to flee when the Rebels approached. Situated on Cemetery Ridge, behind Union lines, the house and outbuildings were close to some of the heaviest fighting. Relatively safe from direct fire, the property became one of the busiest of the front-line hospital aid stations.

By the 1880s monuments and markers were well on the way to commemorating the scenes of battle as well as the units that fought there. The summit of Little Round Top (*above*) was no exception.

For five months after the battle, the only clue to the identity of a dead Union sergeant was the photograph above. Philinda Humiston recognized the image as one she had sent her husband, Amos, just weeks before the battle. The story raised the issue of orphaned children and led to the founding of a home and school for orphaned children in Gettysburg (*below*). Among the first to attend were Humiston's children. Their mother was employed there as a matron.

Albertus screamed for his father, David McCreary, who rushed out and saw the squad of Rebel soldiers. The officer explained, "He is in the army and must come with us."

"Oh, no. He is just a schoolboy," McCreary responded.

Finally the officer was persuaded to release the boy when several neighbors confirmed that the youngster wasn't a Union soldier.[5]

JULY 3 was becoming a steamy day, and the air in town turned fetid. Dead horses bloated under the hot summer sun. Corpses in the field did likewise, as did the mounds and piles of amputated limbs outside the many field hospitals. Outhouses and latrines, overused and filled, could not handle the added capacity. The air around Gettysburg was putrid.

Nevertheless, several women persevered with their baking and food preparation for the wounded. Carefully they carried their edibles to the nearby hospitals. Yet even the shortest trip was perilous, often drawing sniper fire.

At 1 P.M. E. Porter Alexander's 143 cannons opened fire on the Union center. Yankee guns returned fire. The cannonade was the largest ever unleashed on the North American continent. Immediately the townspeople returned to their cellars.

"The scene was indescribably grand," Henry J. Hunt, the Union chief of artillery, said later. "All their batteries were soon covered with smoke, through which the flashes were incessant, whilst the air seemed filled with shells, whose sharp explosions, with the hurtling of their fragments, formed a running accompaniment to the deep roar of the guns."

It was during this cannonade that Union Gen. Winfield Scott Hancock calmly rode among his entrenched men on Cemetery Ridge. "There are times when a corps commander's life does not count," he answered one of his aides who urged him to take cover.

As the bombardment continued, the recoil of the smoking guns dug into the ground and caused the cannon to be aimed slightly higher with each shot. Over time the Confederate guns overshot the Union line, landing shells in the Federal rear. As a result, Meade's headquarters was blasted.

In their underground shelters, civilians could only listen to the bombardment. Some strangely noted the shots with brief commentary such as,

"Their side . . . Our side." To many it sounded "as if heaven and earth were crashing together."

Sarah Broadhead observed, "We knew the Confederates were putting forth all their might and it was a dreadful thought that they might succeed."[6] Sitting in the Troxel basement with others, Broadhead reported that most of the people could not help but think about the soldiers on the battlefield, and their thoughts were not limited to the men in blue. "We knew that with every explosion," she wrote in her diary, "human beings were hurried through excruciating pain into another world and that many more were torn, mangled, and lying in torment worse than death."

Albertus McCreary noted "the vibrations could be felt and the atmosphere was so full of smoke that we could taste the saltpeter."[7]

"The scene on Cemetery Ridge after the battle was something that cannot be described. It was horrible to see the men of the artillery dead and dying against their guns; their dead horses were all about them," Billy Simpson, a native of Mauch Chunk, Pennsylvania, recalled years later. "I witnessed another terrible incident on [the] Baltimore pike during the artillery engagement. Two pieces of Battery K, of the Fifth U.S. Artillery, had been placed on the right of the pike. The firing was so rapid that there was a premature explosion and the man at the sponge staff had both his arms blown off, and he was flung into a ditch. He was a splendid looking fellow before the accident, but a sight to behold afterward. I often wondered what became of him; in all probability, he died. The sight of the battlefield after the battle was something awful."[8]

Pickett's Charge was a failure. Federal troops captured or killed all the Confederates who broke through their lines. More than three-fourths of the attacking force were casualties.

Meade's field commanders proposed a counterattack, but the commanding general was against it. "We have done well enough," he simply told them.

Lee rode into the field to meet the survivors of the ill-fated charge, addressing them with words of encouragement and calm. Within moments a courier arrived and informed him of Jeb Stuart's defeat at the hands of Union cavalry three miles east of Gettysburg. Lee anticipated that Meade's army would counterattack.

THE LATE afternoon of July 3, 1863 was muggy in south-central Pennsylvania: hot, humid, and stifling. Thousands of soldiers required medical treatment. At the same time, Lee knew that he could no longer stay in Pennsylvania. He returned to his headquarters to plan the retreat to Virginia. That evening Lee summoned Gen. John Imboden to his headquarters. Imboden commanded a cavalry brigade that had arrived at Gettysburg that afternoon. It was too late for his unit to do anything in the day's battle. He learned from the general that he would be guiding the wagon train of the wounded back to northern Virginia.

Imboden later recalled the scene of the early morning hours of July 4, 1863, at Lee's headquarters:

> When he arrived there was not even a sentinel on duty at his tent, and no one of his staff was awake. The moon was high in the clear sky and the silent scene was unusually vivid. As he approached and saw us lying on the grass under a tree, he spoke, reined in his jaded horse, and essayed to dismount. The effort to do so betrayed so much physical exhaustion that I hurriedly rose and stepped forward to assist him, but before I reached his side he had succeeded in alighting, and threw his arm across the saddle to rest, and fixing his eyes upon the ground leaned in silence and almost motionless upon his equally weary horse,—the two forming a striking and never-to-be-forgotten group. The moon shone full upon his massive features and revealed an expression of sadness that I had never before seen upon his face. Awed by his appearance I waited for him to speak until the silence became embarrassing, when, to break it and change the silent current of his thoughts, I ventured to remark, in a sympathetic tone, and in allusion to his great fatigue:
>
> "General, this has been a hard day on you."
>
> He looked up, and replied mournfully, "Yes, it has been a sad, sad day to us," and immediately relapsed into his thoughtful mood and attitude. Being unwilling again to intrude upon his reflections, I said no more. After perhaps a minute or two, he suddenly straightened up to his full height, and turning to me with more animation and excitement of manner than I had ever seen in him before, for he was a man of wonderful equanimity, he said in a voice tremulous with emotion: "I never saw troops behave more magnificently than Pickett's division of Virginians did today in that grand charge upon the

enemy. And if they had been supported as they were to have been,—but, for some reason—not yet fully explained to me, were not,—we would have held the position and the day would have been ours." After a moment's pause he added in a loud voice, in a tone almost of agony, "Too bad! Too bad! OH! TOO BAD!"[9]

When the two men later entered the general's headquarters, Lee laid out the requirements for the retreat. "We must now return to Virginia. As many of our poor wounded as possible must be taken home. I have sent for you because your men and horses are fresh and in good condition, to guard and conduct our train back to Virginia. The duty will be arduous, responsible and dangerous," Lee explained with deep concern, "for I am afraid you will be harassed by the enemy's cavalry."

At the same time, Lee's opponent, Meade, was considering several points. First, his army needed time to reorganize. Reinforcements and ammunition had to be brought forward. At the same time, any counterattack would require his troops to cross the same open field over which Pickett's Charge had occurred. He could only assume that Southern gunners still had canister. The Rebels had also positioned an impressive line of extremely deadly howitzers on Seminary Ridge to meet the anticipated Federal attack. After weighing the potential losses against the gains of the day, Meade decided that there had been enough bloodshed at Gettysburg. He elected to hold his current line and pursue Lee at the first opportunity or sign of the Confederates' withdrawal from the area.[10]

Ominous storm clouds rising in the west provided Meade with additional reason to hold off an assault until his army was reorganized and the foul weather cleared. The battle of Gettysburg was the most important ever fought by the Army of the Potomac. It was also Meade's victory, and one he would not blemish by an ill-prepared counterattack. Meade feared, however, that Lee might attack again.

Yet no attack came. With the cover of darkness, both sides attempted to remove their wounded. The staggering number of injured, however, was overwhelming. Because the Federal troops were in charge of the high ground, more of their wounded could be removed. The Confederates simply could not reach many of their men, because they were so close to the Union line. In many instances, there was little they could do except to desert their wounded and dead. This created another problem.

The ferocity of the bombardment prior to Pickett's Charge forced Tillie Pierce and the others who had found safety at the Weikert farm to flee to a farm even farther from the fighting. When the battle subsided, the refugees returned to the Weikert property. It was late.

"Toward the close of the afternoon," Tillie recalled, "it was noticed that the roar of the battle was subsiding, and after all had become quiet we started back to the Weikert home. As we drove along in the cool of the evening, we noticed that everywhere confusion prevailed. Fences were thrown down near and far; knapsacks, blankets and many other articles, lay scattered here and there. The whole country seemed filled with desolation."

Tillie had seen things on July 1 and 2 that few fifteen-year-olds had ever seen, but on July 3 she witnessed the raw terror of war. "Upon reaching the place I fairly shrank back aghast at the awful sight presented," she recollected. "The approaches were crowded with wounded, dying and dead. The air was filled with moanings, and groanings. As we passed on toward the house, we were compelled to pick our steps in order that we might not tread on the prostrate bodies."[11]

Weikert's farm was on the Taneytown road. In July 1863 sixty-six-year-old Jacob Weikert lived and worked the property with Sarah, his sixty-one-year-old wife. A few years earlier he had deeded about seventy-one acres south of the main homestead to his son, Emanuel. Together they farmed the pleasant farmland and raised cows and horses.

The farm was not far from the ferocious fighting on Little Round Top between Col. William C. Oates's Fifteenth Alabama and Col. Joshua Lawrence Chamberlain's Twentieth Maine. Casualties from that engagement, both Union and Confederate, were brought to the farmhouse, which had become an improvised field hospital.

Tillie vividly recalled the sight when she and the Weikerts returned to the battle-scared farm: "When we entered the house we found it also completely filled with the wounded. We hardly knew what to do or where to go. They, however, removed most of the wounded, and thus after a while made room for the family." Smells of war were everywhere. The distinctive odor of blood, perspiration, and ether permeated the place.

Such sights were not limited to the Weikert farm. Another resident noted: "The beds, the floors, the yards, everywhere, where they [were cared] for, and behind them in the lines of battle, in the brush, by the side of the little springs streams where they had so painfully dragged themselves or sometimes been carried by their companions, were the uncollected dead and dying mostly."[12]

At the Weikerts', the small group of civilians did all they could to be of assistance. "As soon as possible," Tillie recalled, "we endeavored to make ourselves useful by rendering assistance in this heartrending state of affairs. I remember Mrs. Weikert went through the house, and after searching awhile, brought all the muslin and linen she could spare. This we tore into bandages and gave them to the surgeons, to bind up the poor soldiers' wounds."

In the field hospitals erected around the battlefield, the surgeons were constantly occupied. Men whose limbs were partially destroyed awaited their turn beneath a surgical saw. Such was the state of medicine. No one knew about bacteriology. Most doctors had no more than two years of medical school; others had less training. Some became surgeons because they were deemed "to be good with their hands." In general, medical care in America was woefully inadequate in 1863. Supposedly the Harvard Medical School did not own a single stethoscope or microscope until after the war.[13]

THE COOLER night air offered some relief from the direct heat of the summer sun. Some Confederates were repositioned from the fields south of town to the town. Many civilians noted the Southerners were "sullen and gloomy." More barricades went up to impede an anticipated Union advance. Several townspeople fretted at the likelihood of street fighting so close to their homes. No one knew what might happen next.

Belle King made some biscuits and took them to Martha Scott's kitchen on Chambersburg Street. When she arrived, she saw two young Southerners standing guard. She offered each a biscuit, but they declined. So she urged them to put some in their haversacks to eat during the retreat. "Oh, we are not going to retreat," one said. "Why yes," she answered matter-of-factly. "McClellan will be here before morning with a big army!" They feared she might be right, so they accepted the biscuits.[14]

Some Confederates knocked at the door of Catherine Garlach, seeking permission to use the cabinet shop to build a coffin for a dead officer. Catherine refused, telling them that the light would attract sharpshooters. Instead, she offered them the necessary lumber and told them to go to Daniel Culp's shop, which was close to the courthouse. The sharpshooters on Cemetery Hill didn't have a view of that area. The Southerners thanked her and went to Culp's shop. They could only begin the work of making a coffin for Gen. William Barksdale; orders came for the retreat. They left the coffin unfinished and unused. The next day Anna Garlach believed it was the one used to bury Ginnie Wade in the garden at the Wade house.

Before withdrawing, Confederates conducted a house-to-house search for Union soldiers. Perhaps tipped off by a Southern sympathizer, they entered homes without knocking. John Will observed that the county had "its share" of sympathizers; such was common in the border counties.[15]

During their search, the Rebels discovered three Federals hiding in the basement of Martin Stoever's house on Baltimore Street. They marched the prisoners down the street. Troops returned shortly to arrest Stoever, but he refused to open the door and pleaded his case from a second-floor window. He said that he was concerned for the women in the house and agreed to report to the provost marshal in the morning. The soldiers agreed, and Stover remained with his family the remainder of the night.[16]

At the Globe Inn, Confederate and Union surgeons who had dined together throughout the battle suddenly were ready to brawl. What had been a pleasant evening turned nasty until it was halted by John Will. Out of respect for Tillie Gillespie, a neighbor who sought safety in the inn during the day's bombardment, the surgeons agreed to settle their quarrel somewhere else in the near future.[17]

An uneasy calm pervaded the night of July 3 as soldiers and civilians went to sleep that steamy Friday evening. Slumber came easier to most, probably out of sheer exhaustion from the day's events.

Part 3

THE DEBRIS OF WAR

•8•

JULY 4

MOST OF THE GUNS were silent on the morning of July 4, but the air was filled with the pitiful cries and groans from the fallen in both the field and in the many hospitals around the countryside and in town. Injured men cried out for help, water, and mercy. Some even begged for another to put them out of their pain and misery. Thousands lay waiting in agony under the broiling summer sun.

One Adams County resident observed: "Rebel and Union lay rotting in the hot sun side by side. People threw open their private houses; the churches, schoolhouses, the public halls and even the barns and stable, rang with the groans of agony from the shot, maimed, and mutilated, that filled apparently every place, and still the field of death and agony could yet furnish more victims."[1]

As the Army of Northern Virginia began to withdraw from the area, Lee's meager resources were focused on getting a fighting force back to northern Virginia. Thus the Southerners left behind their dead—mostly unburied—as well as the many wounded. So the enormous burden of burying the dead and tending the wounded fell to the Union army and the people of Adams County. Fighting had ravaged the area surrounding the little town of Gettysburg, and the town itself was greatly limited in terms of resources due to the previous week's raid and three days of occupation under combat conditions.

Early in the morning on July 4 the first signs of the withdrawal were detected by one of the townspeople. Mary McAllister, dozing in a chair, awoke to the noise of wagons moving west on Chambersburg Street. "I believe the Confederates are retreating," she told Martha Scott.[2]

An animated Rebel ran up the street and woke up the sleeping guards in front of the Scotts' home. "We are retreating!" he told them.

Mary watched as the men gathered their equipment and ran down Chambersburg Street. She considered saying good-bye, perhaps only out of gratitude for their not damaging her property and for their humane treatment of the civilians, but she chose not to do so. "It would have sounded like a mockery," she concluded.

Daniel A. Skelly recalled a small excitement the night before. He was sleeping fitfully and heard something. "About midnight I was awakened by a commotion down in the street," he recalled. "Getting up I went to the window and saw Confederate officers passing through the lines of Confederate soldiers bivouacked on the pavement below, telling them to get up quietly and fall back. Very soon the whole line disappeared but we had to remain quietly in our homes for we did not know what it meant."[3]

Sarah Broadhead was jolted awake at 6 A.M. when she heard the Southerners hurrying past her home. Their commander admonished the men to make quick time or risk being captured.[4]

All around Gettysburg the awareness spread that the Confederates were retreating. Robert McClean heard a horseman outside his house on Baltimore Street around 2 A.M. The man passed on directions to the soldiers to go to the railroad and turn left.

On the east side of Baltimore Street, Agnes Barr also heard the early morning ruckus of the Rebel retreat. Awakened by voices outside her home as the pullout was discussed, she could not go back to sleep. Under a white flag she took the first news of the retreat to Federal troops positioned on Cemetery Hill.[5]

Slowly and stealthily some Union soldiers cautiously advanced into the town. They surprised and captured numerous sleeping Confederates. By the time the Federals reached the square, they had taken more than one hundred prisoners.

Daniel Skelly noted the early appearance of Union soldiers that morning at about 4 A.M. A disturbance on Baltimore Street caught his attention, and he hurried to a window. "Ye gods!" he recalled. "What a welcome sight for the imprisoned people of Gettysburg! The Boys in Blue marching down the street, fife and drum corps playing, the glorious Stars and Stripes fluttering at the head of the lines." While the Federals advanced into town, Skelly noticed numbers of Confederates being double-timed to the rear. All transpired under a summer shower. Skelly dressed but did not go into the street. Later that morning the Skelly family visited their neighbor, "comparing notes and finding out how all had fared during the days we were in the hands of the enemy."[6]

Many residents slept through the Confederate withdrawal. When they awoke, they were pleasantly surprised to see Federal troops occupying the positions held by Confederates the night before.

"None but smiling faces were to be seen," Jennie McCreary noted.[7] The mood of the town was jubilant.

Caroline Horner busied herself on her hands and knees, scrubbing mud and blood from the pavement in front of her home. Others were not long in joining her in beginning the cleanup.

Not all the Confederates, however, had yet departed. Daniel Skelly observed that they had "thrown up formidable breastworks extending from the Railroad Woods clear out along the ridge to Emmitsburg Road and beyond it." It was a rear guard. Despite the general cessation of hostilities, the youngster reported, "As my father's house was on West Middle Street, which extends in a direct line out to Haupt's Hill, which was along the embattled ridge, we were exposed during the whole day to sharpshooters' fire." These breastworks were small matters of earth and rock, sufficient enough to protect the remaining Southerners and "extending down the hill in the direction of town." The Rebels were dedicated to their task, as

Skelly noted: "They lay behind them all day with guns loaded ready to bang away at any suspicious object in the street. Sometime during the morning, several of our officers rode down the street and when about half the length of the square from Baltimore and Washington Street, one of them was hit in the fleshy part of his arm by a bullet, evidently causing a very painful wound, for he yelled at the top of his voice."

A Confederate picket line ran along Stevens Run, a small creek just outside Gettysburg. From there they fired at anything that moved along High, Middle, and Chambersburg Streets. Jacob Gilbert was shot in the arm and treated by Dr. Charles Horner. Seminary student Amos Whetstone was shot in the leg when he tried to warn Mary McAllister of the sharp-shooter danger.

Panic spread through the civilians when a rumor circulated that the Confederates planned to shell the town. Residents returned to their cellars, but no shelling occurred.

Around noon, in the humidity and heat, an anticipated rainstorm struck. It rained heavily. The downpour helped to wash away the thick puddles of blood on the battlefield.

LEE'S PLANNING for the retreat began shortly after the sun set on July 3. Gen. John Imboden was entrusted with moving the wounded back to the relative safety of Virginia. Lee had already plotted his route, sending Imboden west to Cashtown then south to Williamsport, Maryland. In this manner, the awkward wagon train of wounded would be out of the way of the main retreating column, which was ordered to march back by a shorter route. Once in Williamsport, Imboden was to stop only long enough to rest his men and horses. Then he was to ford the Potomac and move as quickly as he could to Winchester, Virginia.

For the wounded, the movement would be especially agonizing as the ambulances and wagons bumped, jolted, and rocked over rough, muddied mountain roads toward the rain-swollen Potomac River. Their venture began in the earliest hours of Saturday morning, but the task of loading the wounded into twelve hundred wagons was enormous and took time. Imboden noted, "It was apparent by 9 o'clock that the wagons, ambulances and wounded could not be collected and made ready to move till late in the afternoon." Therefore the last combat units did not depart Gettysburg until late the next evening. Portions of the Army of the Potomac followed in a close but cautious pursuit.

Regarding the rainstorm that struck around noon, Imboden observed, "The very windows of heaven seemed to have opened." The massive downpour turned the fields into an instant marsh. Jittery horses and edgy mules, already unnerved by three days of heavy shelling, were made frantic by the driving wind and pounding rainfall. They would not be easily calmed. Wagons, ambulances, and artillery carriages became desperately stuck in the deepening mud.

Imboden commented, "The deafening roar of the mingled sounds of heaven and earth all around us made it almost impossible to communicate orders, and equally difficult to execute them." Finally, the column began to move at 4 P.M., and once in action, the wagon train stretched across the countryside for miles.[8] Imboden remained with the last wagons to pull out, personally positioning troops at intervals to protect the departing vehicles. His work was not finished until late that evening.

The walking wounded straggled behind the wagon train, but they were not restricted to the roadway. Imboden described the evening's events:

> After dark I set out from Cashtown to gain the head of the column during the night. My orders had been peremptory that there should be no halt for any cause whatever. If an accident should happen to any vehicle, it was immediately to be put out of the road and abandoned. The column moved rapidly, considering the rough roads and the darkness, and from almost every wagon for many miles issued heart-rending wails of agony. For four hours I hurried forward on my way to the front, and in all that time I was never out of hearing of the groans and cries of the wounded and dying. Scarcely one in a hundred had received adequate surgical aid, owing to the demands on the hard-working surgeons from still worse cases that had to be left behind.
>
> Many of the wounded in the wagons had been without food for thirty-six hours. Their torn and bloody clothing, matted and hardened, was rasping the tender, inflamed, and still oozing wounds. Very few of the wagons had even a layer of straw in them, and all were without springs. The road was rough and rocky from the heavy washings of the preceding day. The jolting

was enough to have killed strong men, if long exposed to it. From nearly every wagon as the teams trotted on, urged by whip and shout, came such cries and shrieks as these:

"O God! Why can't I die!"

"My God, will no one have mercy and kill me?!"

"Stop! Oh! For God's sake, stop just for one minute; take me out and leave me to die on the roadside."

"I am dying! I am dying! My poor wife, my dear children, what will become of you?"

Some were only moaning; some were praying, and others uttering the most fearful oaths and execrations that despair and agony could wring from them; while a majority, with a stoicism sustained by sublime devotion to the cause they fought for, endured without complaint unspeakable tortures, and even spoke words of cheer and comfort to their unhappy comrades of less will or more acute nerves. Occasionally a wagon would be passed from which only low, deep moans could be heard. No help could be rendered to any of the sufferers. No heed could be given to any of their appeals. Mercy and duty to the many forbade the loss of a moment in the vain effort then and there to comply with the prayers of the few. On! On! We must move on.[9]

While the wagon train continued to roll toward the Potomac, the thundering storms continued to drench everything. Imboden observed: "The storm continued, and the darkness was appalling. There was no time even to fill a canteen with water for a dying man; for, except the drivers and the guards, all were wounded and utterly helpless in that vast procession of misery. During this one night I realized more of the horrors of war than I had in all the two preceding years."

"It got very dark," a wounded North Carolinian recalled, "but there was no halt made, a steady trot being kept up all night. I could never tell you how we got along without some accident."

Imboden realized that he had to push the wagon train on throughout the night, for "in the darkness was our safety." Daylight was fraught with Union attacks that continuously harassed the wagon train. The suffering wounded, as they lay defenseless in the wagons, were terrorized during these skirmishes.

The retreating Confederates arrived in Williamsport late on the afternoon of July 5. Occupying the town, Imboden turned it into a giant hospital and ordered the citizens to cook for the wounded. The following day Union cavalry attacked the town in strength, but Imboden's men were able to defend their position successfully.

Regarding the other retreating column being led by Lee, some Union soldiers were able to block its immediate escape by destroying a bridge at the Potomac. Meade had decided not to attack Lee immediately, but rather to pursue the remnants of the Army of North Virginia slowly. Almost ten days later, on July 13 and 14, Lee's army had rebuilt the destroyed bridge near Williamsport and crossed the river. By the time Meade was set to attack, Lee's army had slipped into Virginia and demolished the bridge.

Perhaps one of the best descriptions of the retreat and pursuit comes from Pvt. Allen Rice of the Eleventh Michigan Infantry:

After that thare was to[o] much more fighting, for old Lea began his retreat and we after him. This was on the fourth of July. We rode all day through the awfullest rain and mud that I ever see. Just at dusk we entered the gap and commenced asending the mountain. We rode on prity briskly some 5 or 6 miles when all at once the column halted and my company with three others ware ordered to the frunt with drawn sabirs. Just immagine your self on a dark night, so dark that you could hardly see the next horse to you, to be placed in a narrow road just wide enough for four horses to march abrest with a ledge of rocks on one side and a steap bank on the other and to be called forward with a drawn sabir in hand and ordered to charge, no knowing what you was going in to and when you had gone a short distance have the bulits come whiring about your ears like a lot of beas after honey and your horse rearing and pransing half scart to death.

I say immagine all of this and then you can form some idea of what we trapsed through on the fourth of July night 1863. We faught nearly all night. We captured 250 wagons & ambulants and 1200 prisoners. Our regiment passed over the road that they ware on and it put me in mind of a fourth of July spree to see the wagons all strung along the road, the wheals choped to pieces, tungs cut off, barels of liqer smashed in and the wagons set afire. We took about 40 wagons to a small place some 10 miles from the mountain and examined them, and what things we wanted in the shape of clothing we took and the rest we burnt and that learnt our ofisers something to see the stuff that they had taken in Pensilvania. All the litle trinkets that you could think of litle babies play things not worth 3 sents.

In his memoirs, Isaac Norval Baker of the Eighteenth Virginia Cavalry also described the difficult conditions of the massive retreat:

We came up with General Lee's army at Gettysburg. We guarded Lee's left wing, could see the fighting on Round Top on the 3rd of July, 1863. We laid quiet on the 4th of July till evening, then General Lee ordered our brigade to fetch out his wagon train and General J. D. Imboden got the train ready to move before dark. It was the longest wagon train I ever saw, some said it was 37 or 38 mile long and hauled thousands of dead and wounded soldiers. 'Twas an awful night, it rained all night, one thunderstorm after another. The rain fell in sheets and vivid flashes of lightning and so dark we could not see our hands an inch from our eyes when there was no lightning. The roar of the waters and heavy bursting thunder, the cries of the wounded and dying soldiers made it awful.

The burden of the abandoned enemy's dead and severely wounded caused a huge logistical problem for the Federal commanders. In a series of dispatches from their headquarters, the commanders often mentioned the problem of the Confederate wounded and dead.

On the morning of July 4, many in the North prepared to celebrate the eighty-seventh anniversary of the Declaration of Independence. In Washington, the War Department received a dispatch from Meade highlighting the repulse of Pickett's Charge and concluding, "My cavalry have been engaged all day on both flanks of the enemy, harassing and vigorously attacking him with great success, notwithstanding they encountered superior numbers both of cavalry and infantry."

A retreat in the face of the enemy was a hazardous affair for any army, and Lee issued explicit instructions to his officers on how this withdrawal was to be executed. While the wagon train of Confederate wounded rolled south, the Army of Northern Virginia remained in position on Seminary Ridge. After the wounded had been evacuated, the remainder of the army marched southwest through a rugged South Mountain pass to join up with the wounded at Williamsport. Jeb Stuart's cavalry would provide cover for the army by riding south toward Emmitsburg then cross the mountains and join up with the marching columns.

Meade reported to the War Department: "This morning the enemy has withdrawn his pickets from the positions of yesterday. My own pickets are moving out to ascertain the nature and extent of the enemy's movement. My information is not sufficient for me to decide its character yet—whether a retreat or maneuver for other purposes."

Throughout the morning Meade was not sure if there would be another attack by Lee. He clearly expected one. His army remained in place, and Lee's army was holding its position. A distance of one mile was all that separated the two. At noon Meade sent another status report, noting that "the enemy has abandoned large numbers of his killed and wounded on the field." He realized the Confederates were abandoning the area, but Meade continued reinforcing his positions and resting his men.

The vast, open fields between the Union and Confederate lines were littered with the debris of the great battle: weaponry and horse carcasses, corpses and injured men too weak to move.

Col. Joshua Lawrence Chamberlain, commander of the Twentieth Maine, noted:

> On the 4th, we made a reconnaissance to the front, to ascertain the movements of the enemy, but finding that they had retired, at least beyond Willoughby's Run, we returned to Little Round Top, where we buried our dead in the place where we had laid them during the fight, marking each grave by a head-board made of ammunition boxes, with each dead soldier's name cut upon it. We also buried 50 of the enemy's dead in front of our position of July 2. We then looked after our wounded, whom I had taken the responsibility of putting into the houses of citizens in the vicinity of Little Round Top, and, on the morning of the 5th, took up our march on the Emmitsburg road.

Fifty miles to the east, Gen. John Reynolds was buried in Lancaster with full military honors, and the city was declared to be in a state of mourning in his memory.

Most of the Army of the Potomac remained in place, reinforced and resupplied. The injured were moved to various field hospitals; the dead were buried. The rest waited in the drenching downpour for orders.

Within the town of Gettysburg, Union soldiers replaced the Confederate soldiers. Men in blue now begged for food. The citizens did their best to accommodate, but supplies were running low. Railroad service had not yet been restored. The nearest supply depot, in Westminster, Maryland, was twenty miles away. Food, medicine, and other supplies needed to be hauled by wagon.

Lee proposed an exchange of prisoners, which would make his retreat less complicated. The Confederates held about four thousand prisoners, which he would have obviously preferred not to have to take along on his march back to Virginia. Meade, however, rejected the exchange, later saying he did not have the authority to grant it.

Both sides used some of the same buildings as hospitals. One of those was the Edward McPherson farm on the Chambersburg pike at McPherson's Ridge. McPherson was a journalist and had been elected to the U.S. House of Representatives. At the time of the battle, he was deputy commissioner of internal revenue—appointed by Lincoln to that post. Tenant farmer John Slentz's family occupied the farm at the time of the battle, but the family had fled when the fighting began. Wounded soldiers from both armies used the house, barn, and outbuildings as shelters during and after the July 1 struggle. When the fighting moved closer to town, the McPherson buildings were used as a hospital by Confederate surgeons. On July 5 the Union First Corps established its field hospital on the property. The restored barn is the only structure remaining today.

AFTER SUNSET and under the cover of darkness, A. P. Hill's corps withdrew, followed by Longstreet's men. At 2 A.M. on July 5 Richard S. Ewell's corps pulled out and followed the rest of the army. Seven thousand men, however, were left behind because they were too severely wounded to attempt the journey back to Virginia; they had to be abandoned and left to the care of the Union medical corps.

At the same time there was little the Confederates could do to retrieve and bury their dead. Corpses and carcasses lay in the town streets, some having laid there since the first day of the battle. Other debris was scattered throughout the town. The foul air surrounding the rotting rubble of war was relieved only by the torrential downpours of that Saturday afternoon.

Old Liz, one of the African American residents who had been taken away by the Southerners earlier in the week, was indeed lucky on July 4. She returned to her home, still a free woman living north of the Mason-Dixon Line. Someone commented, "We never expected to see 'Old Liz' again, but the day after the battle ended she came walking in."

Albertus McCreary recorded that the townspeople gathered around the old woman to learn how she had escaped the march to slavery. "The main fact was this," he wrote. "She was marched with the rest down the street and there was such a crowd that when they were opposite the Lutheran Church, in the confusion she slipped into church without being seen, and climbed up into the belfry; she stayed there for the two days without anything to eat or drink."

Sarah Broadhead scribbled in her diary: "It has been a dreadfully long day. The day is ended and all is quiet, and for the first time for a week I shall go to bed feeling safe."

In his small leather diary, Sgt. Matthew Marvin wrote: "Our men are driving the Rebs. It is a gloomy 4th here in the Woods among so many Wounded[.] With the surgeons amputating arms & limbs this morning we were short of Bandages & Rations but got some near nite. Out of 24 Field & Line Officers that went in 16 were killed or wounded."

Marvin's regiment, the First Minnesota, had bravely leveled their bayonets and charged Cadmus Wilcox's brigade on July 2 and brought it to a sudden halt. They tore into the Confederates and were shredded by the action. Of the 262 men who attacked the force of 1,600 advancing Confederates, only 47 returned to Union lines.

Sometime during the day of that horrible action, Marvin inscribed a cautionary last request on the inside cover of his diary: "Should any person find this on the body of a soldier on the field of battle or by the roadside they will confer a lasting favor on the parents of its owner by sending the book & pocket perce [purse] & silver finger ring on the left hand. Taking their pay for trouble out of the greenbacks herein inclosed."

ONE OF the first civilians to visit the field hospital at the McPherson farm was William McClean. He was a prominent Republican attorney who lived on East Middle Street. He wrote,

> I was informed that men were suffering in the McPherson barn, on the Chambersburg Pike. My good wife went to work, baked biscuit, prepared gruel and we gathered fresh Antwerp raspberries in our garden, and loaded up with as much as I could carry, I started, on foot of course, to the barn. As a civilian, I must confess to a little trepidation in going to what was so recently the front, and hearing the firing of artillery, as the retreat was being followed up. There were parties engaged in burying the dead in the fields, where they fell. A dead soldier in blue was lying along the side of the turnpike, black and swollen from the heat and rain, disfigured beyond recognition. When I entered the barn it was crowded with the wounded of both armies, some of them having fallen four days before and without having any food, except in some cases the little hard-tack in their haversacks, and without any surgical attention to their wounds. There was so many of these wounded and so closely packed together, that I was obliged to tramp on some of them in distributing my supplies. You may imagine how pleased and grateful they were for this fresh food, in their famished and suffering condition. One of them told me that as he was lying on the field, Gen. Lee had given him a drink out of his canteen. Lee's headquarters were in this locality. Many of these poor fellows must have died afterwards from gangrene.[10]

Maj. Gen. Carl Schurz also described what he witnessed in the field hospitals: "At Bull Run, I had seen only a very small scale what I was now to behold. At Gettysburg the wounded—many thousands of them—were carried to the farmsteads behind our lines. The houses, the barns, the sheds, and the open barnyards were crowded with moaning and wailing human beings, and still an unceasing procession of stretchers and ambulances was coming in from all sides to augment the number of the sufferers."[11]

Schurz had been born in Cologne, Germany, on March 2, 1829. He immigrated to the United States in 1852. He soon became active in politics, and in 1860 campaigned in many states on Lincoln's behalf. He stood staunchly against slavery and helped recruit German immigrants into the army. Lincoln gave him a political appointment into the army.

Schurz remembered July 4 in Gettysburg: "A heavy rain set in during the day—the usual rain after a battle—and large numbers had to remain unprotected in the open, there being no room left under roof. I saw long rows of men lying under the eaves of the buildings, the water pouring down upon their bodies in streams."

His recollections also include a description of an operating theater:

> Most of the operating tables were placed in the open where the light was best, some of them partially protected against the rain by tarpaulins or blankets stretched upon poles. There stood the surgeons, their sleeves rolled up to the elbows, their bare arms as well as their linen aprons smeared with blood, their knives not seldom held between their teeth, while they were helping a patient on or off the table, or had their hands otherwise occupied; around them pools of blood and amputated arms or legs in heaps, sometimes more than man-high.

The general with thick spectacles, a broad forehead, tousled brown hair, and reddish beard looked more like a college professor than a military commander. He performed several diplomatic functions for Lincoln, and his wife, Margarethe, is credited with opening the first kindergarten in the United States. At just thirty-four years old, the lanky German immigrant was charming and animated, gentlemanly and vivacious. He was a natural orator. He was also very well connected, which brought him power and suspicions. Following the war, he served as a journalist and editor.

No one ever doubted Schurz's courage or that he took his duties seriously, but his first command under fire had been a disaster. At Freeman's Ford during the Second Manassas campaign in August 1862, one of his brigades was annihilated. At Gettysburg he briefly commanded the Eleventh Corps while Oliver O. Howard stepped into the void created by the death of Reynolds. The Eleventh faltered on the first day of fighting, but the men blunted the assault on Cemetery Hill on the third day. It was one of Schurz's greatest moments.

Schurz's word skills are evident in his account of an amputation:

> Antiseptic methods were still unknown at that time. As a wounded man was lifted on the table, often shrieking with pain as the attendants handled him,

the surgeon quickly examined the wound and resolved upon cutting off the injured limb. Some ether was administered and the body put in position in a moment. The surgeon snatched his knife from between his teeth, where it had been while his hands were busy, wiped it rapidly once or twice across his blood-stained apron, and the cutting began. The operation accomplished, the surgeon would look around with a deep sigh, and then—"Next!"

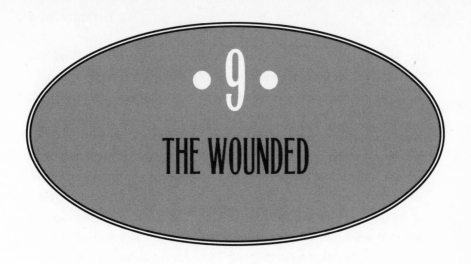

· 9 ·

THE WOUNDED

When I got a little better, I learned that my leg had been amputated by the said Bailey while so drunk that he had to lean against the table to keep from falling; there are many living witnesses to testify to this fact.

LT. J. R. BOYLE

ESPERATE CONDITIONS IN THE field hospitals continued after the battle. A curious preacher—probably one of the battlefield's first tourists—traveled from York Springs to look over the field of battle. July 5 was his second day in the area.

I started out Chambersburg Street on a tour of observation. In looking over the ground many little hillocks could be seen where the dead had been covered with earth just where they fell and died. In the Theological Seminary, I found all the rooms filled with the wounded. Going beyond I passed over the open ground in the direction of a large stone barn on the Chambersburg pike. The landscape here was thickly dotted with those same little hillocks in every direction. As I neared the stone barn and was gazing around indifferently, I heard a voice calling and a man looking over the side of a pigsty.

He beckoned to me with his hand and as I approached cried out: "For God's sake, Chaplain, come and help us; there's no one here to do it." When I examined the situation I found that the barn above and below, the wagon shed, the tenant house, the pig sty, and the open barnyard were all crowded with badly wounded soldiers. . . . At this moment my curiosity was superseded by a sense of duty, and I began what I have since regarded as the best Sabbath day's work of my life. In the retreat during the night these men, who had been in the hands of the enemy for three days, were left behind. No relief had reached them at this early hour and I happened to be the first to come to their assistance. My first work was to carry them water, for the morning was very warm and they were all thirsty. On going to the pump I found two of them trying to fill their canteens. Both were wounded in the arm, which they carried in a sling. One pumped and the other held the canteen using their sound limbs. As the time passed, other persons strolled in and rendered aid, but it was not until about noon that any part of the hospital corps arrived. And then only one surgeon and two assistants came to render their service. In the wagon shed a few boards were laid on some trestles and the work of amputation begun. I was asked to assist in holding the limbs of the subject operated on. The heat was intense and as the men had received no treatment for three days the odor from the wounds was repulsive. One after another was placed on the scaffold, put under the influence of chloroform and while the surgeon dexterously performed the operation, I would hold the limb until it was separated from the body. During all this time I suffered no nausea from the offensive smell or ghastly sight of bloody limbs that lay at my side. In due time the ambulances came and all of these wounded men were removed to the hospital in the town. While mingling among these men at the stone barn, I entered the gangway between the stables and found my way to the rear. A number were lying there in the dark.[1]

Public buildings were in full use as field hospitals. Churches, the train depot, the Lutheran seminary, and other buildings housed the wounded and provided a place for the surgeons to work. Women served as nurses and assisted the surgeons in these spur-of-the-moment hospitals.

Sarah Montford lived on the south side of York Street, two blocks from the train station. She walked to the station with her twelve-year-old daughter, Mary, to help with the wounded. Soon after arriving at the depot and witnessing the vast number of mutilated soldiers, Mary discovered that one of the wounded was her father. Injured in battle, he had a gaping wound in his side, the result of shrapnel.

"Father looked at me and said, 'Mary Elizabeth,' then he closed his eyes," she wrote in her diary.[2] "Mother told me to go home and take care of Grandma and Jennie Ann [her younger sister]." She kissed her father and obeyed.

"The wounds were of every imaginable description, and upon all parts of the person," a volunteer nurse from Philadelphia reported:

> There were wounds in the head, the breast, the abdomen, the legs, the feet, the hands; there were wounds of the flesh merely, and others affecting the vital organism; in some cases legs and arms were swept away so closely to the socket that it was impossible to gather up the cords, and hurts were necessarily cauterized or left to fester and eat away the life; in others, the face would be partially shot away, leaving, perhaps, only a single eye or row of teeth; while in others still, simply an ear, or finger, or part of the nose would be missing.[3]

Another vivid description of the grisly scenes was offered by the Reverend Bellows:

> I found my way, at the earliest moment possible, to this unwillingly neglected scene. The Place was a barn and stable. Every foot of it was occupied by a wretched sufferer, clad in ragged gray or the rebel uniform. Those above in the barn might also be said to be in heaven, as compared to those below in the stable, who might with equal truth be said to be in hell. For upon heaps of dung, reeking with rain, and tormented with vermin, the wounds still undressed, and many longing for amputation, as the happy long for food or drink, lay fair and noble youth, with evidences of gentle breeding in their fine-cast features, and hunger, despair, and death in their bright and hallow eyes. The surgeon had at length got to work among them, and limbs just cut off (one I recollect, with the heavy shoe and stocking still upon it,) lay in dreadful care in full view, about the place.[4]

During the fighting more than 650 medical officers were on duty. According to the chief medical officer of the Army of the Potomac,

Jonathan Letterman, "These officers were engaged assiduously, day and night, with little rest, until the 6th, and in the Second Corps, until the 7th of July, in attendance upon the wounded."[5] Letterman was a pioneer of the care for the wounded of the battlefield. He organized an efficient military ambulance corps and improved sanitary conditions and soldiers' diets.

One of the doctors to whom Letterman referred was Capt. John Shaw Billings, a surgeon with the Second Division, First Corps. In a letter to his wife on July 6, Billings offered a grim account of the cost of the battle: "I have been operating all day long and have got the chief part of the butchering done in a satisfactory manner. I am utterly exhausted mentally and physically, having been operating night and day and am still hard at work. I have been left here in charge of 700 wounded with no supplies and have my hands full. Our division lost terribly. Over 30-percent were killed and wounded."

Four days later Billings wrote his wife: "The orderly has just scrubbed all the blood out of my hair with castile soap and bay-rum and my scalp feels as if a steam plow had been passed through it."[6]

Letterman modestly described the labor performed by these officers as "immense." "Some of them fainted from exhaustion induced by over exertion, and others became ill from the same cause."

Of the medical staff, thirteen were wounded. W. S. Moore of the Sixty-first Ohio (Eleventh Corps) died on July 6 from wounds sustained on July 3.

In general, medical care in America was primitive in 1863. Prior to becoming an army surgeon, most Civil War doctors had never treated a gunshot wound or received any training in treating them. Many doctors had never performed surgery. Medical boards, where they did exist, allowed many to practice who were not qualified. About fourteen thousand surgeons served the armies of the Civil War; roughly, ten thousand in the Union army and four thousand with the Confederacy.

As understaffed, undertrained, often underqualified, and very usually undersupplied as they were, army surgeons performed well. In July 1863 medical knowledge had not yet embraced the use of sterile dressings, antiseptics, or sterile surgery. The medical community had yet to recognize the importance of basic hygiene and simple sanitation. For every soldier who died of battle injuries, two died from diseases such as typhoid or dysentery.

When fighting broke out, field hospitals were set up quickly and without much thought. Many times the aid stations were situated near the front lines. Sometimes the site was only a mile behind the battle lines. In the Union army, hospitals were marked with a yellow flag having a green H. It was common for some of the field hospitals to be "open air" or simply places in the woods. With more than thirty thousand wounded, it was necessary for some wounded to wait several days before a surgeon could examine their wounds and treat them.

As was the practice at the time, Civil War doctors often took over houses, churches, schools, even barns for hospitals. This is what had happened at the Weikert farm near Little Round Top.

"By this time, amputating benches had been placed about the house. I must have become inured to seeing the terrors of battle, else I could hardly have gazed upon the scenes now presented," Tillie Pierce recalled. "I was looking out of the windows facing the front yard. Near the basement door, and directly underneath the window I was at, stood one of these benches. I saw them lifting the poor men upon it, then the surgeons sawing and cutting off arms and legs, then again probing and picking bullets from the flesh. Some of the soldiers fairly begged to be taken next, so great was their suffering, and so anxious were they to obtain relief."[7]

John Shaw Billings was reassigned to the Fifth Corps. He described setting up a field hospital at Gettysburg:

There I established the hospital at a farmhouse on the side of Round Top, perhaps half a mile behind the first firing line. In the house, we found dough kneaded and nearly ready for the baking pans, which had even been greased. There was a fine fire in the stove, but nobody about the house. I got my men to separate that dough into reasonably sized lumps and slip them into the oven. Then we found a big copper boiler which we filled with water and made coffee and some soup.

In about twenty minutes the wounded began to come in, and we had about 850 before 12 o'clock that night. They all got hot coffee and hot soup, but there was not enough bread to go beyond the first hundred. The seriously wounded were in the house, and near it under the trees and in the big barn. The slightly wounded picked their own places on the outskirts. About midnight, Dr. Letterman came in and said that he had just learned that this particular place was going to be shelled early in the morning, and that we should have to move on at once. I found a place a mile to the rear, where there was plenty of water and shade, and we began to move early in the morning. Here I had an ambulance train and the work of moving was safely accomplished. Few shells began to drop near as the first train of ambulances moved off, but no one was injured.[8]

Following his service at Gettysburg, Billings went on to become one of the foremost experts on the importance of public and military hygiene. He is also credited with many other accomplishments that advanced the medical professional in the United States throughout the remainder of the nineteenth century.

Whenever possible chloroform was administered before the surgeries. Most of the screams heard in the field hospitals were from men who had just been informed that they would be losing a limb and from friends who unfortunately witnessed the plight of another under the knife and saw of the surgeon.

Apparently the surgeons at the Weikert farm had sufficient quantities of anesthetic, because Tillie Pierce marveled at the procedure: "I saw the surgeons hastily put a cattle horn over the mouths of the wounded ones, after they were placed upon the bench. At first I did not understand the meaning of this but upon inquiry, soon learned that that was their mode of administrating chloroform, in order to produce unconsciousness." Chloroform was not always effective, however, and Tillie noted that "the effect in some instances was not produced; for I saw the wounded throwing themselves wildly about, and shrieking with pain while the operation was going on."

Amputations were common because the armies used ammunition that tended to wreak severe damage on the human anatomy. These projectiles, known as minié balls, were basically an ounce of lead that was transformed during the firing process into a low-velocity misshapen mass that shattered bones upon impact or tore up a man's insides if it failed to strike bone. If a bone in an arm or leg was broken by one of these bullets, there wasn't much material left to the bone, and surgeons had little choice but to amputate the damaged limb. More than 70 percent of all injuries occurred to the extremities, so amputation was commonly performed. As a result, Civil War surgeons became quite proficient at amputation.

The wounded received care in far less than antiseptic conditions. The medical profession in 1863 did not understand or accept the concept of working on open wounds in an antiseptic environment. It was uncommon for a surgeon to wash his hands prior to touching a wounded soldier.

Blood-spattered surgical instruments were the norm. Doctors' clothing was usually soaked with blood and gore and infectious matter from prior patients. Instruments were rinsed with bloody water. Bloodied sponges or cloths were used as if they were new. Bloody knives served as scalpels. Added to this concoction of infectious bacteria were bloodied bandages, fecal matter, and urine. The result was a septic, germ-laden, deadly operating theater. After the afternoon's heavy, earth-soaking rains on July 4, the open-air field hospitals were muddy and moldy as well.

Wounds were probed with dirty fingers or instruments to determine if the bullet had torn an artery or fractured a bone. If the artery or bone was damaged, the surgeon would amputate the limb. Surgeons performed the procedure on blood-saturated work tables.

Chloroform would be administered, and the surgeon would cut into the skin with whatever scalpel was at hand. The cut would go to the bone, then a similar cut was made from the opposite side, carefully leaving a flap of skin to close over the end of the limb afterward.

Using a bone saw, the surgeon would saw through the bone. The excised end of the arm or leg would then be tossed onto a nearby pile of similarly severed extremities. These piles could become several feet high before they were removed, disposed of in a common grave or pitched into a gully.

The surgeon would tie off the arteries with horsehair, silk, or cotton threads. The end of the bone would be scraped smooth, then the flap of skin would be pulled over the exposed end of the severed arm or leg and sewn closed, leaving a drainage hole. The stump would be bandaged, and the soldier would be set aside to await consciousness. He would awaken in pain, thirsty but alive. By then the surgeon would have continued his grisly work on others. Generally, an amputation required only ten minutes' time.

Doctors operated in blood-soaked, stained coats. Some had their clothes so bloodstained that they preferred to operate bare-chested. Surgeons worked long hours, through the night, until they were exhausted. Water was always scarce, so the surgeons did not wash their hands or their instruments. Any cleansing of the instruments was superficial at best.

If the patient survived the surgery, he stood a chance of developing surgical fever or gangrene. Pyemia was common and deadly, as were blood poisoning, sepsis, and septicemia.

Tillie Pierce's account of her experience at the Weikert farm includes all of this: "To the south of the house, and just outside of the yard, I noticed a pile of limbs higher than the fence. It was a ghastly sight! Gazing upon these, too often the trophies of the amputating bench, I could have no other feeling, than that the whole scene was one of cruel butchery."

The quick work of cold-hearted triage practiced at Gettysburg was described by Capt. John Gregory Bishop Adams of the Nineteenth Massachusetts. He was wounded on July 2 when his regiment was brought up to help save the Third Corps, which was being mauled during the Confederate thrust against the left side of the Union line that day. Adams was carried to the field hospital of the Third Corps. He recalled: "An assistant surgeon was in charge and I asked him to look at my wound. He did, and said that I could not live twenty-four hours. I suggested that he stop the blood, as he might be mistaken, but he had no time to waste on me and went along. Upon examination I found that I was wounded in three places, and all were bleeding badly, but I could not tell where the bullets had entered or come out."[9]

The assistant surgeon's diagnosis placed Adams with those who had mortal wounds. One of the men who had carried him to the aid station heard the report and took it back to the regiment. After a short while, a lieutenant from the regiment visited Adams, bringing him coffee and taking a blanket from a wounded Confederate to make Adams more comfortable. That night he was moved to the Second Corps hospital, because it was farther from the fighting. During the removal, his wounds opened. After withdrawing about a mile, he and some others were placed beside the road and abandoned until noon the next day.

That afternoon, when the Confederate bombardment preceded Pickett's Charge, shots whistled over the cluster of wounded men that included Adams. Shells burst overhead and on all sides. As Adams recalled, "Solid shot ploughed up the ground and I expected my time had come. Many of the wounded could crawl away, but I could not." Suddenly he found himself in the way of a mad rush of civilians from the front and, as Adams termed them, "skedaddlers."

Adams was near a gateway and called out for help. Some who paused to assist him were killed in the shelling. Finally, an officer heard him and had some men fetch him. They carried him to the rear of a barn, placed him in an ambulance, and started for the rear.

At an aid station, Adams was again placed on the ground, this time on a bit of hillside near Cub Run. In charge of the field hospital was Adams's regimental surgeon. When the doctor inspected the wounds, he discovered that one bullet had entered the groin and not come out and another had passed through his right hip. He told Adams the wounds were bad, "very bad."

The Nineteenth Massachusetts was in the center of the Union line for Pickett's Charge. Afterward Adams was joined by seven officers from the regiment, all lying side by side. When Adams had fallen the day before, there were fifteen officers and men in his company. After Pickett's Charge only six remained. Stories of the fighting lifted his spirits, but the next day he was distraught to learn that the surgeon did not expect he would survive his wounds, and so he did not allow Adams to be moved from the hospital.

The only solace Adams received came in the form of another wounded man from his regiment who joined him at the hospital. The two had a direct view of two tables used for amputations and watched as several men they knew were laid on them and removed "minus a leg or an arm."

All around him wounded men groaned constantly, and dead men were lifted up and carried past him. Next to Adams was a young boy in much pain, but the lad barely made a sound. Then one night the youngster told Adams that he believed he might die that night. When Adams awoke, the boy was dead. "He lay by my side until afternoon, before they could find time to take him away," Adams recalled. "I had forgotten to ask his name, and no one knew him. His grave no doubt bears the mark 'unknown' and the records of his regiment say, 'missing in action.'"

Adams himself received little attention, and during the time he lay on the ground, he noted how busy the surgeons were. He stayed there for six days, and the only individuals who treated his wounds were the injured comrades around him. They ensured that his canteen was always full, and he used the water to wash out the wounds, hoping to prevent inflammation. "Do not think that I blame the surgeons," he commented in his 1899 memoir. "No nobler men ever lived than composed the medical staff of the Army of the Potomac; but there were twenty thousand wounded men, Union and Rebel, on the field of Gettysburg, and the cases requiring amputation must receive attention first."

Not all the men who faced amputation did so eagerly. One corporal told his colleague that he would not allow the surgeons to remove his leg, because he did not want to go home to his wife and be a burden for her. Years later his friend noted: "He was certainly earnest in every word he said. When the surgeons went over to him the second time, intending to cut off his leg, he was dead."[10]

Conditions in the field hospitals were often desperate and hellish. Regarding the food given the wounded, Adams commented that the first thing that tasted good to him after six days of convalescence was a pot of chicken broth that two visitors from his regiment brought to him.

ABRAHAM BRIAN was a free black and a widower with five children. In 1857 he purchased a twelve-acre farm on Cemetery Ridge. He married for a third time and, with his wife, Elizabeth, moved his large family into a modest clapboard farmhouse adjacent to Ziegler's Grove. The house had a fireplace and few windows. Brian farmed his land and had a horse and a cow. He raised wheat, barley, and hay in his small but fertile fields and maintained a bountiful apple and peach orchard near his house. His hard work provided a humble lifestyle for his large family.

Union troops appeared on his doorstep late in the evening of July 1 and ordered the Brian family to leave. Several days later Brian returned and found his home ransacked, the walls riddled with bullet and shell holes, the windows smashed, and his meager furniture dragged into the yard. His fences were destroyed, the crops had been trampled and mangled, and the orchard trees were ruined. To top it off, the pasture west of the barn was now a huge graveyard. Despite the hardships involved in repairing and restoring his home, he continued to work and farm the land until 1869, when he moved into town and found work at a hotel.

Brian filed a claim with the government for the damages to his farm property totaling $1,028. Unlike most claimants, he was compensated, but he received only $15. He died in 1875 and was buried in Gettysburg next to his wives.[11]

When Isaac Lightner was finally able to return home, he found his house was being used as a hospital and his family huddled in the barn. When the Lightners were allowed back into their house, the stench was so horrific that they could not live there again.

Lt. J. R. Boyle, Twelfth South Carolina, described his experience in a Confederate field hospital in his diary:

> My driver in the wagon was a full-fledged Irishman, from a Mississippi regiment; he appeared very sorry for me, and when I groaned would say, "Poor boy, I hope we'll soon reach your hospital." We found it at last, I was lifted out and put on a pile of straw. I knew my leg would have to be amputated, but did not wish it done by the surgeon of our regiment, Dr. Bailey. I wanted Dr. Evins, the brigade surgeon, to perform the operation, and, with tears streaming down my cheeks, begging him to do it, which he promised he would; I was given something and laid out until next afternoon—was too near dead to know how the night passed.

Boyle did not get his wound cared for immediately. "The next day I was lifted upon a table, which roused me a little, chloroform was placed to my nostrils and I felt as if I rose up and flew away," he recalled. "When I next remembered anything, I was on a pile of straw on my back in a tent, my right leg gone; some parties were whispering that I was gone, no chance for me; I felt that my time had come and was resigned to my fate, but thought it hard." The young lieutenant listened to the cannonading of July 3, but he had no food until the morning of July 4, when a comrade brought him some nourishment. "The first I had taken," Boyle noted. "And I began to get a little strength."

That morning he realized that the army was withdrawing. "We were left to the tender mercies of five or six well men of our regiment, left to nurse and dress our wounds, until the enemy should take charge of us," he recorded. Then Boyle described his capture: "On the 5th or 6th, a body of awkward Yankee cavalry, with drawn sabres, came charging and captured us in the name of the United States."

Boyle also learned how his surgery was performed:

> When I got a little better, I learned that my leg had been amputated by the said Bailey while so drunk that he had to lean against the table to keep from falling; there are many living witnesses to testify to this fact; I suppose he deemed me a good subject to experiment on—amputated my limb twice, and left me such an imperfect stump that I would never wear an artificial limb, but will go on crutches the balance of my life, having already been on them 25 years.

He described the misery of being a captured.

> We lay nearly naked and starved for some time before the enemy gave us any attention except to capture us; could hear the guns of our men as they sullenly retreated to the Potomac, and our hearts felt sad to think of them; the days were very hot and the nights cool. Our covering consisted of blankets picked up on the battlefield, and so full of lice that we could lie on our backs and see them almost move the covering; we became polluted—hair, beard, rags. I mention these things in order that those who were not there and the children who have grown up since may know what war is, and learn to cultivate peace.

Boyle notes how his comrades would suddenly break into song: "Poor wounded soldiers, there they lay; frequently someone would start to sing, when all who were able joined in, and the little camp resounded with strains of sacred music, praise to the great Creator; the words of a popular piece they sang was 'Joyfully, joyfully onward, we're bound for the land of bright spirits above,' etc."

Finally, Boyle was taken from the field hospital to Baltimore:

> On the morning of the 17th, the Yankees began to move us away; I was placed in an ambulance and driven carefully over a rough turnpike to Gettysburg—if I suffered, it was not the fault of my driver, for he used the utmost care to keep me from jolting; good, kindhearted soul, I hope the Lord blessed him for it.

Arriving at Gettysburg, we were placed in box cars, and while the train was standing, sweet women, ladies from Baltimore, Sisters of Charity, had refreshments of all kinds, distributing to us poor sufferers; buckets of milk punch were passed along the train and every poor reb allowed to help himself, if able—if not, kind hands lifted him up and held it to his dying lips.[12]

During the next several weeks after the battle, Sallie Myers cared for her patients at the nearby church. She also brought some of the less injured men to her home and cared for them during their convalescence. "These were bitter days," she recalled much later. "But memories of them are softened when one considers the friendships that were made."

Just three days after the Confederates retreated from Gettysburg, the U.S. Christian Commission took over Schick's store to use for a supply and distribution center. During this time, the Stoevers fed a countless number of hungry soldiers in their backyard.

In his 1891 memoirs, Maj. John H. Brinton described the scene at Gettysburg when he arrived:

Immediately after the battle of Gettysburg, I was ordered by the Surgeon-General to go there on special duty. . . . Arrived at Gettysburg . . . and busied myself for several days in visiting the hospitals in the towns, in the churches and public buildings, and also the large field hospitals which had been organized outside of the town. These hospitals were generally in good condition and accommodated large numbers of wounded. A good many of the enemy's wounded were gathered in one hospital under the care of their surgeons. . . . Operations were being performed at the operating tent under the trees. He [a Confederate surgeon] was about to amputate a limb. . . . I was very warmly received by the Confederate surgeon . . . whom I was glad to meet with. Our loss at Gettysburg was heavy but as the battle was fought on our land and as we remained masters of the field, we had every opportunity for care for the wounded in large hospitals and for their proper transportation.[13]

Unlike so many other surgeons, Brinton had been formally educated and trained, having been graduated from the University of Pennsylvania and Jefferson College. He went on to serve on U. S. Grant's staff.

Because of the continuing clashes between the two armies, there was a never-ending stream of wounded soldiers. As the number of wounded grew, more and more buildings were pressed into service as hospitals. From churches and the courthouse to farmhouses and barns and even open fields, anyplace and everyplace was used to shelter both the wounded and the work of the army surgeons.

The Army of Northern Virginia carried very few hospital tents, so the Southerners relied more on barns, farmhouses, outbuildings, sheds, houses, and public buildings as places to care for their wounded. When Lee ordered the retreat from Gettysburg, more than sixty-eight hundred wounded soldiers were left behind. The total number of Confederates wounded in the battle is debatable because surgeons were under orders not "to report slight wounds not preventing duty."

After Lee's army withdrew, about eighteen hundred wounded Confederates were added to the Union field hospitals. The Second Corps hospital received about one thousand of these soldiers; the rest were scattered throughout the other corps hospitals. The other five thousand Confederates were left in about twenty-five field hospitals strewn across the fields around Gettysburg and farther west and north of the town.

Union army surgeons practiced a form of triage. A surgeon or assistant surgeon assessed the wounded as they were brought into the field hospital. He determined who would likely benefit from medical treatment. Patients fell into three categories: (1) minor injuries; (2) injuries to the legs, feet, arms, and hands; and (3) severe injuries to the head or torso. The middle group received the immediate attention of the surgeons, because these were the injuries most in need of the surgeon's craft—that is, amputation.

Injuries to the head or torso (category 3) were considered mortal wounds, and those injured soldiers were moved to an area where they might be as comfortable as they could while they died. Minor injuries (category 1) were treated after the more severely wounded patients had been treated.

Unlike the temporary hospitals set up in the public buildings, churches, and homes in the town of Gettysburg, which had basic supplies for the care of the wounded, field hospitals were not usually well supplied. On July 7 it was reported that the wounded from both armies were lying "around in the woods, with scarcely a blanket to cover or lay under them, and all soaked with the daily drenching rains, with not even a sheltering tent to protect them from the weather, and many of them perfectly helpless from wounds."[14] Scattered about Adams County in about a twenty-five-mile area surrounding the town, many of these temporary field hospitals lacked much, including potable water.

The Second Corps field hospital was positioned about three miles south of Gettysburg. On July 4 more than four thousand wounded were clustered here for medical attention. It might be hours or even days before a wound was examined then dressed or treated.

Field hospitals in barns featured the always pungent smell of animal wastes, which was a natural breeding ground for horseflies, mosquitoes, and maggots—all of which did their share to spread infectious bacteria. Add to that the putrid odors of rotting human flesh and smelly body odors. From the accounts of both Confederate and Federal soldiers who were treated at these makeshift camps, it is clear that the conditions were horrific at best.

Although there were competent doctors at some of these hospitals, the evidence indicates that there were others who should not have been permitted anywhere near a wounded man. Misdiagnoses occurred often.

Dr. W. W. Keen of Philadelphia described the conditions of a Civil War–era operation:

> We operated in old blood-stained and often pus-stained coats, the veterans of a hundred fights. . . . We used undisinfected instruments from undisinfected plush-lined cases, and still worse, used marine sponges which had been used in prior pus cases and had been only washed in tap water. If a sponge or an instrument fell on the floor it was washed and squeezed in a basin of tap water and used as if it were clean. Our silk to tie blood vessels was undisinfected. . . . The silk with which we sewed up all wounds was undisinfected. If there was any difficulty in threading the needle we moistened it with bacteria laden saliva, and rolled it between bacteria-infected fingers. We dressed the wounds with clean but undisinfected sheets, shirts, tablecloths, or other old soft linen rescued from the family ragbag. We had no sterilized gauze dressing, no gauze sponges. . . . We knew nothing about antiseptics and therefore used none.[15]

Personal hygiene was poor at the field hospitals. Latrines were supposed to be dug, and each day the collected material was to be covered with six inches of soil. This procedure, however, was not routinely followed. It did not take long for human waste to contaminate the area. Fresh springs or small streams, potential sources of drinking water, became quickly contaminated.

This rural Pennsylvania area experienced a sudden influx of 150,000 men and countless animals. It was more than the region's resources could accommodate. Potable water was in short supply.

In this unbalanced environment, insects spread diseases of all kinds. While the minié bullets were destructive and took many lives, disease was the real enemy of the Civil War.[16] Bugs of all kinds—from maggots to flies, fleas to lice, were part of the everyday life of the Civil War soldier.

Insects were a factor in food spoilage, yet the soldiers still ate it. Regularly soldiers reported their meals were seldom motionless, routinely filled with insects that had already devoured their share of the food. If a soldier's meat ration was not infested when he received it, it was soon likely to become bug-ridden. One Yankee soldier related, "Fresh-killed beef . . . had to be eaten with the odor and warmth of blood still in under penalty of finding it flyblown before the next meal."[17]

Of course, meat was not the only food likely to attract insects. One disgruntled Union soldier complained, "We live so mean here the hard bread is all worms and the meat stinks like hell . . . and rice two or three times a week & worms as long as your finger. I liked rice once but God damn the stuff now."

Probably the most noted havens for those pesky insects during the war were simple flour-and-water biscuits or crackers known as "hardtack." One variety of hardtack was moldy or wet, a condition that likely resulted unintentionally from exposure to the weather prior to distribution or from being packaged too soon after baking. The second variety of the food was rock-hard, which was the ration's namesake. The third variety was issued complete with insects. Soldiers called them "worm-castles." They were infested with worms, weevils, or maggots. One man commented: "These weevils were, in my experience, more abundant than the maggots. They were a little, slim brown bug an eighth of an inch in length, and were great bores on a small scale, having the ability to completely riddle the hardtack. I believe they never interfered with the hardest variety."[18]

Sometimes the soldiers heated the hardtack as a way to kill the bugs, which took care of the weevils, but they did not budge from their position. Soldiers preferred to eat their hardtack at night so they could not see the bugs. Those who dunked the hardtack into their coffee soon found bugs swimming across the top of the liquid.

Bugs were common at the field hospitals. Compounding matters was the sheer number of corpses and carcasses rotting under the hot summer sun and drenched by the regular rains. The humidity was perfect to send the insects into a feeding frenzy, all the while spreading diseases.

Maggots were common on meat, hardtack, and other rations. Maggots also fed off the wounds of the soldiers. Surgeon C. S. Wood of the Sixty-sixth New York wrote of the problems his patients had with flies and maggots in the hospital wards: "In 12 hours the wound is literally covered with maggots and in 24 hours the stump looks as though a swarm of bees had settled into it." Another surgeon noted: "The maggot does damage in the wound, not by attacking living tissue, but by the annoyance created by the continued sensation of crawling."

Unknown at the time to the Union surgeons were the benefits of these maggot infestations. Doctors and caregivers tried their best to eradicate the flies. They used netting and chloroform injections into the stumps of amputees. Confederate doctors tending gangrene cases in a prison stockade at Chattanooga did not have these supplies, but they made an important observation: maggot-infested wounds healed quickly.

It did not take long for maggots to find decaying flesh. At Gettysburg, their next meal was always nearby, and they often found their dinner before a wound could be treated. Capt. John Gregory Bishop Adams recalled: "My wounds were in a frightful condition. They had not been dressed, and the maggots were crawling into them."

While offering her services as a nurse to the wounded soldiers, Sarah Broadhead commented: "I procured a basin and water and went into a room where there were seven or eight. . . . I asked for his wound and he pointed toward his leg. Such a horrible sight I have never seen and I hope never to see again. His leg was all covered with worms."[19]

Under such conditions it is no surprise that dysentery,[20] diarrhea, dyspepsia,[21] enteritis,[22] and other such diseases played havoc with the lives of the soldiers. Nor were officers exempted from such misery. Robert E. Lee himself was described as being extremely ill with dysentery during the entire battle of Gettysburg. He was said to be so weak at times that he could not ride his horse. Some have argued that his health may have affected his decisions throughout the battle.

Dysentery was listed as the cause of death for many soldiers. During the war, the Union army reported 1,739,135 cases of diarrhea and dysentery with 44,558 resulting deaths. Confederate records are not as exact.

As EARLY as the evening of July 1, medical director Jonathan Letterman had supplies, tents, and provisions shipped to Adams County. He allowed his regimental surgeons to perform their grisly work at the many temporary field hospitals, but he realized that the numerous hospitals made support difficult on an already overburdened supply train from Maryland. On July 5 Letterman ordered the establishment of a general hospital in the Gettysburg area. The orders provided transportation and supplies to the site for treatment of both Union and Confederate soldiers.

The army selected the George Wolf farm as the site for the general hospital. The Wolf property was about one and a half miles east of Gettysburg on the York pike (Route 30). The farm was adjacent to the railroad tracks and the main road. Arriving trains could deliver a continual flow of supplies for the camp and transport convalescents to hospitals in Philadelphia, Baltimore, and Washington. Wolf's land had good drainage, water, and a readily available source of firewood. Work on the camp commenced, and it was named in honor of the medical director—Camp Letterman.

The hot, muggy weather, the moans of the wounded, the shortages of food and supplies, the missing residents, the disruption of regular services like mail, telegraph, and the railroads all affected the massive recovery work that was undertaken. "The private houses of the town were, many of them, hospitals; the little red flags hung from the upper windows," one nurse said.[23] And there was so much more to do.

• 10 •

THE SECOND WEEK OF JULY

Our horses could hardly be made to proceed on account of the horrid objects lying about them—dead men and horses here and there; men digging graves and others bring[ing] the bodies to them! There was a little group sitting over a fire, trying to cook their meat, in the midst of all these scenes.

SISTER MARIE LOUISE CAULFIELD

ON THE MORNING OF July 5 some straggling Confederates made their way to Emmitsburg, Maryland. About ten miles southwest of Gettysburg, just below the Mason-Dixon Line was the home of the Daughters of Charity of Saint Vincent de Paul.[1] The retreating Rebels stopped at the central house.

While they savored the warm breakfast offered to them there, the Southerners described for the sisters and Father James F. Burlando the massive battle that had just occurred at Gettysburg. The news of the fighting was not a total surprise, as everyone had heard the massive cannonading from the north for the past several days.

Father Burlando and Mother Ann Simeon Norris decided that some of the sisters should go to Gettysburg to do what they could for the recovery effort. They gathered bandages, sponges, clothing, and other things for the wounded, placing them in baskets, and readied a wagon for the trip. A total of fourteen sisters left for Gettysburg in two vehicles—Father Burlando rode in a carriage with two sisters. Twelve sisters followed, riding as comfortably as they could in a long wagon over the muddy, bumpy road. The recent rains as well as the heavy usage of the roadways by the armies made the road nearly impassible for the vehicles.

Two miles from Gettysburg the small party found that Federal troops had blocked the road. Trees had been chopped down to make a zigzag fence in the road. Suddenly Union soldiers ran to a fence along the road and raised their rifles, ready to fire. When they realized the travelers were nuns, they lowered their guns.

Father Burlando, a white handkerchief tied to his cane, approached the pickets. After a short while, the troops permitted him and the sisters to pass. The soldiers removed their caps and bowed their heads as the nuns passed. Within a short distance the sisters witnessed the massive destruction, the fields filled with horror. They saw men lying dead along the road. Some lay dead by the side of their fallen horses. The wagon driver had to maneuver the teams carefully so as not to roll over the corpses in the road.

"The rains had filled the roads with water, and here it was red with blood: our carriage wheels rolling through blood!" Sister Marie Louise Caulfield recalled. "Our horses could hardly be made to proceed on account of the horrid objects lying about them—dead men and horses here and there; men digging graves and others bring[ing] the bodies to them! There was a little group sitting over a fire, trying to cook their meat, in the midst of all these scenes."[2]

The band of sisters most certainly had to be overwhelmed with the tragic scene before them: acres of beautiful farmland now filled with devastation, bodies of soldiers and horses strewn about with thousands of guns, swords, and accoutrements. For as far as they could see from their wagons, there was little more than ruin everywhere.

Sister Camilla O'Keefe observed, "The Battlefield was a very extensive space on either side of the road, the east was General George Meade's stand, the west General James Longstreet's. On both sides were men digging pits and putting the bodies down by the dozens. One newly made pit contained fifty bodies of Confederates. By a large tree in another spot might be pointed out where the body of such a General lay until removed to another location. In this frightful condition we found the Battle grounds of that fearful Battle of Gettysburg."

Despite the devastation and difficulty of travel, the Daughters of Charity pressed on. By 1 P.M. they had arrived in town. They stopped at McClellan's Hotel in the northeast corner of the town square.[3] The hotelkeepers gave the nuns immediate use of the parlors.

The sisters wanted to start work immediately, and accompanying Father Burlando, they went to the nearby hospitals. They visited the courthouse, the churches, and the public schools. They bandaged the wounded, offered drinks, and tried to comfort the injured.

Afterward they returned to McClellan's. Father Burlando decided that he would return to Emmitsburg with two of the sisters. Twelve would remain in Gettysburg to continue their work. They took total control of the parlors of the hotel, using them as nursing quarters. After an evening meal, the nuns returned to the wounded.

"Impossible to describe the condition of those poor wounded men, the weather was warm and very damp for some days after the battle," Sister Camilla said. "They were covered with vermin and actually that we could hardly bear this part of the filth."[4]

When the sisters returned to the hotel, they slept on the floor of the parlor but did not get much sleep. The next day, Mother Norris sent beds and coverings as well as food, which included cooked hams, coffee, and tea. Soon nuns from Baltimore and the surrounding areas arrived at Gettysburg and joined the Emmitsburg sisters in tending the wounded. Daily operations at a number of nearby schools were suspended, which allowed the nuns to respond to the emergency in Gettysburg and be available for help with the wounded.

For days the sisters worked in the temporary hospitals. One of these hospitals was the Gettysburg Catholic church, Saint Francis Xavier, on the north side of West High Street. The hospital was filled with mutilated men whom the nuns nursed and tended. In the church the wounded lay on the pews, in the aisles, and under the pews.

Sister Marie Louise noted, "All kinds of filth and stench, added to their misery, for already gangrenous wounds had begun to infect the air, but no complaint came from these poor men!"[5]

Many of the men had piles of maggots on them. Lockjaw also set in on several men. The nuns used spoons to give them liquids.

The sisters traveled through Gettysburg and the surrounding area to the scattered field hospitals. They requested dry straw from the area farmers so that the soldiers would not have to lie on the muddy ground. They used jellies to make drinks and provided, of all things, combs. The nuns used hair combs to remove the lice and maggots. It was not long until some of the sisters had the vermin on their clothing.

"We noticed one large man whose leg had to be taken off. No other part of his body was in such a condition that the big maggots were crawling on the ground on which they crept from the body," Sister Camilla noted.[6]

Many surgeons who knew of the sisters preferred them as their nurses. Because of their skill and experience in caring for the wounded, the nuns provided better care than a civilian nurse or another wounded soldier who was recovering from his wounds. When the sisters arrived at one of the field hospitals, the surgeon in charge took them to the other ladies attending to the wounded and announced: "Ladies, and you men nurses also, here are the Daughters of Charity, come to save our men. They will give all the directions here: you are only required to observe them."

The Daughters of Charity were not without their critics. Rumors quickly circulated through the town and the countryside that the sisters were baptizing or converting the wounded to Catholicism—and they were—but their charity and caring were more often recognized and appreciated. It was also noted that they cared for the wounded of both armies, indifferent to the color of anyone's uniform, only concerned with providing aid and comfort to the wounded.

"What? Good God! Can those Sisters be the person whose religion we always run down?" an elderly man asked John McClellan. He had come to town shortly after the battle to look for his soldier son. He feared his son had been wounded or killed.

"Yes," McClellan told the visitor. "They are the very persons that we often run down by those who know nothing of their charity."

The old man sat on a bench in front of the hotel with other bystanders and watched as the sisters worked feverishly, loading a wagon with supplies, clothing, and food for delivery to the wounded in a field hospital.

McClellan often heard such remarks from those who witnessed the nuns' work with the wounded. They always swore that they would never again believe anything "wrong of persons doing what those Sisters have been doing around the battle grounds of Gettysburg."

As part of their mission of caring and nursing the wounded, the sisters spoke of their religion and inquired of baptism. They were not proselytizing the soldiers but rendering pastoral care and spiritual assistance as they responded to requests from the wounded men for reading material and religious articles.[7]

A dying old soldier rebuffed a nun every time she showed any kindness toward him. Finally, as he weakened, her perseverance caused him to show some civility. Realizing he was in danger of dying, the sister spoke to him of baptism. The old soldier was immediately displeased and told her he was too old to be plagued in that manner. During the next two weeks, at every possible occasion, the nun mentioned baptism. Each time he rejected her.

On the last evening of his life, the sister was ready to leave him. With her rosary in hand, she removed the medal of Mary she wore and slipped it quietly under his pillow without the old soldier seeing her. As she left him, she prayed, "I can do no more for this man; I leave him to you."

The next morning the nun returned, and he asked her for a drink. Then he said, "Sister, I want no breakfast today, but I wish to be baptized."

"Well," the sister said. "Be very sorry for your sins."

"Oh," he said. "I have cried over them all the night, and also for my obstinacy toward your kindness. Will you forgive me?"[8]

Tears filled his eyes as the nun baptized him. Then he slipped away.

The sisters baptized many soldiers from both armies while they were in Gettysburg. At the requests of the soldiers, the nuns baptized the wounded men into the Catholic Church. "There were 60 of the Confederates that were baptized," Sister Camilla said.

The nuns soon learned how to get supplies from the commissaries. It amused them when they were asked if they wanted the supplies for the Catholic Church hospital.

"'No,' they replied. 'We want them for the Methodist Church Hospital.' The officer would look at them with a kind of smile, but also a look of surprise on his face."[9]

As the days went on, the sisters' work of caring for the wounded steadily progressed. Wounded Confederates, when well enough, were taken under guard as prisoners to a holding area. The Union wounded were transported to other hospitals.

The nuns were granted passage wherever they wanted to go by the provost, including the prisons. "Yes the Daughters of Charity have my confidence," he said. As a result, a great many of the convalescing soldiers and officers were reading Catholic books, obviously gifts from the sisters.

The Daughters of Charity from Emmitsburg remained in Gettysburg until most of the wounded were transferred to the newly established Camp Letterman or transported by railroad to hospitals in Baltimore, Philadelphia, and other cities. As their work ended, the sisters boarded a wagon to return to Emmitsburg. Through their work of caring and nursing the wounded of both armies, the nuns earned respect for themselves and their religion from many of the town's residents and the soldiers and officers of both armies.

The Daughters of Charity was just one example of aid that began to pour into Gettysburg. As word spread about the battle and its aftermath, supplies and assistance were sent from across the region.

DOCTORS WORKED with a shortage of supplies at the field hospitals, at least during their initial first few days. John Shaw Billings described the shortages at his field hospital:

> As usually happens, about the second day it began to rain and rained continuously for five days, and the supplies were slow in coming. Various State auxiliary associations brought fresh bread, mutton, fruits, etc., for their State regiments, but there were none for the regular troops. Finally, there came along a wagon from the Fire Department of Baltimore. They said: "This is just the kind of place we want to find, that don't belong to any State." Baltimore was rather neutral. After the wagon had been unloaded, they informed me that they had packed one box for the surgeon. I got the benefit of that box, and it was most judiciously packed.[10]

As the commissions set up and offered their services, to a large degree the burden was lessened on the women of Gettysburg who volunteered for nursing duties. This supplemental aid also relieved them from many cooking and baking chores.

Both the U.S. Sanitary Commission and the Christian Commission arrived on the scene soon after the battle ended. In addition to bringing in supplies for the military casualties, the commissions provided food for the civilians. Fannie Buehler recalled, "For some days, fresh meat was not to be had, but those that had wounded could order from the Sanitary Commission and get as much as they needed, by paying for it."[11]

Yet the lack of food was a persistent problem at the field hospitals. Generally speaking, feeding the wounded was an afterthought. "A great difficulty always exists in having food for the wounded," Jonathan Letterman observed. On July 4 more than thirty thousand rations were made available for the wounded in the hospitals. By July 5 more food was delivered to the injured and convalescent. Letterman noted, "Some of the hospitals were supplied by the commissaries of the corps to which they belonged."[12]

On July 1 two supply wagons of the Sanitary Commission had arrived with the headquarters' train at Cemetery Hill. They carried brandy, beef soup, sponges, chloroform, lint, and bandages. The vehicles were moved to the field hospitals to which the wounded were first being brought. After they were emptied, the wagons were taken to Frederick to resupply.

Supplying the hospitals had been inadvertently complicated by Meade. He ordered that the medical supplies be kept in the rear, because he was determined to keep the ammunition supply lines open. Thus medical supplies were kept well back from the front. On July 2 a medical officer returning from Washington with supplies was ordered away from the battlefield.[13]

Although the fighting at Gettysburg ended July 3, tents for the hospitals established in the open fields and woods were not generally available until two days later. The lack of supplies and additional shelters required the doctors and surgeons to rely solely on the smaller medicine wagons that accompanied ambulances.

The Twelfth Corps, however, inexplicably avoided or ignored the restrictions placed on the rest of the Army of the Potomac. Its record after Gettysburg suggests what might have been accomplished had the rest of Meade's army not been handicapped by his order to keep the medical wagons to the rear. The Twelfth managed to hold on to its normal complement of hospital wagons; none were held back from the battlefield. As a result, the medical officers of the Twelfth Corps were able to evacuate their wounded from the field, bathe, dress, and feed them, all within six hours at the end of the fighting on July 3.[14]

Although Meade's restrictions limited the quantity of medical supplies available during the fighting at Gettysburg, ambulances worked freely. According to Jonathan Letterman, of the more than 14,000 wounded, none who were within Union lines were left on the field. The 650 officers and 3,000 drivers and stretcher-bearers of the ambulance corps went about their tasks under fire. Of this number of men, only 5 were killed and 17 wounded. In removing the 12,000 from the battlefield where the ambulances could reach them, a total of eight vehicles were damaged and a number of horses were either killed or wounded. Nevertheless, Letterman noted that since the battle lasted three days, the work of the ambulance corps was not as intense as it had been at the 1862 battle of Antietam and no serious difficulties developed.[15]

By July 22 the Reverend Dr. Gordon Winslow of the U.S. Sanitary Commission had visited twenty-four Confederate camps and recorded a total of 5,452 wounded Southerners receiving treatment. In most cases their wounds were considered severe. Winslow stated, "Amputations and resections are frequent." He evaluated the Confederate surgeons as "intelligent and attentive," but the conditions of the treatment facilities were deplorable: "The hospitals are generally in barns, outhouses, and dilapidated tents. Some few cares are in dwellings. I cannot speak favorable of their camp police. Often there is a deplorable want of cleanliness. Especially in barns and outhouses, vermin and putrid matter are disgustingly offensive."

Dr. Theodore S. Dimon of Auburn, New York, responded to the call for surgeons to care for the wounded. From Philadelphia he traveled by rail to Columbia. The bridge there had been burned several weeks earlier to prevent Jubal Early's army from crossing the Susquehanna River. Dimon was ferried across the river in a rowboat. He arrived in Gettysburg on July 12 and noted:

The first thing I noticed on arriving at the town was the relief tents of the Sanitary Commission. The station house of the railroad was burned. Such wounded as could bear transportation were brought to the trains in ambulances, there were subjected to delay before the trains were ready, sometimes even being taken back again to the field hospitals, some miles distant, when they were too late or some occurrence prevented the arrival or departure of the expected train.

The Sanitary Commission, in default of any provision by the Government to remedy this, pitched relief tents at the station and provided bedding, food and surgical attendance so that the wounded could remain comfortably at the starting point without being again and again moved over the roads in ambulances or kept waiting in uncomfortable positions, and without opportunity for relief of evacuations and other necessities of their condition.[16]

Dimon was sent to the United States Hotel in town where about two hundred soldiers, mostly from New York, were convalescing. "There were beds in most of the rooms and the regular cooking arrangements of a hotel with a supply of hydrant water. But every part and parcel of the premises were disordering and filthy inside and outside of the building," he observed. These men had been wounded on July 1, but their wounds had been neglected until July 5. Finally they were collected in this building and were receiving care from two nurses from the Christian Commission. Dimon remained in Gettysburg for several weeks, caring for the wounded and noting the need for better burials for those who succumbed to their wounds.

In the meantime, work progressed at Camp Letterman. The army's general hospital was ready by mid-July and staffed with surgeons, nurses, cooks, quartermasters, and supply clerks. Infantrymen were detailed as camp guards to watch over both supplies and hospitalized Confederate prisoners.

Each tent in Camp Letterman held nearly forty folding cots with mattresses and linens. This simple bedding was a luxury to the wounded who had lain on the hard ground for days. Nurses bathed and fed their patients. A large cookhouse was set up in the woods in the middle of the camp and supplied soups, stews, and warm bread. The army erected warehouse tents near the railroad to accommodate the supplies arriving by railroad.

A steady stream of ambulances brought injured Federal and Confederate soldiers to the camp. Each wounded man was assigned to a bed. Sophronia Bucklin was one of the first nurses posted to Camp Letterman:

The hospital lay in the rear of a deep wood, in a large open field a mile and a half from Gettysburg, and overlooking it, the single file of rail which connected the battletown with the outer world. . . . The hospital tents were set in rows, five hundred of them, seeming like great fluttering pairs of white wings, brooding peacefully over those up between these rows in order that they might dry quickly after summer rains. The ground, now sodded, soon to be hardened by many feet, was the only floor in the wards.[17]

The army also established a temporary morgue and cemetery near the camp. An army chaplain quickly managed soldier deaths and conducted a Christian burial for each man who died.

Agents of the U.S. Sanitary Commission and U.S. Christian Commission arrived at Camp Letterman to provide both nursing care as well as religious comfort. Surgeons continued to work around the clock while treating the seriously wounded. Ambulatory cases were set aside for transfer to hospitals in nearby cities.

By late July Camp Letterman was filled to capacity, eventually housing more than sixteen hundred patients. Hundreds more were still treated by the army medical staff in some of the temporary field hospitals in Gettysburg's churches and homes.

Despite the ever-present threat of infection and the effects of poor diet, most of Camp Letterman's patients endured the surgeon's knife and survived their ordeal. While the army medical staff labored in the camp, members of the Sanitary Commission worked near the temporary railway depot. They assisted in transporting the wounded bound for city hospitals, but transportation was limited because only one railroad line served Gettysburg, and there were long waits between train arrivals.

A Sanitary Commission volunteer described the care given the wounded at Camp Letterman:

The surgeon in charge of our camp, with his faithful dresser and attendants, looked after all their wounds, which were often in a most shocking state, particularly among the rebels. Every evening and morning they were dressed. Often the men would say, "That feels good, I haven't had my wound so well dressed since I was hurt." Something cool to drink is the first thing asked for after the long dusty drive, and pailfuls of tamarinds and water, "a beautiful drink," the men used to say, disappeared rapidly among them. After the men's wounds were attended to, we went round giving them clean clothes, basins and soap and towels, and followed these with socks, slippers, shirts, drawers, and those coveted dressing gowns. Such pride as they felt in them! Comparing colors and smiling all over as they lay in clean and comfortable rows ready for supper, "on dress parade," they used to say. And then the milk, particularly if it were boiled and had a little whiskey and sugar, and the bread, with *butter* on it, and *jelly* on the butter—how good it all was, and how lucky we felt ourselves in having the immense satisfaction of distributing these things. Two Massachusetts boys, I especially remember, for the satisfaction with which they ate their pudding. I carried a second plateful up to the cars, after they had been put in, and fed one of them till he was sure he had had enough. Young fellows they were, lying side by side, one with a right and one with a left arm gone.

ELIZABETH MASSER THORN did not return to the Evergreen Cemetery gatehouse until July 7. As she was returning to the cemetery with her parents and her family, she encountered the president of the cemetery, David McConaughy, who told her, "There is more work for you than you are able to do." When the gatehouse came into sight, she saw that none of the windows had any glass and some of the window frames were laid out next to the pump shed. The family's valuables in the basement were foremost in her mind, though:

> I went to the cellar to look for the good things I had put there on the first night. One chest was packed with good German linen, others packed with other good things,—everything was gone, but three featherbeds and they were full of blood and mud. After I had dragged them out of the cellar I asked an officer who was riding by, if I would ever get any pay for things spoiled like this. He asked me what it was, and I told him bed clothes that were in the cellar, and he said in a very short way: "No!"

The first order of business was to fix the pump. After it was repaired, Thorn sought the assistance of three women. "We washed for four days. . . . Then I got a note from the president of the Cemetery, and he said: 'Mrs.

Thorn, it is made out that we will bury the soldiers in our Cemetery for a while, so you go for that piece of ground and commence sticking off lots and graves as fast as you can make them.'"

The work fell squarely on the backs of Thorn and her father—a woman six months pregnant and a sixty-three-year-old man: "Yet for all the foul air, we two started in. I stuck off the graves and while my father finished one, I had another one started."

Such back-breaking work continued for days until someone suggested she ask for help:

> Two came, but one only stayed two days, then got deathly sick and left. The other stayed five days, then he went away very sick, and I had to pay their fare here and very good wages for their work. By that time we had forty graves done. And then father and I had to dig on harder again. They kept on burying the soldiers until they had the National Cemetery ready, and in that time we buried one hundred five soldiers. In front of this house there were fifteen dead horses and beside the Cemetery there were nineteen in that field. So you may know it was only excitement that helped me to do all the work, with all that stench.

Three months after the battle, Thorn gave birth to a girl. The child was not very strong and was sickly all her life.

Despite her hard work, Thorn was never compensated any more than her husband's salary of less than thirteen dollars a month. Both Peter and Elizabeth Thorn died in 1907 and are buried at Evergreen Cemetery.[18] "In my older days," she reflected, "my health has been better, but those hard days have always tolled on my life."[19]

HELP FOR GETTYSBURG

Gettysburg cannot be called a town, but a large collection of hospitals.

PVT. GEORGE R. FRYSINGER

TECHNOLOGICAL ADVANCES HELPED BOTH sides during the war. The armies used the railroads to move soldiers and supplies rapidly. The telegraph provided fast communication, allowing both the North and the South to synchronize military movements on expansive fronts. By the end of the battle, however, Gettysburg lacked both. Nevertheless, news from the battlefield went out to the surrounding areas by courier, and from there was telegraphed on to Washington and beyond.

While the situation at Gettysburg progressed, it became clear to the War Department that casualties were high. Supplies were dispatched to Gettysburg long before the last shot was fired.

When word reached Baltimore of the conditions in nearby Gettysburg, Gen. Robert C. Schenck communicated with Secretary of War Edwin M. Stanton, seeking his approval to hire civilian surgeons:

I learn that the suffering near the battle-field at Gettysburg is terrible, in the want of sufficient medical attendance, food, and other help. The food we can supply, but I understand that the medical director of the Army of the Potomac has objected and perhaps very properly, to civilian surgeons being indiscriminately admitted.

Cannot I authorize my medical director or purveyor to organize and employ a corps of 10 to 12 able loyal surgeons from civil life to go up and give their services? Barns, houses, and yards are full of these sufferers. Pennsylvania is not taking care of them, not withstanding the governor's notice to the public that she should.

While officials authorized relief efforts for Gettysburg, families came to the area to search for loved ones. If they found them, they often stayed to care for them. In some instances, special accommodations were made to facilitate the reunion of the wounded with family members, usually through the generosity of the townspeople.

In the meantime, the commander of the Department of the Susquehanna, Darius N. Couch, was able to look beyond the defense of Harrisburg to the military situation around Gettysburg and toward the Maryland border. So many Pennsylvanians responded to Gov. Andrew Curtin's call for troops that it took time to assemble the men and transport them to Harrisburg. Most were not mustered into service until after the battle at Gettysburg had ended. Couch ordered some of these new troops to guard railroads, river crossings, and state and federal property throughout Pennsylvania. Many units were pushed forward through the Cumberland Valley and joined the Army of the Potomac in Maryland, which was posed for an anticipated fight near Williamsport. Lee's army, however, withdrew into Virginia on July 13 and 14.

Couch also ordered two militia regiments to Adams County to help with the massive recovery effort. The Thirty-sixth Pennsylvania Emergency Militia set out for Gettysburg on July 7, traveling first by rail to Carlisle and then on foot from there, arriving in the area on the afternoon of July 9.

Pvt. George R. Frysinger described the march to his father, the editor of the *Lewistown Gazette*:

We have had a severe trial for young soldiers. We left Harrisburg on Tuesday last in the Cumberland Valley cars, rode to Carlisle, then marched that same evening to Mt. Holly, encamped just in the rear of brother's church, but the rain commenced pouring down about 9 o'clock, flooding us out, when we sought shelter in schoolhouse, barns and dwellings. It rained very hard all night, and in the morning our camping ground was almost inundated; we had to wade to get to our arms, which were stacked near the creek bank. We got ready to march over the creek bridge, just at Mullen's Paper Mill, and took a road over a small hill, (the road we were to go was flooded, so that we could not march over it,) but getting to a point where we were to recross, we found the creek had risen so rapidly as to render it impassable. A carriage was swept away at this point, but the horse and men were saved. We were detained on that side, about half an hour, when it was reported that the bridge was in danger of being swept away, whereupon the regiment turned about, and a half "run" to get across the bridge again took place. The current nearly swept us off our feet; several fell down, and three or four who did not get over in time were thought to have been drowned, but fortunately, the apprehension proved unfounded. The creek rose about two feet in half an hour, and a short time after the regiment got over, the three bridges were carried away by the swelling tide. A small house near the mill was also taken down, with boxes, ladders, fences, logs innumerable, trees, &c. The houses were flooded completely. It kept raining all the while. I sought shelter in an empty log house, built a fire, took off everything, and dried myself thoroughly. While sitting by the fire, the water rose so as to crowd me and the old fire place very close together. I concluded to wade out. At this juncture I learned that the regiment was preparing to move by another route to Gettysburg, where the Colonel was ordered to report that evening, and which brought about 15 miles more of a march than the direct road from Mt. Holly. The march was commenced in the afternoon, and away we went through the mud and rains, and wading through the once diminutive but now swollen rivulet, nearly waist deep, and which was sometimes 30 yards wide. We pressed through, however, and between marching, wading, resting, &c.,— arrived here yesterday afternoon, having marched a distance of 35 miles. Of course we were wearied, foot sore, and "about played out," as the boys express it. So here we are, limping around with blistered feet, and quartered in this building, which it was little thought at the day of its dedication would ever be used to serve the purposes of war. But such is its character that destruction of life, &c., are not the only result, but also of our religious institutions. Perhaps we will not deface it much, as our Capt. takes good care of everything else, as he does of his men.

By the heading of my letter you will learn of our being detached from the regiment (it is encamped just out of town) to serve as provost guard of Gettysburg. Gettysburg cannot be called a town, but a large collection of hospitals.

Even Pennsylvania College has not escaped the necessity of being converted into a resting place for the wounded soldiers, which amount to about six thousand in and for sixteen miles around the town.

The town is full of civilians, who visit the battlefield in large crowds.

I visited Lieut. Frank Wentz yesterday, who lies in the 1st Corps hospital. He is wounded just above the knee and does not know how it will turn out. It will be a long time in healing. He was feverish and had a headache yesterday, but otherwise is doing well.

The church in which we are quartered is built after the style of our own Lutheran building. The gallery is in the same position, and the melodeon and seats bring to our mind reflections connected with my Zion at home, which is now to me like distant Jerusalem was to the ancient Jews. But instead of the attentive congregation, the familiar face of Uncle L . . . at his musical post, I see the pews occupied by forms moving amid the din and clanging of arms, which the soldiers are brightening up for duty; and instead of singers on the gallery, boys writing letters to their friends far away from this varied scene. Everything remains in the church seemingly just as the congregation left their last Sabbath's service. Hymn books are scattered through the pews, spittoons and footstools remain in the aisles, and the altar and pulpit carpeted with Brussels. Even the clock hangs suspended, ticking the hours as they fly, and which, instead of meeting the minister's eye, now catches the eye of the sergeant of the guard as he says "Fall in, second relief."

The bell no more calls together the people of God on sweet Sabbath eve, with its hallowed chime.

The greens prepared for an extra occasion are still suspended around the church, which gives it a festive appearance. Tell M I eat a meal at one of his Sunday School scholar's residence, at Mt. Holly, and let them know who I was. The woman said her little boy was a favorite of his.[1]

Col. H. C. Alleman, commander of the Thirty-sixth Pennsylvania, served as the military governor of the district that included the battlefield area and all of the hospital sites in the county. His men provided basic security, police services, and logistical support for the care of the wounded.

On July 5 supplies from the U.S. Sanitary Commission arrived from nearby Frederick, Maryland. The railroad was still unusable, so everything came by wagon. In the beginning, several vehicles were captured by retreating Confederates. Doctors and laborers were taken prisoner, and the supplies were confiscated. Sanitary Commission agents rushed to get more supplies to Gettysburg. Five wagons arrived by July 6.

Railroad service to Gettysburg was restored in the middle of the week, which greatly increased the flow of supplies. Large quantities of meat and vegetables were sent daily from Philadelphia in "refrigerating cars," as they were called, or boxcars that had been converted into moving icehouses.

A Sanitary Commission report noted: "Car-load after car-load of supplies were brought to this place, till shelves, and counter, and floor up to the ceiling were filled, till there was barely a passage-way between the piles of boxes and barrels, till the sidewalk was monopolized, and even the street encroached upon. This abundant overflow of the generous remembrance of those at home to those in the Army was distributed in the same generous manner as it was contributed."[2]

Each morning divisional and corps supply wagons carted loads of supplies to the hospitals. The commission shipped "tons of ice, mutton, poultry, fish, vegetables, soft bread, eggs, butter, and a variety of other articles of substantial and delicate food." These supplies were "provided for the wounded, with thousands of suits of clothing of all kinds, and hospital furniture in quantity to meet the emergency."

According to one tally of the material distributed by the Sanitary Commission to the wounded, the perishable articles included 11,000 pounds of poultry and mutton, 6,430 pounds of butter, 8,500 fresh eggs, 675 bushels of vegetables, 48 bushels of berries, 12,900 loaves of bread, 20,000 pounds of ice, 3,800 pounds of beef soup, 12,500 pounds of milk, 7,000 pounds of "farinaceous food," 3,500 pounds of dried fruit, 2,000 jars of jellies and conserves, 116 boxes of lemons, 46 boxes of oranges, 850 pounds of coffee, 831 pounds of chocolate, 426 pounds of tea, 6,800 pounds of sugar,

785 bottles of syrup, 1,250 bottles of brandy, 1,168 bottles of whiskey, 1,148 bottles of wine, 600 gallons of ale, 134 barrels of biscuits and crackers, 500 pounds of preserved meat, 3,600 pounds of preserved fish, 400 gallons of pickles, 100 pounds of tobacco, 1,621 pounds of meal, 3,848 pounds of codfish, 582 cans of canned fruit, 72 cans of oysters, 302 jars of brandied peaches, 42 jars of ketchup, 24 bottles of vinegar, and 43 jars of ginger.

This assistance, however, also included dry goods, such as 5,310 pairs of woolen drawers, 1,833 pairs of cotton drawers, 7,158 woolen shirts, 3,266 cotton shirts, 2,114 pillows, 254 pillow cases, 1,630 bed sacks, 1,007 blankets, 274 sheets, 508 wrappers, 2,659 handkerchiefs, 3,560 woolen stockings, 2,258 cotton stockings, 10,000 towels and napkins, 2,300 sponges, 1,500 combs, 250 pounds of soap, 7,000 tin basins and cups, 110 barrels of linen for bandages, 46 water coolers, 225 bottles of cologne, 3,500 fans, 4,000 pairs of shoes and slippers, 1,200 crutches, 350 pounds of candles, 300 square yards of canvas, and 648 mosquito nets.

Supplementing the work of the Sanitary Commission was the Christian Commission, which had been organized in November 1861 by many of the same people who had founded the Young Men's Christian Association. Whereas the Sanitary Commission was supported by celebrities, politicians, and other prominent citizens, the Christian Commission was funded by churches that raised the money through member donations. During the first year of operation, the Christian Commission used most of its budget to provide Bibles for the soldiers. As the physical needs of the wounded became more urgent, the Christian Commission sought to provide food, clothing, medicines, and bandages to the armies at the front.

Thus the Christian Commission also sent supplies and personnel to Gettysburg. Christian Commission volunteers relieved the tired women of the town, taking over the cooking and caring for the wounded. It was the first respite the townspeople had had since July 1.

The Sanitary Commission and Christian Commission turned supplies over to the field hospitals without charge. Yet, according the Fannie Buehler, the people of Gettysburg who provided shelter for the wounded had to pay for supplies. Albertus McCreary recalled that the supplies provided by the Sanitary Commission kept his family from starving.

· 12 ·

BURYING THE DEAD

Men wounded in almost every conceivable shape, and writhing under the most
excruciating pain.

CHARLES P. COLE

WHILE THE WOUNDED LAY in homes and schools and churches and
tents, thousands of bodies still lay in the fields around Gettysburg.
Someone estimated that twenty-four hours of fighting occurred during the
seventy-two hours between July 1 and 3. Only after the last shot was fired
was priority given to treating the wounded. A seemingly lesser concern was
the burial of the dead.

Before the Confederate army retreated, some Southerners buried a
small portion of their dead. Pvt. Louis Leon of the Fifty-third North Carolina noted in his diary on July 4: "No fighting to-day, but we are burying the
dead. They have been lying on the field in the sun since the first day's fight;
it being dusty and hot, the dead smell terribly."

The next day, July 5, Tillie Pierce and some friends climbed to the crest
of Little Round Top to survey the battlefield below. She described what she
saw there:

By this time the Union dead had been principally carried off the field, and those that remained were Confederates.

As we stood upon those mighty boulders, and looked down into the chasms between, we beheld the dead lying there just as they had fallen during the struggle. From the summit of Little Round Top, surrounded by the wrecks of battle, we gazed upon the valley of death beneath. The view there spread out before us was terrible to contemplate! It was an awful spectacle! Dead soldiers, bloated horses, shattered cannon and caissons, thousands of small arms. In fact everything belonging to army equipment was there in one confused and indescribable mass.

J. Howard Wert commented on a similar vista of the battlefield: "Death in its ghastliest and most abhorrent forms everywhere. Festering corpses at every step."[1]

Many of Gettysburg's residents returned after the battle to find that their lives had changed forever. Most of them never forgot the sickening sights of the blackened, grimaced faces of the dead. Flies buzzed about the decaying bodies and did the work that nature dictated. Bloated bodies reeked an indescribable smell that stayed forever in people's memories. Insects roamed around swollen faces, in and out of nostrils, eating at eyes, tunneling into ears, and entering mouths. Hands swelled into bearlike claws.

On Tuesday, July 7, attorney John B. Linn arrived in Gettysburg. An amateur historian, he described the scenes he witnessed:

Three miles before we got into town we could see the marks of Cavalry skirmishes, passed some dead horses which were slowly burning up. Two miles this side of town we left our conveyances and walked in: took into the fields to the left of the road. Here I picked up some town Confederate money, we kept on to the South of town and soon came among the debris of the battle-field, any quantity of shells lying about, under an oak tree was a grave marked; W.P.D. 2nd Louisiana, his little tin bucket cartridge box coat contents of his haversack were lying about and near the fence the shell that killed him. I took a cartridge out of his cartridge box. Further on we mounted a hill and came upon a number of dead horses, a blown up caisson marked position of a rebel battery. The stench of the horses was horrid, I picked up a box marked "3

Second fuses Richmond Arsenal." Here I saw a knapsack marked "E.P. Scone Co. E". We then crossed down over the creek by a rocky fording and came to a rebel cannon-wagon apparently concealed in the woods. . . . After ascending from the creek and passing through some fields we came upon the 2nd Cav. encamped by town. Their camp seemed to be on a very hotly contested part of the battle, coats, knapsacks etc. lying about and the stench awful. As we passed up the alley behind the church I noticed the fences perforated with balls. Here Early's brigade lay before supporting Stonewall Jackson's Brigade in their charge upon the Cemetery on Friday. As we passed up into town, the smell of putrefied blood was very disagreeable to me.[2]

The task of burying the dead was well under way when the armies departed the area. A notice appeared in the local newspaper: "Men, Horses, and Wagons wanted immediately, to bury the dead and to cleanse our streets, in such a thorough way as to guard against pestilence. Every good citizen can be of use by reporting himself, at once, to Capt. W. W. Smith, acting Provost Marshall, Office, N.E. Corner Centre Square."[3]

Lt. George Kitzmiller accompanied Beckie Weikert and Tillie Pierce on their trip to the summit of Little Round Top:

As our Lieutenant's company was raised from our town, and as one of my brothers was a member of the company, I eagerly inquired whether he had also been in this battle. He informed me that my brother had been taken very sick on the Peninsula, and was still in the hospital at Washington. It was a great satisfaction to know he was still living, though I was very sorry to hear of his sickness.

While we were climbing up Little Round Top we met one of the Pennsylvania "Buck Tails", who walked with us and pointed out the different places where the bodies lay among the rocks. . . .

Here again, I had the advantage of a field glass, for there were also some officers present who kindly gave me an opportunity of thus viewing the field.

On account of the confusion everywhere abounding, and the impassable condition of the roads, it was thought best for me to remain at Mr. Weikert's for several days after the battle, and especially since my folks knew I was safe.

Sometime during the forenoon of Tuesday, the 7th in company with Mrs. Schriver and her two children, I started off on foot to reach my home.

As it was impossible to travel the roads, on account of the mud, we took to the fields. While passing along, the stench arising from the fields of carnage was most sickening. Dead horses, swollen to almost twice their natural size, lay in all directions, stains of blood frequently met our gaze, and all kinds of army accoutrements covered the ground. Fences had disappeared, some buildings were gone, others ruined. The whole landscape had been changed, and I felt as though we were in a strange and blighted land. Our killed and wounded had by this time been nearly all carried from the field. With such surroundings I made my journey homeward, after the battle.

We finally reached and passed through the Evergreen Cemetery, and beheld the broken monuments and confusion that reigned throughout that heretofore peaceful and silent city of the dead.[4]

Time was the problem now. The hot July weather in Pennsylvania accelerated decomposition. Skin turns slightly green within twenty-four to thirty-six hours after death. This discoloration spreads to the shoulders, neck, and head. The head swells after that, and skin takes on a marbling look as blood vessels become visible. Bloating and decomposing begin within sixty to seventy-two hours. The body turns greenish black; the original skin color is nearly impossible to discern. Bloody fluids pass through the nostrils and other body openings. Skin and hair slippage occurs within four to seven days. The rate of decomposition is largely a matter of temperature, humidity, and insect activity.

In July 1863 in southern Pennsylvania, all the elements of nature combined to accelerate the process: heat, high humidity, and massive insect infestations. Hunger also proved to be a factor in the process. The stench of rotting flesh attracted wild animals who freely roamed the countryside since almost all fencing had been destroyed during the fighting. In addition to cows, goats, and chickens, hogs rambled around the area and gnawed at the bodies of soldiers and the carcasses of horses.

"Swine were found reveling in the remains in a manner horrible to contemplate," J. Howard Wert observed. The matter was brought to Gov. Andrew G. Curtin's attention by attorney David Wills that there were "several places where the hogs were actually rooting out the bodies and devouring them."

One of Gettysburg's weeklies, the *Compiler,* noted: "Judging from the numerous inquires made after stray cows, hogs, &c., a large number must be running at large throughout the county. Persons should make known at once any strays that may be under their notice, so that the owners may recover them as speedily as possible."[5]

HUMAN SCAVENGERS also preyed on the dead, stealing any items of value that might be in the pockets of a fallen soldier. Such petty thefts often ended any chance of identifying a corpse.

Attorney John Linn's diary records his encounters with these battle-field looters. He described a July 8 journey on the Emmitsburg road during which he "came to marks of a fearful contest, hats with holes in them, rebel canteens, over-coats, torn clothing, dead horses, broken gun cartridges, letters, torn knapsacks and haversacks strewed on the road." Nearby was the grave of Col. J. Wasden of the Twenty-second Georgia. His July 3 grave was marked with a Masonic symbol.

"There was on the left of the road, a little further on and more to the left were 15 unburied rebels. We walked up to look at them, they were swollen large as giants, black in the face, but seemed to me to have an individuality which would render recognition by their friends even then possible. They had shirts, yellow pants, and a leather belt on. Pockets of their pants were turned out, have been rifled by someone probably," Linn recounted.[6]

In 1886 an entrepreneur published a collection of photographs of the battlefield, *Stereo Gems of Gettysburg Scenery.* Among them was an image of a "battlefield vulture" known as "Godfor." The identification was briefly elaborated: "one of those inhuman creatures who follow in the wakes of armies, robbing the field of blankets, clothing, turning the pockets of the dead, &c."

One such case of emptied pockets was detailed by Pvt. Isaac Kelly of the First New Jersey. On Saturday, July 4, Kelly found the mangled body of his brother, Thomas. Later that night, he wrote a pain-filled, heartbreaking letter to his parents:

> It is with great sorrow that I write you these few lines, but I can't refrain from it, I must let you know it. It is the death of my Dear Brother Thomas. He was

wounded on Thursday in the Breast. While leading his Company to Victory, his regiment was flanked and had to fall back. Therefore he was left on the Battle field. Mortally wounded, yesterday during the Battle he had his both legs shot off and I suppose he died right away after he had his legs shot off. All his Company's are very sorry about him. He had nothing left in his Pocket except a little flag, which I send you. Please save it as a memento for the family. I just seen him. He will be buried in the morning; his Company will try to send him home after the Battle is over. I am very well and hope this will find you all well. I can not write any more for my Breast is bursting with Sorrow. Write soon.[7]

In a postscript, Kelly added: "He was Robbed of every things else."

Pictures of the Rebel dead dressed in ripped and punctured butternut and gray lying on the battlefield show their pockets turned out. Shoes had been removed. "On the Codori farm there were still some dead Confederates who had not been buried. They were lying on their backs, their faces toward the heavens, and burned as black as coal from exposure to the hot sun," Daniel Skelly recollected. "One of the saddest sights of the day's visit on the field I witnessed near the Devil's Den, on the low ground in that vicinity. There were twenty-six Confederate officers, ranking from a colonel to lieutenants, laid side by side in a row for burial. At the head of each was a board giving their names, ranks and commands to which they belonged."[8]

The Gettysburg teenager added:

A short distance away was another group of thirteen arranged in the same way. They had evidently been prepared for burial by their Confederate companions before they had fallen back, so that their identity would be preserved, and they would receive a respectable burial. Among the hundreds of graves on the battlefield there was but one whose headboard had the Masonic emblems on it. I saw it for the first time this day and often stopped to look at it afterward. It was close to the southern end of the Codori barn along the Emmitsburg Road [and] was the grave of a Confederate colonel.[9]

By holding the field on July 4 while the Confederates withdrew toward the Potomac River, many in the Union army at Gettysburg were involved in burying fallen comrades. Col. Patrick Kelly of the Eighty-eighth New

York Infantry reported: "The 4th and a portion of the 5th were spent in burying the dead, attending to the wounded, and collecting arms and equipments." One of Kelly's subordinates, Capt. Denis F. Burke, confirmed: "We held our position until the evening of the 5th, details in the meantime being engaged in burying the dead and attending to the wants of the wounded left of the battle-field." The burial parties dug graves without regard to landowners and along the roadways.

The remains of 1,242 Confederates were buried in a long trench along the Second Corps front. Among them was placed the body of a woman dressed in a uniform. Her identify was never discovered, but some have speculated that she had followed her husband into Confederate service. Likely both perished during the battle.

Burial details created cemeteries near the field hospitals and the larger divisional hospitals. They used the triangle of land between the Peter Frey farmstead, the Abram Bryan farm, and the Jacob Hummelbaugh farm—despite the many rocks and boulders—for at least 163 graves.

Brig. Gen. Alexander S. Webb's Philadelphia Brigade laid out a cemetery for their dead. They buried at least ten men in the fields of the G. Herling (or Herting) farm. The First Brigade of the First Division buried at least three of their dead on the farm of the J. Bair family. The Third Division field hospital at the Jacob Swisher house buried at least eight men from the Second Corps behind the farmhouse, including two troopers of the Sixth New York Cavalry, which was serving as the corps headquarters guard.

Bodies were dumped almost anywhere. On one farm on Herr's Ridge several bodies were dropped in a well, a quick and easy way to dispose of them and much easier than digging a grave. Only later, after people became sick from drinking the water, were the bodies discovered. When the well was cleaned out, in addition to the bodies, body parts from amputations were also removed.

The Jacob Schwartz farm near Rock Creek was soon the site of four cemeteries (or yards) near the three divisional hospitals. Yard A was a Union cemetery adjacent to the farm buildings, in a field to the northwest of the barn and house. Yard B, holding both Union and Confederate soldiers, was southwest, between Schwartz's buildings and those of his neighbor, Louis A. Bushman, whose farm was on the western side of Rock Creek.

Yard C was positioned on a hill along Rock Creek, in the woods on a ridge known as Red Hill. Yard D was placed along a lane through a cornfield, near a walnut tree. Soldiers from both armies were buried in Yards C and D. Outside these four official yards were a series of other unofficial cemetery plots. At least nine soldiers from the Third Corps, along with at least one lonely Confederate, were buried under the breezy shade of a grouping of maturing walnut trees along a farm lane. The Third Division Hospital, a half-mile south of the other two divisional facilities, placed at least twenty-three graves along Michael Trostle's "Walnut Row."[10]

At the hospitals clustered along Granite Schoolhouse Road between the Taneytown road and the Baltimore pike, soldiers dug small cemeteries on impulse. The Second Corps used Sarah Patterson's property for burials. On the William Patterson farm six were buried in various recognizable places, such as near a fortification, a cedar tree, or the Second Corps hospital.

When some of Gettysburg's African Americans returned home, they found soldiers buried on their property. A total of forty-five Confederates had been buried around Basil Biggs's house. When James Warfield returned home, he discovered fourteen Confederate bodies buried in his garden. Two Southerners were interred in the AME church cemetery in town.

The burial parties, however, did not always bury just the dead. In one case a soldier named White, of the Twentieth Massachusetts, was carried with two of his comrades to a grave. White "revived under the rude shock with which the stretcher was set down, and looking down into the open grave in which lay a brave lieutenant of his own regiment, declared, with grim fun, that he would not be 'buried by that raw recruit,' and ordered the men to 'carry him back.' This man, though fearfully wounded in the throat, actually lived and recovered."[11]

In addition to the dead, the fields around Gettysburg were littered with the debris of the armies. Work details were dispatched to retrieve usable materials. One member of such a group noted:

> The morning of July 4th was fair and cool. We were encamped nearly two miles from the battlefield, among great rocks and boulders. . . . I went up to the hospital and saw the boys, and then went over to view the battlefield. . . . [T]hey were gathering and burying the dead as quickly as possible. There was no firing

of any kind. . . . I went over the wall in front of our position and found the ground covered with muskets. Upon picking one up, I found it loaded and cocked. . . . I called out to some soldiers nearby and told them to be careful with the guns, then stuck the one I had in the ground. I did the same to a number of muskets, and when I left . . . [the area] resembled a large field of bean poles, as everyone who picked up a musket, after looking at it, stuck it in the ground. The enemy appeared to be in about the same position as on the 2nd and 3rd. . . . A detachment from our battery went over to bury our dead, but found they had already been buried by Battery C of our regiment.[12]

Neither army carried coffins into combat. The dead were interred in a hole in the ground, and the graves were marked with whatever board a comrade might find on which to scratch the name of the deceased. Frequently, the boards either disappeared or disintegrated. Coffins were a luxury. In general, the Confederate government lacked the funds to provide coffins, and the Union army might supply coffins to hospitals in the larger cities.

After the battle of Gettysburg there were no coffins in the town. In fact, a town the size of Gettysburg relied on its local cabinetmaker to construct coffins as they were needed. The immediate need after July 3 was beyond the ability of all the cabinetmakers in the several surrounding counties. As a result, the fallen received a quick soldier's burial and a crude marker to designate the grave.

Burial details dug the graves as close as possible to where a man fell in battle. Not surprisingly, the evidence suggests that Union soldiers received better burials than Confederates.

Union soldiers were buried first. This is seemingly confirmed insofar as only two photographs exist of any Federal corpses on the Gettysburg battlefield. By the time photographers arrived on the scene, the majority of the Northern soldiers had been interred. Meanwhile, Confederate corpses were laid out for mass graves, granting the photographers the opportunity to record the images of their bloated bodies lying in the battlefield.

The practice of burying Union soldiers first did not go unnoticed by newspaper correspondents visiting the battlefield. "Our dead have all been buried, but the rebel dead are strewn over the field by thousands," one newspaperman reported on the afternoon of July 5.[13]

The graves dug for the Confederates were often shallow. In many instances it was only a matter of time until some of the bodies surfaced. The mass graves for the Southerners were only as deep as the terrain and the tools available to the soldiers allowed.

Many of the burial parties were supplemented with civilians who were caught stealing from the dead or snatching government property. The grisly work was not pleasant. The stench was unbearable, and the swollen, blackened corpses were horrific. Many of those buried were already beyond recognition. Flies swarmed around the bodies.

Burials of those men who died behind their own lines, often at field hospitals, were less gruesome. Even so, these dead were not always buried quickly. Understaffed medical personnel were harried and focused on caring for the recovering wounded. Many soldiers could recall a corpse "lay by my side [from the early morning] until afternoon, before they could find time to take him away."

AT THE time of the battle, Peter and Susan Rogers lived in a small house on the Emmitsburg road with twenty-three-year-old Josephine Miller. During the fighting, Josephine had baked bread for the soldiers. Situated between the two armies on July 3, artillery fire severely damaged the farmhouse. During Pickett's Charge, the house was overrun by the divisions converging on Cemetery Ridge. More than sixteen hundred Confederates who fell during that attack found their final resting place around the Rogers farm. A Rebel sharpshooter was killed on top of the house and tumbled down in front of the door. Another died from exhaustion on the steps. Many more were found dead in the yard. In a field behind the house several were buried. The feet of one buried Confederate stuck up through the ground. After the battle, Rogers collected more than three hundred pounds of lead from his property.

Burial details were routine for both armies. In his account of the fighting, Capt. William D. Stauffer of the Thirtieth Pennsylvania noted the kind of gallant gesture not uncommon during the war:

> The next day [July 3] the regiment was in the grand charge and flank movement by which many of the enemy, were captured, and also a flag. They were

driven off the field, a burial party was taken by surprise and a number were captured. They left in great haste leaving many of their dead all ready for burial, which duty our men completed for them, for which those who were present as prisoners were very thankful.[14]

J. C. Williams of the Fourteenth Vermont offered another description of the burials of some Confederate soldiers: "I shall never forget the many ghastly scenes which met my gaze—the dead in piles and heaps, horses and riders mingling in the same mass. In one trench dug by the rebels I saw seventeen officers, and a number of other trenches were filled with the rebel dead but remained uncovered, showing that the enemy had commenced to bury his dead, but was obliged to effect a hasty retreat."[15]

The battlefield interments of most of the Union dead were completed, based on most of the accounts of various soldiers, by July 5. Yet more corpses still lay in the fields and woods in and around Gettysburg. Those burials were left to the residents and the Pennsylvania militia.

MANY OF the dead were never identified. Those who died on the battlefield were less likely to be identified than those who died in a field hospital. Since neither army issued identity tags to the soldiers, the only way to identify a corpse was by the items found on the body: letters, rings, Bibles, books, or some item that carried a name. Friends often identified comrades.

As a result, graves were marked as best as possible. Markings were often only in pencil on a board salvaged from an ammunition box. Carved inscriptions were rare because such work took time, which was not an option for burial details working in the rain in the expansive fields around Gettysburg. Rocks, trees, fence boards, and any other material at hand were used to mark the graves of men whose identities were known.

Most of the time, the men in the burial details knew the men who had fallen in a fight. At Gettysburg, however, the interment task eventually fell from the units that fought there to troops who had no point of connection with the men in the field other than that they wore the same uniform.

Perhaps the most well-known unknown of the battlefield was Sgt. Amos Humiston of the 154th New York. His corpse was found in the side yard of Judge Samuel Russell's home. The body was in a sitting position in a field near the intersection of Stratton Street and the railroad tracks. In his hand was an ambrotype of three children.

Had it not been for the thoughtful act of John Francis Bourns, a Philadelphia physician who responded to the call for medical assistance after the battle, the story of the soldier and the children might have remained only part of the local lore about the battle. Bourns gave the story to the Philadelphia newspapers and asked that anyone who knew anything about the children might contact him. Newspapers lacked the technology to reproduce photographs, so the appeal was limited to a description of the image.

The *Philadelphia Inquirer* published the story on October 19 with the headline "Whose Father Was He?" Other papers ran the story in the weeks to come. A religious journal, the *American Presbyterian*, reprinted the *Inquirer* story in its October 29 issue. In Portville, New York, Philinda Humiston realized that the described ambrotype was the same one she had sent to her husband in May of that year. She wrote to Bourns, and he sent her a copy of the image to confirm. Amos Humiston was no longer an unknown casualty of Gettysburg. The Humiston story generated national concern for the plight of war-orphaned children and started a movement to provide care.[16]

CORRESPONDENTS VISITED the battlefield on July 4 and 5. One reported his first glimpse of the battlefield:

> Most of the dead have been buried where they fell, or gathered in little clusters beneath some spreading tree or beside clumps of bushes. Some of the rebel dead are still uncovered. The first that meets my gaze I come upon suddenly, as I descend a bank, some three or four feet in height, to the side of a small spring. He is lying near the spring, as if he had crawled there to obtain a draught of water. His hands are outspread upon the earth, and clutching at the little tufts of grass beneath them. His haversack and canteen are still hanging on him, and his hat is lying near him. His musket is gone; either carried off by his comrades, taken by some relic seeker, or placed in the accumulated heap by our own soldiers.
>
> The body of another rebel attracts my attention by a singular circumstance. The face is discolored in the extreme. . . . The hands are as delicate as

those of a lady and of snowy whiteness. With the exception of the face, the body is but little swollen, and there are no signs of the commencement of decomposition. Several bodies that I find show blackened faces, but no others than this display such a contrast between the color of the face and hands. Near a small white house on the rebel line lies the body of an officer, evidently a lieutenant or captain. His right arm is extended as if to grasp the hand of a friend. All possible positions in which a dying man can fall can be noticed on this field.[17]

DURING THE morning of July 5 a three-man team led by photographer Alexander Gardner arrived on the battlefield. Gardner's group came up the Emmitsburg road, first glimpsing the scene of the fighting near the George Rose farm, which was one of the last areas of the battlefield to be cleared of the dead.

Photography in 1863 required significant daylight to acquire reasonable images. With Gardner were James Gibson and Timothy O'Sullivan. They wasted no time. Twenty images were taken the first day. The next day they focused on Devil's Den and Big Round Top. On July 7 their work was concentrated in the town and Evergreen Cemetery.

Gardner pioneered battlefield photography. His images of the Antietam battlefield had been the first of their kind and drew an enthusiastic response from the public, which was both horrified and fascinated by his pictures of the dead in the field. At Gettysburg, Gardner's crew decided to pose the bodies in a way to make their images more evocative. They moved bodies and debris to compose salable pictures. The photographers brought props of their own, since few rifles were still in the field.

Less than forty-eight hours after the final shots had been fired between the two armies, photographers roamed the battlefield, looking for opportunities to capture dramatic images that would tantalize the public again. The grim tasks of cleanup and burial were well under way as the photographers moved from site to site.

Most of the best-known photographs of dead soldiers at Gettysburg were produced by Gardner's crew. The fact that these were staged would not be determined until more than a century later. One of these is an image of a dead Confederate lying in the rocks at Devil's Den. Gardner and his associates positioned the corpse and dressed up the scene with battle relics that had been scattered about the area. The final touch was a rifle leaning against the barricade; Gardner used the same weapon in many photographs.

Gardner's team also took photographs of a single scene from opposing angles, creating multiple views of the same subject. This technique allowed him to market the different views.

Although some of Gardner's photographs would not meet certain ethical standards today, one should keep in mind that Gardner was creating a new kind of photography: photojournalism. Within the context of the standards of his day, he used his camera to offer moral comment on the war. At the same time, the historic value of his images alone is staggering. For the first time, photographs revealed and preserved the horrors of combat.

Working as quickly as possible, the Gardner photographic crew first captured the stark reality of Confederate dead gathered and laid out in rows for burial in mass graves. They also photographed a small group of dead Union soldiers lying scattered in a field. These Northerners were untouched, except by those (presumably Confederates) who had removed their shoes, equipment, and the contents of their pockets. Gardner's two photographs of the dead Federals lying on the battlefield are the only two known to exist.

Some of Gardner's photographs depict horrific deaths. One shows a Confederate on his back, his abdomen ripped open, with a musket (complete with bayonet) perfectly posed across his legs at his knees. The gaping, gruesome wound shows the severity of combat injuries, although it is unknown whether the man was disemboweled by a shell or, some say more probably, by wild pigs.

WOUNDED AND suffering from a bullet bruise, on July 6 Lt. Frank Haskell of the Sixth Wisconsin observed: "The spade and shovel, so far as a little earth for the human bodies would render their task done, had completed their work—a great labor, that. But still might see under some concealing bush, or sheltering rock, what had once been a man, and the thousands of stricken horses still lay scattered as they had died."[18]

The dead horses Haskell described were all over the battlefield. Their disposal was the foremost public health problem for the people of Adams

County. Swarms of green flies hovered around the rotting carcasses. Too many and too large to bury, the dead animals were dragged by mule or horse teams into piles and then torched. There are many different accounts of the number of animals that were killed as a result of the battle; the actual number was never known. The stench of the burning animals polluted the air for miles.

Daniel Skelly recalled the scene of the horse carcasses on July 6:

> The sight around Meade's headquarters along the Taneytown Road was terrible, indicating the exposed position it occupied, subject to every shot and shell that came over the ridge above it. Around the house and yard and below it lay at least 12 or 15 dead horses. . . . A short distance below the house there was a stone fence dividing a field. Across this was hanging a horse which had been killed evidently just as he was jumping the fence, for its front legs were on one side and the hind legs on the other. In the road a short distance away was another horse which had been shot down while drawing an ambulance.[19]

As wounded horses and mules were wrangled and examined, those that could be treated and were likely to recover were herded into pens. Those that were beyond recovery were shot and destroyed.

William T. "Billy" Simpson was a drummer boy with the Twenty-eighth Pennsylvania. He recorded: "I was mighty glad to get away from that field. I assisted in gathering some of the dead and the wounded, and it was anything but pleasant. The dead horses were burned and the odor from the burning horse flesh made our departure smell like an escape from a hateful charnel house."[20]

NO MATTER how horrendous the event or how ghastly the sights, people tend to congregate at the scene to see for themselves the grisly gore. Little time passed after the Confederate army disappeared before sightseers appeared at Gettysburg.

The house and barn of Jacob Hollinger stood at the intersection of York and Hanover Streets. His daughter Liberty recalled the scene shortly after the battle: "The town began to fill with friends and strangers, some intent on satisfying their curiosity, and others, alas! to pick up anything of value to be found. Blankets, sabers, and guns and many other articles were thus obtained and smuggled away or secreted."[21] Some people claimed to know the Hollingers just to have access to the area and a place in which to stay.

Some of the sightseers were area farmers, taking advantage of the opportunity to view an indescribable scene. As they stood on the knolls and looked over the vast valley, the destruction was everywhere. Others came out of curiosity to see the macabre sights of death and destruction.

The fields and woods were also filled with booty and loot. Not until the authorities took control of the entire battlefield area would the morbid sightseeing and scavenging stop.

Retrieving munitions and weapons from the battlefield was dangerous business. Uncollected weaponry posed a problem in 1863. Samuel Warner from York was instantly killed while handling a gun just picked up from the battlefield. The weapon accidentally discharged, and the bullet passed through his heart.[22]

The problem only grew. Within two weeks a notice from the provost marshal was published in the *Sentinel and General Advertiser:* "Citizens visiting the battle-field are warned against carrying away any Government property, and all those having taken such property, either Federal or Confederate, are directed to return the same without delay, to my office in Gettysburg, thereby saving themselves from arrest and punishment."

Daniel Skelly noted that the town filled up every day with people from all over the country. These were not always sightseers. Skelly observed "fathers, mothers, brothers, sisters hunting their wounded or dead."[23]

With regard to the influx of visitors, hotel owner John C. Will reported: "We had no place for men. They occupied the carpets and floors of the parlor, even the loft in the stable. Women occupied all of our rooms."[24]

On July 7 a correspondent described in detail both the battlefield and the spirit of the wounded Rebels and Yankees and the heart of the people of Gettysburg:

On Tuesday evening after the fight, we found ourselves among the crowd of visitors to the battle field of Gettysburg. There were many whose sad faces and anxious inquiries proclaimed their errand. Others, again, were busily attending to the necessities of the wounded; but perhaps in every breast there was felt something of that strange feeling which instinctively draws us to a battle field. It is not a morbid curiosity as some would claim. It is with a feeling more akin to reverence that we draw nigh to the broad and bloody altar, on which thousands of our fellow beings have so freely laid down their lives for our redemption. Such spots are shrines to which true patriots will ever make their pilgrimages; and we may rest assured that the nation is nigh destruction when it can forget or walk thoughtlessly over its battle grounds. It was with much feeling that we stood on the now historic heights of Gettysburg. The sun was just setting as we began our walk, and the silence of coming night seemed best calculated to impress the scene. A friend who had witnessed the fight walked along, and through his vivid descriptions the whole battle seemed to rage before us. The rising fogs of evening were not unlike the smoke of battle as we had seen it before; and as they hung over the hills on the rebel lines, fancy could easily picture on this misty background, marshaled lines and charging columns. It is exceedingly difficult, as every one is aware who has made like visits, to arrive at the truth concerning the details of the fight. Each soldier claims for the point where he stood, special importance. Never was there so fierce an assault as the one repelled by his brigade. But there are certain points that tell their own story. The deep ruts made by the artillery wheels, the broken fragments of shell, the shrubbery cut down as with the scythe of the mower, the trampled caps and haversacks that no soldier comes to claim, and the graves, thick as if sown broad-cast on the hillside, need no interpreter. There are many such places at Gettysburg, but there is one which will ever claim special interest. It is Cemetery Hill, occupied by our centre. It was, as Gen. Lee said in his address to his soldiers, "the key to the whole position, and the Confederacy expected them to take it." Standing on it one could realize as never before the magnitude of the issues at stake in this one battle. That little hill alone stood between the hosts of the rebels and victory. It was all that seemed to interfere between us and disaster and humiliation to the whole North. But it was peopled that day with heroes; it fairly bristled with cannons and bayonets. The tide of battle swept up to its foot, then back, then forward and partly up its sides, leaving them in its fearful ebb, covered with mangled and bleeding bodies; but still like some bold headland mocking the waves the hill held out.

On the top you can still see the field works marked with the wheels of the cannon. Just on the brow of the hill, was a square field, enclosed by a stone wall. This made two parallel walls to stretch between the patriots on the hill and the rebels; and behind [illegible] long lines of eager soldiers waiting for the coming of the foe. The tops of these walls are now ragged; in some places broken quite to the ground. There is good reason for it, for first the artillery, from those woods opposite, played on them, and then a column, the forlorn hope of the charge, stormed over them. They passed the first with a yell; broken, but not dispirited, they reached the second and clambered over it. They sweep to the brow of the hill, and over it, and at last lay their hands on those cannon behind the field works. But there were men with those guns who scorned to fly. Bravery was met with equal bravery, and they flew to embrace each other in the fearful struggle of death. A rebel laid hold of an artillery man, and in the struggle threw him to the ground, and then seized a limestone to beat out his brains. A patriot lieutenant sprang to aid his comrade; then a rebel officer joined in the fray. It was a brief struggle—a shot, a snapping stab with a bayonet, and two more traitors passed to their doom. This was the way they fought around these guns. For a few brief minutes the enemy held the batteries, then broke and fled in disastrous rout down the hill. Few reached the meadow below. They lay upon the hillside crushed by the pitiless storm that overtook their flying feet. Behind the second wall lay a company of Texians, unable to move forward or backward. They could not lift their heads, so fierce and incessant was the fire that swept over them. They were afterwards taken prisoners. Next morning after the assault a man might have walked from the muddy stream below, up to the very muzzles of the cannon above, on dead and bleeding bodies. All this occurred just outside the gates of the Cemetery. It seems as if war in cruel mockery of death, had flung a thousand victims at his door. We walked back through the Cemetery, and on all sides were traces of this most sanguinary conflict. Artillery horses had trampled the flower which the hand of affection had planted over the dead; monuments were overturned, and the green sod of graves torn by bursting shells. We noticed one monument shattered by a cannon ball. It was one marking the grave of a young soldier who fell at the battle of Fair Oaks. His last words: "Tell my father I died for my country," were chiseled on the marble, and it seemed, as if for these words, the bitterness of rebellion would disturb his last resting place. But he sleeps on a field of victory after all. To give an account of a walk along the whole line of battle, without entering into a detailed history of the conflict, would be to repeat what has been written. Each hill top has its story of desperate assault and gallant defence; and alike are baptized with patriot blood.

But in order to obtain a correct conception of the sanguinary character of this battle, one must visit the hospitals. The dead are soon covered from the sight; the scarred earth, washed by pitying rains and nursed by the sunshine, quickly recovers from its wound, but men must bleed and groan and die for long days after the shock of battle is over, and the shattered columns have swept away to other scenes. The multitude of such sufferers at Gettysburg is appalling. There are literally acres covered with them, while in the town every available building is turned into a crowded hospital. As we were there early in the week, it was too soon to find much done to relieve their wants. The citizens of the place were doing all in their power, and so far as our personal knowledge goes, we can assert most positively that the charges of extortion and indifference preferred against them are altogether unfounded. The Christian Commission were already present and actively at work. Too much praise cannot be awarded them for their labor of love. Dressing wounds, administering cordials, sponging a parched face, writing letters, or administering a few words of comfort to the dying, thousands of grateful soldiers will bless their names and the charity that sent them. The sufferings of the rebel wounded, for the first five days after the battle, were indescribable. Abandoned by their friends lying under trees and sheds, without any adequate medical attendance, or supplies of any kind, they remained. The gnawing of hunger soon added to the pains of their neglected wounds, while the drenching rains that followed the battle increased the discomfort of their condition. Every effort was made as soon as possible to relieve their wretched state. They were gathered up and conveyed to a convenient locality on the Chambersburg pike, where tents and supplies were furnished them.

At this point, the fields look as if an army were still encamped there; but a closer look is enough to move the hardest heart. Pity turns away to weep, while indignation bursts out afresh against the wicked leaders who betrayed these misguided men to such horrible sufferings. Maimed, wounded, covered with gore, and writhing in agony they lie there to mark the pathway the monster secession has trodden. There is a most remarkable contrast between the wounded of the opposing armies. We need not allude to the outward appearance, for the filth and squalid attire of the rebels are proverbial. It is also to be expected from the result of the battle, that one party would be dogged and sullen while the other would be cheerful. However, the contrast may be traced in the cheerfulness and patience with which the men bear their wounds. I have yet to hear a regret from our brave soldiers that they entered the army, or that they had sacrificed too much for their country, while among the rebels one could hear without inquiry, most hearty wishes that they were out of the army and safe at home. Frequently did we hear the desire expressed that the "war might soon be over and the Union restored as before." A dying rebel from Georgia, the son of a wealthy planter, sent for a minister in the town to beg of him that he would see him decently buried and write to his friends of his death. He stated that he had been driven into the army by the bayonet, and that his father had offered fifteen hundred dollars for a substitute but none were to be had at any price. Others expressed their sorrow that they had taken up arms against the Union, but who can point out a soldier in our army, sorry for the part he has taken in subduing this rebellion.

The debt the North owes to the Army of the Potomac is one we can never repay. But for it, we would to-day, be lying helplessly in the power of the insurgents. Surely then no appeal need be made to our generosity, to send all necessary supplies to the suffering soldiers at Gettysburg. The number is so great that it will require continuance in well doing on our part to supply their need. It will be months before this vast army of sufferers can be discharged. We might add indefinitely, to what has been written, but every one is busy repeating the story of how they fought at Gettysburg. Nor will it now grow old. History shall record it on her pages, and generations yet unborn, shall read it with throbbing pulses, and with glowing words bring their tribute to the memory of those who have bled and died for their country's redemption.

Many would visit the battlefield and hospitals in the days after the battle. "The scenes at the hospitals were sickening in the extreme. Men wounded in almost every conceivable shape, and writhing under the most excruciating pain," commented editor Charles P. Cole of the Cortland, New York, *Gazette & Banner*.[25]

•13•

MILITARY MEDICAL CARE

He was deranged and would die without doubt.

JOHN LINN

D URING THE WAR, THE medical services on both sides learned much about how to provide better care for wounded soldiers. For the North, one of those improvements was an increase in the number of doctors. In 1860, the year before the war started, the U.S. Army consisted of 16,000 men, of which there was a surgeon general, 30 surgeons, and 83 assistant surgeons. When the war started, 24 of these 114 physicians left the army to "go South," and the Union army promptly dropped 3 assistant surgeons as "disloyal." Thus, at the beginning of the war the Union medical corps totaled only 87 men. By the end of the war, both sides employed more than 15,200 surgeons: 12,000 in the Federal army and 3,200 in the Confederate ranks.

Within the Union army, ranks were assigned in conjunction with the physicians' level of expertise. Surgeons were given the rank of major, and assistant surgeons rated as captains or first lieutenants. In addition to the regular army surgeons, civilian doctors served in the hospitals or with a regiment in the field. Many of these acted as assistant surgeons, but they were not commissioned as officers and worked under a contract,[1] often on a part-time basis. Part-time surgeons could wear uniforms if they wanted, but they were usually restricted to general hospital duty far away from the front lines.

Numbers, however, did not translate into a uniform level of care. The vast suffering at Gettysburg overwhelmed both volunteers and visitors to the various hospitals scattered around town. At the Catholic church, the Third Division's hospital, attorney John Linn encountered Samuel Hassenplug with a severe wound in his side. In his diary, Linn recorded:

> He was deranged and would die without doubt. Saw him with his great black thick head gazing about wildly as if in great pain, during the night in his paroxysms he injured the other wounded who lay about him as close as they could be placed on boards stretched over the top pews. The doctor in attendance seemed to be a brute, he stepped about smoking and swearing, and paying no attention whatever to the frequent appeals made to him, and for the sake of appearing to do something commenced sweeping out the house which any one else could have done better. One soldier appeared to be in great agony and on enquiry said a shell had burst over his head, no examination was made of him until a volunteer surgeon came in, who not satisfied with his insane raving ripped off his coat and shirt and found a wound through his shoulder in which were maggots already.

Competence and care were not consistent in either army. In the Union army, however, the matter improved over the course of the war. Part of that advancement was in proportion to the funds allocated for medical needs. In 1860 the U.S. Army's Medical Department had a total budget of $90,000. In 1863 that amount increased to $11,594,000. By the end of the war, the War Department expended $47,000,000 on the Medical Department.[2] The additional expenditures provided for more surgeons, assistants, and supplies.

Another improvement was the use of ambulances. When the war started, the concept of an ambulance was new and not used. The idea of rapidly removing wounded soldiers from a battlefield via vehicle to a field hospital for examination and treatment by a surgeon was novel. When wounded on the battlefield, soldiers still able to walk made their way back to the surgeon with or without assistance. Reportedly, after the battle of First Manassas, none of the casualties reached Washington in ambulances; some of the wounded had to walk twenty-seven miles to reach the city.

Those unable to walk were carried by their comrades, often with improvised litters. Some soldiers made stretchers by passing poles or even rifles through coats or improvising hammocks of blankets. Ordinary chairs were frequently used to carry wounded men over short distances. Of course, animals were sometimes available, and sometimes these were used in conjunction with traverses. Gates, shutters, ladders, and planks were also used. Whenever possible, wagons were utilized.

As the battles involved more and more men, it became apparent that ambulances were needed. The earliest consisted of horse-drawn wagons and both two- and four-wheel units. Most used a team of two horses, but some of the larger vehicles employed a team of four horses. In the Union army, the two-wheel models were called Finleys, and the four-wheel vehicle was called a Tripler (named for the army's first medical director). The Southerners dubbed their ambulances Chisolms.

At first, any soldier could be detailed to drive the wagon or be a stretcher-bearer. Often the most unfit soldiers were assigned this duty. Because they were not very good soldiers or fighters, they were not much better as care providers. During the first year of the war, these soldiers had a reputation for getting drunk on medicinal liquor and ignoring their wounded comrades so as to avoid enemy fire.

The failure of the army's medical services to transport the wounded efficiently to field hospitals caused many unnecessary deaths. Surgeon Gen. Charles S. Tripler commanded the Medical Department of the Army of the Potomac. He implemented a series of changes to remove casualties from the field safely and efficiently, but when his efforts failed to reduce needless suffering, Tripler was replaced on July 4, 1862, with Jonathan Letterman.

Letterman organized the ambulance service into corps and division units. Medical Department officers handpicked the ambulance crews and drilled them regularly. Each ambulance crew contained a sergeant, two stretcher-bearers, and a driver. Ambulances were assigned to specific divisions and moved with their division. Letterman also devised a three-tier evacuation plan that is still in use today. Stage one was to get the wounded from the fighting to a field aid station for bandaging and triage; stage two was to get the severely wounded to a field hospital for emergency surgery; and stage three was the final movement of the injured to a hospital for long-term care and recovery.

Letterman's transportation system quickly proved successful. By the September 17, 1862, battle of Antietam, the performance of the ambulance corps had improved significantly. The battle, considered to be the bloodiest of the war, lasted twelve hours. Within twenty-four hours all of the wounded had been removed from the battlefield for treatment.

In his report after the battle of Gettysburg, Letterman offered high praise for his ambulance corps: "The ambulance corps throughout the army acted in the most commendable manner during those days of severe labor. Notwithstanding the great number of wounded, amounting to fourteen thousand one hundred and ninety-three, I know, from the most reliable authority and from my own observation, that not one wounded man of all that number was left on the field within our lines early on the morning of the 4th of July." He added:

> A few [wounded] were found after daylight beyond our farthest pickets, and these were brought in, although the ambulance men were fired upon, when engaged in this duty, by the enemy, who were within easy range. In addition to this duty, the line of battle was of such a character, resembling somewhat a horse-shoe, that it became necessary to remove the most of the hospitals further to the rear, as the enemy's fire drew nearer. This corps did not escape unhurt: one officer and four privates were killed, and seventeen wounded, while in the discharge of their duties. A number of horses were killed and wounded, and some ambulances injured. These facts will show the commendable and efficient manner in which the duties devolving upon this corps were performed, and great credit is deservedly due to the officers and men for their praiseworthy conduct. I know of no battle-field from which wounded men have been so speedily and so carefully removed, and I have every reason to feel satisfied that their duties could not have been performed better or more fearlessly.[3]

Medical supplies were another matter, however. They were transported in a variety of ways. Surgeons and assistants often carried medicines in their saddlebags, haversacks, and even their pockets. On the march, drugs were transported in boxes, sometimes called panniers, which were stowed in the ambulances. An innovative wagon known as the Autenrieth was specially designed with shelves and counters designed to function as a "pharmacy on wheels." Without doubt, the Union army was better equipped and supplied than the Confederate army.

The problem during the three days of fighting at Gettysburg was that most of the supplies—as well as the ambulances—were not in the immediate vicinity of the battlefield. Twenty-five wagons of supplies were no closer than Taneytown. Letterman's report confirmed, "The supply of Dr. [Jeremiah B.] Brinton reached the field on the evening of July 4." Without supplies, surgeons were greatly limited in the treatment they could render during the three days of battle.

A volunteer nurse, Mrs. R. H. Spencer, reported such a situation at a church four miles from Gettysburg that was being used as an aid station: "They had sixty wounded undergoing every variety of suffering and torture. The church was small, having but one aisle, and the narrow seats were fixtures. A small building adjoining provided boards which were laid on the tops of the seats, and covered with straw, and on these the wounded were laid. The supply train had been sent back fourteen miles. A number of surgeons were there, but none had instruments, and could do very little for the wounded."[4]

As was noted earlier, Meade ordered the medical wagons to the rear so as not to impede the flow of ammunition to the front lines. The Letterman report did not take issue with the army commander for this decision, but it enumerated the ramifications:

> On July 1, the trains were not permitted to go farther, and, on the 2d, were ordered farther to the rear, near Westminster.
>
> On the 1st, it was ordered that "corps commanders and the commander of the Artillery Reserve will at once send to the rear all their trains (excepting ammunition wagons and ambulances), parking them between Union Mills and Westminster."

On the 2d, these trains were ordered still farther to the rear, and parked near Westminster, nearly 25 miles distant from the battlefield. The effect of this order was to deprive the department almost wholly of the means for taking care of the wounded until the result of the engagement of the 2d and 3d was fully known. I do not instance the effect of this order, excepting to show the influence of it upon the department. The expediency of the order I, of course, do not pretend to question, but its effect was to deprive this department of the appliances necessary for the proper care of the wounded, without which it is as impossible to have them properly attended to as it is to fight a battle without ammunition. In most of the corps the wagons exclusively used for medicines moved with the ambulances, so that the medical officers had a sufficient supply of dressings, chloroform, and such articles until the supplies came up, but the tents and other appliances, which are as necessary, were not available until July 5.

Letterman's report, however, lauded the efforts of surgeon John McNulty, medical director of the Twelfth Corps, who reported that all the wounded of his corps had their wounds dressed within six hours, and those requiring surgery had their operations completed within one day. Letterman contributed this successful care of the wounded to the ambulance system. The army's medical director concluded:

[I]t is with extreme satisfaction that I can assure you that it enabled me to remove the wounded from the field, shelter, feed them, and dress their wounds within six hours after the battle ended, and to have every capital operation performed within twenty-four hours after the injury was received. I can, I think, safely say that such would have been the result in other corps had the same facilities been allowed—a result not to have been surpassed, if equaled, in any battle of magnitude that has ever taken place.

Feeding the wounded was another logistical problem. It seems apparent that after treatment, at least for some time, wounded soldiers were unfed. "A great difficulty always exists in having food for the wounded," Letterman observed. "By the exertions of Colonel [Henry F.] Clarke, chief commissary, 30,000 rations were brought up on July 4 and distributed to the hospitals. Some of the hospitals were supplied by the commissaries of the corps to which they belonged. Arrangements were made by him to have supplies in abundance brought to Gettysburg for the wounded; he ordered them, and if the railroad could have transported them they would have been on hand."

MUCH CREDIT goes to both sides for quickly evacuating so many of their wounded from the battlefield during the fighting. This is not to say that all the wounded were evacuated from the field, because there are innumerable stories of the many cries from the men still in the field after the fighting died down. Yet both armies retrieved wounded men and brought them to field hospitals for some kind of treatment. From all reports, Union and Confederate field hospitals began receiving the injured shortly after the fighting commenced. To their credit, the surgeons in the field labored non-stop until they collapsed from exhaustion.

If gathering the wounded was not easy work, assessing who would be treated and in what sequence was no easier. Within Federal lines the Union wounded received attention before any Confederate captives received care. In a poignant letter, Lt. William Wheeler of the Thirteenth New York Battery described what it was like to treat an enemy as well as a friend:

> I went over a part of the battle-field that night, and did what I could to make the wounded comfortable; but very soon this seemed a hopeless undertaking; our wounded were removed in ambulances as fast as possible, but the rebel wounded, who were almost all of them in our hands, received extremely little attention, and lay scattered over the field in groups of twenty, fifty, or even a hundred, trying to help each other a little. Our men could not help it; most of them were too much worn out to raise a hand and the regular Ambulance Corps could not begin to attend to our own wounded boys. I was glad to do a little something for them, even if it were only to turn them on their side, and give them a glass of water.
>
> Utterly as I detest a living active rebel, as soon as he becomes wounded and a prisoner I don't perceive any difference in my feelings towards him and towards one of our own wounded heroes. I suppose this is very heterodox, but I can't help it. I found a Colonel of a Mississippi Regiment shot through the

breast, a man of stately bearing, and a soldier of his regiment told me that he was judge of the Supreme Court of that State. Now here was a man, evidently one of the real old original Secesh; but I forgot that, took him into a barn, made him a straw bed, fixed a pillow for him, got him a cup of coffee, and ignored the fact that he gave me no word of thanks or farewell when I left him.[5]

Some wounds were gaping, horrendous, untreatable. They were so gruesome that the sight left tremendous, lifelong impressions on those who witnessed them. One of these sightings was recalled by a battle-hardened veteran:

> One of the saddest sights I ever witnessed was on the field of Gettysburg. We had captured some fifteen hundred prisoners and I was one of the guard marching them to the rear. Passing along where there were hundreds dead, wounded and mutilated I saw a soldier with a North Carolina regiment mark in his cap leaning against a fly tent. A fragment of a shell had struck him above the breast bone and tore the whole stomach lining away leaving exposed his heart and other organs which were in motion and he seemed alive and conscious. I lingered a moment for I had never seen any thing so shocking before nor have I seen the countenance of a dying man so peculiar and unearthly.[6]

Letterman reported that the greater portion of necessary surgeries were completed before the army left Gettysburg: "The time for primary operations had passed, and what remained to be done was to attend to making the men comfortable, dress their wounds and perform such secondary operations as from time to time might be necessary."

When the Federals marched out of Gettysburg, 106 medical officers were all that remained behind. "No more could be left," Letterman commented, "as it was expected that another battle would, within three or four days, take place; and, in all probability, as many wounded be thrown upon our hands as at the battle of the 2d and 3d, which had just occurred." Recognizing the glaring need for physicians in Gettysburg, Letterman on July 7 asked the surgeon general for twenty to be assigned to the area. He also ordered that each corps leave six ambulances and four wagons behind "to convey the wounded from their hospitals to the railroad depot for transportation to other hospitals."

Three months after the battle, Letterman reported that the total Federal wounded at Gettysburg totaled 14,193. The number of Confederate casualties that were left to be cared for by the Union army totaled 6,802.

FROM THE close of battle on July 3 until July 22, care for the wounded was provided at field hospitals throughout Gettysburg. On July 22 the army established Camp Letterman. Within two weeks, ambulances transported the remaining patients to this camp on the York road.[7]

Although the spread of disease was not an issue during the first few days after the battle of Gettysburg, it became a serious matter as the wounded convalesced. The filthy conditions of many field hospitals were prime incubators for disease, compounded greatly by their close proximity to the battlefields and recent graves. Dead animals also nurtured the carriers of disease.

In the summer heat, insects persistently assaulted the living and the healing. Soldiers trying to convalesce were covered with flies and bugs. One Southerner reported: "Great green flies in swarms of millions gathered in the camp, grown unnaturally large, fattened on human blood. Fever-smitten, pain-racked, there came to us another terror: we were to be devoured while living by maggots—creeping, doubling, crawling in among the nerves and devouring the soldier while yet alive."[8]

Despite the hardships, the septic conditions, and the brutal misery of the battered soldiers, most of the men injured at Gettysburg survived their wounds. The survival rate was quite remarkable, about 75 percent, especially considering the factors of short supplies, septic conditions, and the number of surgeons with questionable skills.

• 14 •

PRISONERS OF WAR

Tears rolled down the pale face of the young man, but he had not a hand to wipe them away. We wiped the tears from his eyes and gave him some water, when he looked up, and said "Thank God, I am going to die beneath the stars and stripes." We could not help turning away and weeping.

CHARLES P. COLE

A T THE CONCLUSION OF the battle of Gettysburg, both sides surprisingly had about the same number of prisoners. Although the precise number is not known, each side claimed to hold fifty-one hundred prisoners.

As Lee prepared for the retreat, he proposed an exchange of prisoners, but Meade declined. To minimize the impediment involved in guarding so many men and to reduce the drain on his army's resources to feed a large number of captives, Lee paroled fifteen hundred Union prisoners and left wounded Federals in the field. Many of those who were not wounded or injured, he took with him to Virginia.

In his report to Jefferson Davis, Lee said, "There were captured at Gettysburg nearly 7,000 prisoners, of whom about 1,500 were paroled, and the remainder brought to Virginia."[1] Not mentioned in Lee's report was the fact that, in addition to the soldiers, his captives also included captured civilians. Among these was George Codori, who remained a captive until

187

almost the end of the war. He died of pneumonia in March 1865, three days after his release and return to Gettysburg.

SHORTLY AFTER the war commenced, the U.S. and Confederate governments negotiated a parole system for prisoner exchange. Parole meant that prisoners gave their word to not take up arms against their captors until they were formally exchanged for an enemy captive of equal rank—a private for a private, a sergeant for a sergeant, and so on.

Under this system, paroles were supposed to occur within ten days of a prisoner's capture. In common practice, it was granted within a few days, especially after a major battle. Some parolees went home to await notice of their exchange, others waited near their units for the paperwork to be processed. As the war dragged on, the parole system became increasingly confused and chaotic. The idea of going home was quite appealing to many, so many tried to be captured. Some parolees, despite notice of their exchange, simply chose not to return to their units.

To combat this development, the Federal army established detention camps and used parolees as guards. Many parolees were assigned to non-combatant duties, and others were sent west to fight the tribes on the frontier. Technically, parolees were not to be reassigned to duties that would free other soldiers for combat; the military courts upheld that interpretation. The detention camps were the forerunner of prison camps. Soldiers held there habitually lacked both clothing and food. The camps also had poor sanitation. Shortly after these camps were opened, a criminal element developed and victimized the men being held. Paroled men often became pawns. Both sides denied parole to officers until formally exchanged. The Union refused to parole or exchange guerrillas. The North realized that the parole and exchange system was prolonging the war, since the Confederate army's principal method of maintaining troop strength was facilitated by paroles. The Federal army could fill its ranks easier than the Confederates could. As the war continued, both sides used the parole system less, instead sending captives to prison camps.

During the entire war, approximately 675,000 soldiers and sailors were taken prisoner.[2] Nearly 56,000 died in captivity. Of the 8 percent who died, most died from diseases while less than 1 percent died from their wounds.

For days after the battle of Gettysburg, stragglers were collected from across Adams County. Col. H. C. Alleman of the Thirty-sixth Pennsylvania Militia reported that "3,006 Southern unwounded prisoners and a large number of stragglers" were collected.[3]

Being a prisoner of war in a Federal hospital was far better than being a wounded soldier in a Confederate hospital. One Southern newspaper reported the Confederate soldiers' preference in August 1863:

> In the hospitals at Gettysburg there are, by the statement of a correspondent of the New York Herald, about 8,000 wounded Confederate soldiers, and 10,000 Yankee. There were more cases of amputation with our soldiers than with the enemy, and they have been more fatal. This correspondent says that their hospitals are much better managed than ours are. He says: "The wounds of the patients were inflamed and the bandages dry. When asked where their nurses were, they said they only had one or two to each floor, and they could not attend them all. In each corner was a pile of dirt, and the floors were wet from the careless spilling of water when the wounds were wet. We went into the yard, and there were some two hundred slightly wounded and convalescent rebels, able to draw and cook their own rations, eating their breakfasts. In our hospitals, these would have been made to take their watches with the helpless as nurses; but they would not raise a hand to help their more unfortunate fellows. So true is this that many of them express the most ardent desire to get into Union hospitals, where they will have proper attendance."[4]

Editor Charles P. Cole of the Cortland, New York, weekly *Gazette & Banner* had traveled to Gettysburg on July 6. He said that one of the most heart-rending experiences he had at a field hospital was an encounter with a young Georgia captain, a wounded prisoner of war. The Southerner had lost his arms and legs and was lying on a blanket on the floor. A day or so before the battle, he had received a letter from his wife but had not had the time to read it:

> The letter was filled with assurances of prayers and blessings for the Southern army, and urging her husband to fight gallantly for the cause of the South. Alas! He had fought his last fight! A moment after, the surgeon addressed

him, saying: "Captain, we can do nothing for you; you can live but a short time." Tears rolled down the pale face of the young man, but he had not a hand to wipe them away. We wiped the tears from his eyes and gave him some water, when he looked up, and said "Thank God, I am going to die beneath the stars and stripes." We could not help turning away and weeping.

On July 3 Franklin Horner noted in his diary the capture of some Confederates: "[W]e charged sugar loaf mountain last night and took possession without firing a shot part of our Regiment got lost and got out side of our Pickets but we got back again and now are on the hill and have rifle pits we stayed on the hill all day without fighting any the battle last all day the heaviest artillery fight commenced at two P.M. and lasted for two hours the rebs got the worst of the fight they [lost] a great many prisoners."[5]

BECAUSE OF the limited rail service to Gettysburg after the battle, the Southern prisoners were marched to Westminster, Maryland, then moved by rail to Baltimore. Many ended up in Forts McHenry and Delaware, the rest were scattered to other prisoner-of-war camps throughout the North. Because Fort McHenry was becoming overcrowded, a new prison camp was established in July 1863 at Point Lookout, near Annapolis, Maryland. Eventually more than ten thousand Southern prisoners were held there. Wounded Confederates received treatment in hospitals until they were well enough to be transferred to a prisoner-of-war camp.

The Union men taken prisoner at Gettysburg were marched to Williamsport, Maryland, by what was left of George E. Pickett's division. The prisoners then crossed the Potomac and marched to Richmond. Most of the officers remained in detention there while the Confederates dispersed the rest to camps throughout the South.

For weeks after the battle of Gettysburg, Federal troops, Pennsylvania militia, and armed civilians rounded up Confederate stragglers. Whether lost, misdirected, hiding, or deserting, Southerners were collected from Adams, Cumberland, Franklin, and York Counties. Some captures netted wagons and supplies as well as looted goods. One of these occurred twelve miles north of Gettysburg, at Bendersville, on July 9 and involved one hundred Confederates and ten wagons.

Civilians played a role in collecting prisoners. Tillie Pierce's father was involved in such an episode. On the morning of July 4 he was returning home where he "saw a musket lying on the pavement. He picked it up, and just then spied a Rebel running toward the alley back of Mrs. Schriver's lot." James Pierce chased him then shouted for the man to halt.

The man surrendered, claiming that he had deserted his army. Pierce commented, "Yes, a fine deserter you are! You have been the cause of many a poor Union soldier deserting this world." He marched the man back to the Pierce home. Along the way he saw two more Southerners and captured them. Near his home, Pierce turned the men over to some Union troops.

As soon as he was inside, Pierce grabbed his own rifle and went out into the alley behind his house. There he found another Confederate and marched him to the street, where he encountered and captured two more Southerners. Pierce found some Federals to take the three men off his hands. On his way back home, Tillie's father realized that his weapon was not loaded.[6]

For a while the prisoners were held at the intersection of Baltimore and High Streets. They fell into three groups. The first was comprised of Union soldiers who were deserters, bounty jumpers, disciplinary problems, or criminals. The largest of the three groups was made up of captured Confederates, who were confined until they could be transferred or exchanged. The third group entailed political prisoners: civilians arrested under the suspension of the writ of habeas corpus.

Fort McHenry was the primary destination for most of the Gettysburg prisoners. Prior to 1861 the late eighteenth-century seacoast fortification was the most famous fort in American history because of its role as the birthplace of "The Star-Spangled Banner" during the War of 1812. Thus far into the war, the War Department utilized the fort as a military prison, coastal artillery post, hospital, and supply depot for the Eighth Army Corps.

On July 11, Maj. Gen. Robert C. Schenck, commander of the Middle Department and Fort McHenry, reported: "Have received in this month of July at Fort McHenry 6,795 prisoners of war, captured in Maryland and Pennsylvania." The large number of prisoner arrivals included both Gettysburg captives and prisoners from the Vicksburg campaign. The ongoing work of the Pennsylvania Thirty-sixth Emergency Militia in rounding up prisoners and stragglers in Adams County maintained a continuous flow into the prison camp at Fort McHenry.

Severe overcrowding led to the transfer of many Confederate prisoners to Fort Delaware. Among these was Gen. James J. Archer. By August 1863 there were 12,500 prisoners there, which led to horrific conditions. Food was scarce and water puttrefied. Scurvy, malnutrition, and smallpox resulted.

To avoid the deprivations of prison life, some Confederate prisoners renounced their allegiance to the South and swore a loyalty oath to the North. In some circles they were called "Galvinized Yankees." Many were sent to the frontier rather than posted to Union armies in the South.

Medical care for captives was addressed as soon as the Union army found it practical to do so. On July 11, General Orders No. 42 for the Eighth Army Corps in Baltimore stated:

> Suitable and comfortable hospital accommodations will be provided for sick and wounded prisoners of war, the same as for soldiers of the Union.
>
> On the arrival of wounded or sick rebel officers or soldiers in Baltimore, whose injuries or condition are such that in the opinion of the proper medical authority, they should not be confined or sent for exchange with other prisoners, they will be immediately assigned and conveyed to hospitals designated for them, there to remain on parole, until are sufficiently recovered to be removed for imprisonment or exchange. No other paroles of prisoners of war will be taken or recognized.
>
> No rebel officer or soldier can be received or entertained in any private house, or in any place other than the hospital to which he is regularly assigned by proper medical authority.
>
> Separate hospitals for prisoners of war will be established.
>
> No person not thoroughly loyal will be permitted under any circumstances to visit or have access to any military hospital.
>
> If any persons or person, within this Department, be found harboring, entertaining or concealing any rebel office or soldier, in his or her house, or on his or her premises, or in any place, after twenty-four hours of the publication of this order, the person so offending will at once be sent beyond the Union lines in the rebel States, or otherwise punished, at the discretion of the military authority.

Part of the crew that worked on building the Soldiers Monument at the national cemetery established at Gettysburg.

The four panels above form the written invitation from David Wills to Abraham Lincoln, asking him to attend the dedication of the cemetery.

The two panels to the right are Wills's invitation to the president to stay at his home while at Gettysburg.

Facing page: The crowd at the dedication of the Soldiers National Cemetery.

Below: The only known photo of Lincoln at Gettysburg.

Above: An artist for *Frank Leslie's Illustrated Newspaper* created this panoramic view of the dedication ceremony of November 19, 1863.

The familiar gatehouse of the Evergreen Cemetery in 2003 looks very much like it did in 1863, although the structure has been enlarged with the addition to the right. It was from here that Elizabeth Masser Thorn, her parents, and her children fled during the battle. When they returned, the building was damaged and their home had been looted.

Several tombstones in Evergreen Cemetery were damaged by Confederate artillery. Much of the damage is still visible today.

The graves of Peter and Elizabeth Thorn in the Evergreen Cemetery. He was caretaker of the cemetery, but military service called him away from Gettysburg at the time of the battle. She acted as caretaker in his absence and was six months pregnant when shot and shell sounded in the near distance.

Amid the markers in the Soldiers National Cemetery are these for the many unknown soldiers interred here.

Facing page (top): The Diamond in Gettysburg today. Still the center of town, it was the center of much activity during and after the battle of Gettysburg. The large, light-colored building was the home of attorney David Wills. Lincoln spent the evening here before delivering his address. He stayed in the second-floor bedroom marked with the bunting.

Facing page (bottom): Looking west on Chambersburg Street today. This street was used heavily throughout the ordeal of July 1–3. Prior to the battle, Confederate Gen. Jubal Early marched his men down this street and into the town. Days later Union Gen. John Buford ventured west on this roadway to the seminary buildings for a better view of the fighting. Early on the morning of July 1 Gen. John F. Reynolds rode out of town on this street to meet his death.

Below: Looking south on Baltimore Street today. Along this street Federal sharpshooters on Cemetery Hill fired at any suspicious movement during the battle.

Above: Looking east on Chambersburg Street toward the Diamond, the narrow street was the scene of much activity during the battle. Confederates barricaded the street, and the citizens quickly darted between buildings to avoid being shot. *Left:* In 1863 this building was the home of the John and Martha Scott family and Martha's sister, Mary McAllister. *Below:* Many buildings that survived the battle are marked with a plaque like this one.

Above: The home at 303 Baltimore Street belonged to James Pierce. His fifteen-year-old daughter, Tillie, saw much of the battle and years later published her memories of the experience. After the battle the Pierce family nursed severely wounded Col. William Colvill of the First Minnesota to a successful recovery.

Right: Built in 1860, this house was the residence of George and Henrietta Schriver. At the beginning of the battle, Henrietta took her two children and neighbor Tillie Pierce to her family's farm near Little Round Top. Confederate sharpshooters used the home to fire on Cemetery Hill. A neighbor recalled that Union sharpshooters "killed two up in Mr. Schriver's house."

Situated on the south side of the first block of
Chambersburg Street, the Christ Lutheran Church was one
of the first buildings to be used as a field hospital. Across
the street from the Scott and McAllister home, it was the
scene of the killing of a Federal chaplain—Horatio
Stockton Howell of the Nineteenth Pennsylvania—by a
Confederate who saw him as a combatant and demanded
his surrender.

The Saint Francis Xavier Catholic Church stands at 43 West High Street and served as a hospital during and after the battle. Twelve nuns from the Sisters of Charity at Emmitsburg, Maryland—later remembered as the "Angels of the Battlefield"—began their work here on July 4. The sisters cared for the wounded at several of the field hospitals in and around the town. This church sheltered 250 soldiers. An operating table was positioned inside the main entrance, providing daylight for the surgeons during the grisly amputations.

Above: Ginnie Wade, the only Gettysburg civilian killed during the battle, was born in this house in 1843. This house is at 242 Baltimore Street. The day she was killed, Wade was at her sister's residence farther south on Baltimore Street and closer to Cemetery Hill.

Above: The First Shot marker is to the left of a house and on the embankment above Route 30. The five-foot granite shaft (*right*) was erected in 1886 by the three men involved in firing the first shot of the battle: Levi S. Shafer, Marcellus E. Jones, and Alex Riddler.

Left: Built in 1858 in the fashionable Italianate villa style, Gettysburg's railroad depot with its telegraph line afforded transportation and communication. On July 1 the depot and platform were commandeered for use as an army hospital. After the battle, the U.S. Sanitary Commission set up tents across the tracks from the rear platform.

On the grounds of the Gettysburg Fire Company on Stratton Street, a new memorial marks the position where Sgt .Amos Humiston of the 154th New York was killed on July 1, 1863. The sergeant's identity was unknown when his body was discovered with a photograph of his children clutched in his hands. After the widespread distribution of the picture and story, his widow identified the photograph as one she had sent to him shortly after the battle of Chancellorsville.

Facing page (top): The building that came to house the Gettysburg Academy was erected at 66-68 West High Street in 1813–14. At first the structure served as the first building of the Gettysburg Lutheran Theological Seminary and Pennsylvania College. In subsequent years it became the home of the Reverend David Eyster, who died in 1860. His widow operated a young women's academy here at the time of the battle. An artillery shell is still embedded in the upper wall of this building.

Facing page (bottom): This is the only building remaining on the McPherson farm just west of town—and the scene of the first fighting at Gettysburg. At the time of the battle the farm was being worked by tenant farmers, the John Slentz family. They fled shortly after the fighting began, and the buildings were used by the Confederates as hospitals.

Above: A marker about one mile east of Gettysburg along Route 30 is all that commemorates Camp Letterman.

Left: The land on which Camp Letterman was set up after the battle was recently offered for sale. To the consternation of preservationists, the tract has been approved for commercial development.

> The medical director of the Middle Department and provost-marshal of the Eighth Army Corps are charged to see that this order is strictly executed.

When he saw the numbers of Confederate prisoners swell, Abraham Lincoln believed he glimpsed the end of the war. August 8 was declared to be a day for national thanksgiving, praise, and prayer, because "it had pleased Almighty God to hearken to the supplications and prayers of an afflicted people, and to vouchsafe to the army and navy of the United States, on the land and on the sea, victories so signal and so effective as to furnish reasonable grounds for augmented confidence the Union of these States will be maintained, their constitution preserved, and their peace and prosperity permanently secured."[7]

THE PENNSYLVANIA Thirty-sixth Emergency Militia had been mustered into service for ninety days or less and was mustered out by Special Orders No. 54 on August 4, 1863. The unit was replaced with the Fifty-first Pennsylvania Militia. On August 11 the men of the Pennsylvania Thirty-sixth returned to their homes.

The Fifty-first Pennsylvania Militia was also known as the Second Coal Regiment. Its colonel was Oliver Hopkinson, who had formerly served as the lieutenant colonel of the First Delaware Infantry, but he had resigned from that command on December 14, 1862. Hopkinson became the commander of the post at Gettysburg, and his lieutenant colonel, Michael A. Burke, was installed as provost marshal. They performed their duties for less than a month: The Fifty-first was mustered out on September 1, 1863.

•15•

LIFE AS A NURSE

I feel assured I shall never feel horrified at anything that may happen to me here-after. . . . I do not know when I shall go home—it will be according to how long this hospital stays here and whether another battle comes soon.

CORNELIA HANCOCK

P ROFESSIONAL NURSES DID NOT exist prior to the Civil War. In the begin-ning of the war, the nurse's task fell to soldiers who were deemed unfit for regular duties, having reported to the hospital for sick call. Ambulatory patients performed the nursing duties and chores. They were present only as they convalesced. These men had no training in medical care and were of little practical use. Most of their time was occupied with comforting patients rather than addressing their medical needs. Civilians assisted in taking care of the daily tasks like collecting and distributing supplies and food, cleaning, washing, keeping records, and communicating with the relatives and friends of the wounded.

Dorothea Dix was named the Union's superintendent of female nurses. A noted social reformer, Dix crusaded for more than twenty years toward improving treatment for mentally ill patients and for better prison condi-tions. Softspoken yet autocratic, Dix volunteered her services to the Union after the attack on Fort Sumter and received the appointment in June 1861. At the age of fifty-nine, she was in charge of all women nurses working in army hospitals. Serving in her newly created position without pay throughout the war, Dix quickly molded her vaguely defined duties. Her general responsibilities included screening volunteers and establishing the rules for hospital duty.

She had strict requirements for her nurse volunteers.[1] She rejected women whose cheeks she thought were too rosy. She knew what she wanted and what she did not want in her nursing applicants. Her requirements stated: "No woman under thirty need apply to serve in government hospitals. All nurses are required to be plain looking women. Their dresses must be brown or black, with no bows, no curls, no jewelry, and no hoop skirts."[2]

At the time, female nurses were not accepted as a necessary part of medical care. Dix convinced skeptical military officials, unaccustomed to female nurses in the midst of their armies, that women could perform the work well. As acceptance of female nurses grew, she then began recruiting women. She strove to ensure that the ranks of her nurses were not inundated with undependable and marriage-minded young ladies.

With Dix's strict and arbitrary requirements in place, more than three thousand women served as Union army nurses. As the war continued, some of her requirements relaxed. Dix looked after the welfare of both the nurses, who labored in an often brutal environment, and the soldiers to whom they ministered, obtaining medical supplies from private sources when they were not forthcoming from the government. She was nicknamed "Dragon Dix" by some. She was often stern and curt. Dix clashed frequently with the military bureaucracy and sometimes ignored administrative details. There is no doubt, however, that the wounded of Gettysburg received better care because of Dix's strict policies.

CORNELIA HANCOCK served as a volunteer civilian nurse at Gettysburg. A Quaker from Hancock's Bridge, Salem County, New Jersey, Hancock often visited her sister, Ellen, in Philadelphia. During those visits she developed an interest in nursing. Accompanying her brother-in-law, Dr. Henry T. Child, to Gettysburg, Hancock wrote often to her sister.

Hancock's brother had gone to war, and she wanted to do her part by helping to care for the wounded. Her being at Gettysburg was not without opposition. Dorothea Dix objected to her accompanying the Philadelphia doctor because Hancock was twenty-three years old—too young per Dix's criteria—and because she deemed the girl to be pretty. Hancock, however, did not accept the rejection of her service. She appealed and joined her brother-in-law, not waiting for a decision regarding the appeal.

They arrived in Gettysburg on July 6. Once Hancock was in Gettysburg, no one questioned her credentials or purpose, and she gained the respect and affection of the soldiers and the medical staff. She immersed herself in the care of the wounded, and she reported the vivid horrors of war that she witnessed when she wrote to her relatives in descriptive, heartfelt letters.

There was such an overwhelming need for medical assistants that Hancock's capabilities were never questioned. She soon became a trusted aide and was well respected among the medical providers. This allowed her to obtain an agreement that the surgeons in charge of the field hospitals could appoint whomever they wished to work under them "irrespective of age, size or looks." This cherished agreement made it possible for Hancock to circumvent Dix's authority and continue her work as a nurse.

Hancock's vivid letter of July 8 to her sister describes the situation and task in Gettysburg:

We have been two days on the field; go out about eight and come in about six—go in ambulances or army buggies. The surgeons of the Second Corps had one put at our disposal. I feel assured I shall never feel horrified at anything that may happen to me hereafter. There is a great want of surgeons here; there are hundreds of brave fellows, who have not had their wounds dressed since the battle. Brave is not the word; more, more Christian fortitude never was witnessed than they exhibit, always [they] say—"Help my neighbor first he is worse." The Second Corps did the heaviest fighting, and, of course, all who were badly wounded, were in the thickest of the fight, and, therefore, we deal with the very best class of the men—that is the bravest. My name is particularly grateful to them because it is Hancock. General [Winfield Scott] Hancock is very popular with his men. The reason why they suffer more in this battle is because our army is victorious and marching on after Lee, leaving the wounded for citizens and a very few surgeons. The citizens are stripped of everything they have, so you must see the exhausting state of affairs. The Second Army Corps alone had two thousand men wounded, this I had from the Surgeon's head quarters.

I cannot write more. There is no mail that comes in, we send letters out: I believe the Government has possession of the road. I hope you will write. It would be very pleasant to have letters to read in the evening, for I am so tired I cannot write them. Get the Penn Relief to send clothing here; there are many men without anything but a shirt lying in poor shelter tents, calling on God to take them from this world of suffering; in fact the air is rent with petitions to deliver them from their sufferings. . . .

I do not know when I shall go home—it will be according to how long this hospital stays here and whether another battle comes soon. I can go right in an ambulance without being any expense to myself. The Christian Committee support us and when they get tired the Sanitary is on hand. Uncle Sam is very rich, but very slow, and if it was not for the Sanitary, much suffering would ensue. We give the men toast and eggs for breakfast, beef tea at ten o'clock, ham and bread for dinner, and jelly and bread for supper. Dried rusk* would be nice if they were only here. Old sheets we would give much for. Bandages are plenty but sheets very scarce. We have plenty of woolen blankets now, in fact the hospital is well supplied, but for about five days after the battle, the men had no blankets nor scarce any shelter.

It took nearly five days for some three hundred surgeons to perform the amputations that occurred here, during which time the rebels lay in a dying condition without their wounds being dressed or scarcely any food. If the rebels did not get severely punished for this battle, then I am no judge. We have but one rebel in our camp now; he says he never fired his gun if he could help it, and, therefore, we treat him first rate. One man died this morning. I fixed him up as nicely as the place will allow; he will be buried this afternoon. We are becoming somewhat civilized here now and the men are cared for well.

On reading the news of the copperhead† performance, in a tent where eight men lay with nothing but stumps (they call a leg cut off above the knee a "stump") they said if they held on a little longer they would form a stump

---

* A light, soft, often sweetened bread or biscuit.
† Southern sympathizers.

brigade and go and fight them. We have some plucky boys in the hospital, but they suffer awfully. One had his leg cut off yesterday, and some of the ladies, newcomers, were up to see him. I told them if they had seen as many as I had they would not go far to see the sight again. I could stand by and see a man's head taken off I believe—you get so used to it here. I should be perfectly contented if I could receive my letters. I have the cooking all on my mind pretty much. I have torn almost all my clothes off of me, and Uncle Sam has given me a new suit. William says I am very popular here as I *am* such a contrast to some of the office-seeking women who swarm around hospitals. I am black as an Indian and dirty as a pig and as well as I ever was in my life—have a nice bunk and tent about twelve feet square. I have a bed that is made of four crotch sticks and some sticks laid across and pine boughs laid on that with blankets on top. It is equal to any mattress ever made. The tent is open at night and sometimes I have laid in the damp all night long, and got up all right in the morning.

The suffering we get used to and the nurses and doctors, stewards, etc., are very jolly and sometimes we have a good time. It is very pleasant weather now. There is all in getting to do what you want to do and I am doing that. . . .

Pads are terribly needed here. Bandages and lint are plenty. I would like to see seven barrels of dried rusk here. I do not know the day of the week or anything else. Business is slackening a little though—order is beginning so things will be right. One poor fellow is hollow—wounding fearfully now while his wounds are being dressed.

There is no more impropriety in a *young* person being here provided they are sensible than a sexagenarian. Most polite and obliging are all the soldiers to me.

It is a very good place to meet celebrities; they come here from all parts of the United States to see their wounded. Senator [Henry] Wilson, Mr. [Elihu B.] Washburn, and one of the Minnesota Senators have been here. I get beef tenderloin for dinner.—Ladies who work are favored but the dress-up palaverers are passed by on the other side. I tell you I have lost my memory almost entirely, but it is gradually returning. Dr. Child has done very good service here. All is well with me; we do not know much war news, but I know I am doing all I can, so I do not concern further. Kill the copperheads. Write everything, however trifling, it is all interest here.

Cornelia Hancock wrote often to her family and friends in Salem County and Philadelphia. She constantly asked them for food, clothing, bandages, sheets, and blankets. They responded generously to all her requests. The wounded in Hancock's charge were often better cared for than others because of the constant flow of these additional supplies from her contacts.

In a letter written just after she arrived at Gettysburg, Hancock noted:

I am very tired tonight: having been in the field all day—went to the 3rd Division 2nd Army Corps. I suppose there are about five hundred wounded belonging to it. . . . There are no words in the English language to express the suffering I witnessed today. . . . The men lie on the ground; their clothes have been cut off them to dress their wounds, they are half naked, have nothing but hard tack to eat only as the Sanitary Commission, Christian Association, and so forth give them. I was in that Corps all day, not another women within a half-mile. . . . You can tell Aunt that there is every opportunity for "secesh" sympathizers to do good work among the butternuts; we have lots of them here suffering fearfully. . . . [F]our surgeons . . . were busy all day amputating legs and arms. I gave to every man that had a leg or arm off a gill of wine, to every wounded in Third Division, one glass of lemonade, some bread and preserves and tobacco . . . for they need it very much, they are so exhausted. I would get on first rate if they would not ask me to write to their wives; that I cannot do without crying. . . . I do not mind the sight of blood, having seen limbs taken off and was not sick at all. Women are needed here badly, . . . but nothing short of an order from Secretary [Edwin M.] Stanton or General [Henry W.] Halleck will let you through the lines. . . . [I]f we had not met Miss Dix at Baltimore Depot we should have not gotten through.

Hancock always described in great detail the conditions at the field hospitals at Gettysburg in her correspondence. From the Third Division, Second Corps hospital, she wrote on Sunday, July 26:

There is nothing to cook with, hence, I have nothing to do, and, therefore, the time to write. Such days will come here that we have to see our wounded men fed with dry bread and poor coffee. . . . I would give anything to have a barrel of butter and some dried rusk. . . . I wish you would get something of the kind and have Mrs. Jones requested to forward to me. I have eight wall tents full of amputated men. The tents of the wounded I look right out on. . . . The most painful task we have to perform here is entertaining the friends who come from home and see their friends all mangled up.

On a more personal note, on August 6, she wrote, "I expect I shall be able to draw twelve dollars from the government now, but if thee can draw any money for me, send it along, for it is a poor place to be without money."

Hancock also cared for wounded Southerners, although she seemed less enthusiastic about that. On August 8 she wrote: "Sallie S I hear has passed away. But surely as I live it does not seem to me as if I should ever make any account of death again. I have seen it disposed of in such a summary manner out here. I have one tent of Johnnies in my ward, but I am not obliged to give them anything but whiskey."

She worked long hours at Camp Letterman, as she reported in an August 14 letter: "I cannot explain it, but I feel so erect, and can go steadily from one thing to another from half past six o'clock in the morning until ten o'clock at night, and feel more like work than when I got up at home."

Hancock earned the respect of the wounded by her hard work. They presented her with an inscribed silver medal: "Miss Cornelia Hancock, presented by the wounded soldiers 3rd Division 2nd Army Corps. Testimonial of regard for ministrations of mercy to the wounded soldiers at Gettysburg, PA—July 1863."

GEORGEANNA MURISON WOOLSEY was among the first nurses trained by the Women's Central Association of Relief. From New York, after just one month, she was assigned to Washington, D.C., and given the task of receiving new nurses. Woolsey traveled to Gettysburg with the U.S. Sanitary Commission to serve as a nurse. Her observations were originally printed for private distribution among a few soldiers aid societies.

Woolsey reported that the Sanitary Commission had its "camp set up in town by the railroad depot. Here we set up two stoves, with four large boilers always kept full of soup and coffee, watched by four or five black men who did the cooking under our direction, and sang (not under our direction) at the tops of their voices all day."

She also noted that many blacks came to Gettysburg under a government contract to repair the railroad:

> Every night, they took their recreation after the heavy work of the day was
> over, in prayer meetings. . . . We went over one night and listened for an hour,
> while they sang, collected under the fly of a tent . . . men only,—all very black
> and very earnest. They prayed with all their souls, as only black men and
> slaves can: for themselves and for the dear white people who had come over to
> the meeting, and for "Massa Lincoln" for whom they seemed to have a rever-
> ential affection. . . . Very little care was taken of these poor men. . . . They
> were grateful for every little thing.

Woolsey recalled that she and some friends went into town and hunted up several dozen bright handkerchiefs, hemmed them, and sent them over to be distributed after the next meeting.

> They were put on the table in the tent, and one by one the men came up to
> get them. Purple and blue and yellow, the handkerchiefs were, and the desire
> of every man's heart fastened itself on a yellow one. . . . When the distribution
> was over, every man tied his head up in his handkerchief and sang one more
> hymn, keeping time, all round, with blue and purple and yellow nods and
> thanking and blessing the white people . . . as much as if the cotton handker-
> chiefs had been all gold leaf. One man came over to our tent, next day, to say:
> "Missus, was it you who sent me that present? I never had anything so beauti-
> ful in all my life before;" and he only had a blue one, too.

NURSES AT Gettysburg did more than dress the wounds and assist the surgeons during surgery. Their duties were varied, including everything from
washing to cooking. Most of the wounded were as far away from their
homes as they had ever been in their life. In the strange yet beautiful
countryside of Adams County, many longed for the simple life they had
known before the war. This is best illustrated by the request of one of the
soldiers when he asked a camp nurse to sing a hymn. "O yeas," the
woman replied. "I'll sing you a song that will do for either side." A nearby
doctor recalled:

There, in the midst of that band of neglected sufferers, she stood, and with a look of heavenly pity and earnestness, her eyes raised to God, sung, "When this cruel war is over," in a clear, pleading voice, that made me remove my hat, and long to cast myself upon my knees! Sighs and groans ceased; and while the song when on pain seemed charmed away. The moment it stopped one poor fellow, who had lost his right arm, raised his left and said, "O ma'am, I wish I had my o'her arm back, if it was only to clap my hands for your song."[3]

Comfort also included cooking. Yet, for some reason, feeding the wounded seemed to be a low priority to the army. The nurses took up the task. To do so meant getting up very early each day. Volunteer nurse Charlotte McKay commented: "My program for a day at Gettysburg was to rise as early as possible in the morning, and send out everything that was available in the way of food to the wounded. An item for one morning was a barrel of eggs, and as it was impossible to cook them all, they were distributed raw, the men who had the use of their hands making little fires in front of their tents, and boiling them in tin-cups, for themselves and their disabled comrades."[4]

As time went on, the soldiers recovered enough to travel home or they succumbed to their injuries. For those who died in the field hospitals, a nurse prepared the body for burial. She cleaned the body, straightened the soldier's clothing, then wrapped him in a blanket. Few coffins were available, but one could be found if there was enough money in the pockets of the dead man or if friends donated sufficient funds to purchase one. These coffins, however, were little more than crude pine boxes.

The body would be carried to a nearby cemetery, and some words were recited from a burial book. Prayers were offered in a simple service, then the burial party—often friends of the dead soldier—lowered the corpse into the grave. There was no grand ceremony, no band, no honor guards or military splendor and pomp. Then the burial party shoveled dirt into the hole, and the grave might be marked with whatever piece of wood was available.

Nurses rarely attended burials. They were busy elsewhere with the men who still had a chance at life. In the evening, however, many nurses walked through the cemeteries, reading the markers, and grieving quietly over the graves of soldiers whom they could not save.

Spiritual matters also, to some degree, fell to the nurses. L. P. Brockett and Mary C. Vaughan observed: "Another part of her work and one of special interest and usefulness was the daily and Sabbath worship at her rooms, in which such of the soldiers as were disposed, participated. The contrabands were also the objects of her sympathy and care, and she assembled them for religious worship and instruction on the Sabbath."[5]

Many women from Gettysburg nursed the wounded until they were able to travel to Camp Letterman or another destination. From changing dressings to baking, Gettysburg's women cared for the wounded throughout the ordeal.

For three weeks Georgeanna Woolsey worked at Camp Letterman and at the Gettysburg depot in the lodge set up by the Sanitary Commission to feed the many Union and Confederate wounded who waited for the next train out of town. The days were long and tedious, but she persevered.

Afterward, she wrote about her experiences, praising the women of Gettysburg for their faithfulness and charity to the wounded as well as to the strangers who came to town. She did not have the same impression of some of the men who lived in Adams County. Woolsey recalled a visit to the camp by a curious farmer:

> Few good things can be said of the Gettysburg farmers, and I only use Scripture language in calling them "evil beasts." One of this kind came creeping into our camp three weeks after the battle. He lived five miles only from the town, and had "never seen a rebel." He heard we had some of them, and came down to see them. "Boys," we said, marching him into the tent which happened to be full of rebels that were waiting for the train; "Boys, here's a man who never saw a rebel in his life, and wants to look at you;" and there he stood with his mouth wide open, and there they lay in rows, laughing at him, stupid old Dutchman.
>
> "And why haven't you seen a rebel?" Mrs.—— said; "why didn't you take your gun and help to drive them out of your town?"
>
> "A feller might'er got hit!"—which reply was quite too much for the rebels. They roared with laughter at him, up and down the tent.[6]

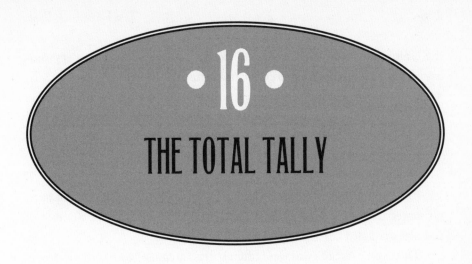

• 16 •

THE TOTAL TALLY

It is believed that the enemy suffered severely in these operations, but our own loss has not been light.

ROBERT E. LEE

WITHIN AN AREA OF about 25 square miles, the battle of Gettysburg was fought with more than 172,000 men and 500 cannons. When the fighting was over, the Army of the Potomac had suffered 23,049 casualties. The Army of Northern Virginia reportedly had 28,000 casualties. The total of 51,000 casualties was the highest toll of any single engagement in American history.[1]

Although there is no consensus regarding the total casualty figures of the war, generally speaking the number of fatalities was at least 618,000.[2] It should be noted that some scholars state the total death toll reached 700,000. The total number that seems most often quoted is 620,000.[3]

Similarly, there are many estimates on the number of casualties suffered during the battle of Gettysburg.[4] Of the estimated 51,000 casualties, the Union army suffered 23,000, the Confederates 28,000. These approximate numbers have been broken down further:

	KILLED	WOUNDED	MISSING	TOTAL	% OF ARMY
Union	3,155	14,530	5,365	23,050	27
Confederate	4,500	18,750	5,250	28,500	37

Exact numbers will never be known. Confederate casualties have been estimated as high as 30,000. In general, many concur that the number of casualties equaled at least one-third of Lee's army.

The word *casualties* was (and often still is) an ambiguous term. It generally includes any soldier who deserted or was missing, wounded, captured, or killed. If a soldier was not present at roll call, he was most likely counted as a casualty.

Many incorrectly believe that more than fifty thousand soldiers were killed at Gettysburg. There were more than fifty thousand casualties but approximately seventy-five hundred deaths. Of the more than thirty thousand wounded, approximately 10 percent died from their injuries. Adding those to the total killed, ten thousand additional deaths are attributable to the battle.

In a letter to Jefferson Davis on July 4, Lee discussed his losses and emphasized the number of general officers who had been killed or crippled or captured in Pennsylvania:

It is believed that the enemy suffered severely in these operations, but our own loss has not been light. General [William] Barksdale is killed. Generals [Richard] Garnett and [Lewis A.] Armistead are missing as prisoner. Generals [William D.] Pender and [Isaac] Trimble are wounded in the leg, General [John Bell] Hood in the arm, and General [Henry] Heth slightly in the head. General [James L.] Kemper, it is feared, is mortally wounded. Our losses embrace many other valuable officers and men. General Wade Hampton was severely wounded in a different action in which the cavalry was engaged yesterday.[5]

Unfortunately, there is no breakdown of the number of wounded or killed per day. Because many of the wounded could not be gathered from the field immediately following an engagement, any attempt to account for the injured on one day or another is impossible.

Nevertheless, at the end of the battle, there were more than fifty thousand men killed, wounded, or missing. Of those men, more than thirty thousand were wounded and required immediate medical attention.

The Army of the Potomac began the battle with more than eighty-three thousand men. All the army's corps except the Sixth had long casualty lists. The First and Third Corps were so badly decimated during the battle that they were later combined with the Second Corps. Of Meade's initial corps commanders, Maj. Gen. John F. Reynolds was dead and Maj. Gens. Daniel E. Sickles and Winfield Scott Hancock were both seriously wounded (although Hancock returned to duty).

Lee had brought about seventy-five thousand men across the Potomac River into Maryland and across the Mason-Dixon Line into Pennsylvania. His unsuccessful attempts to punch a hole through the Union lines had cost him more than twenty-eight thousand casualties. His army suffered a heavy loss of field-grade officers, which proved a detriment to him for the remainder of the war.

REMEMBERING AND COMMEMORATING

•17•

RETURNING TO NORMALCY

We could not open our windows for weeks because of the terrible stench.

NELLIE AUGHINBAUGH

As THE DAYS PASSED after the battle, Gettysburg began to return to a level of normalcy. Those who had fled just before the Confederates arrived returned now to their homes. Businesses reopened, and the county's farmers tended their crops. Although the disruption caused by the battle was immense, over the next several months, life in Gettysburg returned to its routine. While the battle affected everyone somehow or someway, the demands of everyday life mandated a return to ordinary existence. Some of Gettysburg's black residents, however, never returned.

Shortly after she returned to town, Catherine Ziegler commented, "Pen cannot describe the awful sights that met our gaze."[1] She remarked about the stench of the dead animals. When she and her family arrived at their home near the Lutheran seminary, the sights were shocking: "It was ghastly to see, some of the men were lying in pools of blood on the bare floors where they had been placed on July 1st, many having received no

211

care whatsoever." The Zieglers cleaned up their living quarters and tended the wounded in their building.

The summer heat persisted with steamy days and nights. Only occasional thunderstorms offered temporary relief and quenched thirsty crops. The town's three newspapers resumed publication, railroad service was restored, and school, college, and seminary classes reconvened.

Water service, however, was becoming a huge problem. Wells, springs, streams, and cisterns were low. The problem only worsened. The hastily established latrines, the dead buried in shallow graves, animal wastes, and the runoff from the battlefields contaminated the remaining potable water. Heavy rain only worsened the situation, polluting regular water sources.

Under the summer sun the putrid odors of the battlefield lingered in and around the town. "We could not open our windows for weeks because of the terrible stench," Nellie Aughinbaugh recalled.[2] The odors were so wretched that residents carried fragrance bottles to offset the smell. "Everyone went around with a bottle of pennyroyal or peppermint oil," Albertus McCreary noted.[3]

For weeks after the fighting, hastily buried soldiers began to rise from their shallow graves. Thunderstorms excavated many burial sites, uncovering bodies. Under the sun, the emerged bodies rotted, adding to the unpleasant air around the town.

Flies massed in the area to feed on the decaying flesh. Fearful of disease, chloride of lime was spread on the streets to disinfect the mud, puddles, manure, and dirt. The strange smell of disinfectant and death hung in the air, making it just about breathable but still sickening.

Residents kept their windows closed as much as possible, shutting out the odor but keeping in the summer heat. "When you opened the windows for the morning air, you would be assailed by the foul odors," William McClean commented. "We citizens became gradually acclimated to it, but some visitors became ill, left for home and some died."[4]

On the positive side, the food crisis passed. Supplies arrived daily and regularly. Although many crops had been destroyed, some food became available from the nearby farms as their surviving crops matured. Meanwhile, the population of wounded men gradually declined, making food less of a problem.

The Sanitary Commission also moved quickly to alleviate the food crisis. "Beside our own men at the Lodge, we all had soldiers scattered about whom we could help from our supplies; and nice little puddings and jellies, or an occasional chicken, were a great treat to men condemned by their wounds to stay in Gettysburg, and obliged to live on what the empty town could provide," Georgeanna Woolsey recalled.[5]

THE PEOPLE of Gettysburg and Adams County had a long tradition of partisan politics. Republicans were considered pro-Union while, by inference, Democrats were considered anti-abolitionists. Republicans often labeled Democrats as unpatriotic, and in this area of southern Pennsylvania, a group formed a Union League Chapter. Its purpose was to stir patriotic sentiment in favor of the war. Now that the threat from the Confederate army was gone, strong partisan feelings erupted.

The animosity between the two parties surfaced with the sudden arrest of Charles and John Will, proprietors of the Globe Inn and staunch Democrats. They were reported to have been "harboring Confederates" during the battle. Attorney J. Cassat Neely successfully argued on behalf of the Wills that they treated the Southerners the same as they would have treated any paying guests at their inn. No aid or favor was unduly bestowed, but rather the Wills were shown to have suffered losses of supplies at the hands of their Confederate guests. The innkeepers argued that the charges brought against them were political. A provost marshal heard the case and agreed. "I am convinced there are political feelings between you people," he said and dropped the charges.

Henry J. Stahle was the editor of the *Compiler*, a vigorously Democratic weekly newspaper, and charges were filed against him, too. On July 1 Stahle went to the courthouse to find a surgeon to treat Union Col. William W. Dudley. A Confederate surgeon accompanied Stahle back to his home to examine and treat the man's leg wound. After the battle, Stahle's act was construed as aiding the enemy in apprehending a Union officer. The accusation was made by a prominent citizen and staunch Republican, attorney David Wills. Despite eyewitness testimony, including that of Colonel Dudley, the charge was pressed. Stahle was incarcerated in Baltimore at Fort McHenry.

A week later, Stahle's case was reviewed and labeled a sham. He was released and returned to Gettysburg, where he was promptly arrested again but then quickly released. He returned to Fort McHenry to face the new charges, which were again dismissed. Stahle returned to Gettysburg and resumed publication of his newspaper.

Other newspapers widely reported Stahle's arrest and condemned it. Robert G. Harper, editor of the competing, pro-Republican *Adams Sentinel*, condemned the arrest. The *Franklin Repository* in nearby Chambersburg published the following account:

Henry J. Stahle, of the Gettysburg *Compiler*, was arrested by Gen. Meade as soon as he gained possession of the town, and sent as a prisoner to Fort McHenry. We cannot form any judgment as to the guilt of Mr. Stahle from the statement and denials on the Gettysburg papers. It is alleged that he gave the rebels information where the Union troops and property were concealed, and rendered himself in other respects useful to the enemy.

We trust that Mr. Stahle has not been arrested and imprisoned without a purpose. If he has been guilty of the charges preferred against him, he should be promptly tried by a military court, convicted, and shot,—if innocent, he should be allowed an early opportunity to establish it and be discharged. It is high time that military arrests should be understood as meaning something beyond imprisonment without notice of charges and release without explanation. Had Daniel Dechert, of Hagerstown, been tried, convicted and inexorably executed, as he richly deserved, when he was detected as a spy within our lines, corresponding with and furnishing maps to bring the enemy to his own home, justice would have been vindicated and a wholesome practical lesson would have been learned by semi-traitors along the entire border. We insist that military arrests shall mean the prompt trial and conviction or acquittal of the accused, and that the penalty of treason, when clearly shown to extend to positive acts of hostility to the Government, shall be death. It is alike just and humane to the loyal people of the North that they shall not be the victims of cowardly spies and traitors at home; and if Mr. Stahle has by his acts brought himself within that class, he should die. But if he is the victim of personal or political prejudice, or of the inflamed public feeling naturally resulting from the shock of battle between the great armies at Gettysburg, he should have early and ample opportunity to vindicate himself, and be discharged to prove his devotion to the Government by an earnest support of the prosecution of the war. In this particular, we must confess, he has room for improvement.[6]

Politics in Gettysburg and Adams County continued to be antagonistic. The town remained a Republican stronghold, and the county populace remained Democratic. As weeks passed, Democrats grew more open in their attacks. They pointedly opposed emancipation, conscription, and the suppression of civil liberties. In the later fall election, the town supported Governor Curtin's reelection bid, but the county supported his Democratic challenger. Politics turned bitter. Lines were clearly drawn between the two parties, and politics was fiercely discussed and practiced. Gettysburg continued to support Republican candidates, and the following year, would support Lincoln against George B. McClellan. There were some local Democratic victories, including one of three positions on the town council.

ON A more human scale, notices began appearing in the newspapers shortly after the battle seeking information about loved ones or family heirlooms that may have been lost in the battle. One such notice appeared in the *Sentinel:* "Information Wanted: Any person at Gettysburg, who can give information of the exact burial place of Liet. Humphreville, of the 24th Michigan Inf., will confer a favor upon [his] Sister. Address Mrs. J. S. Whitcomn, Chicago, Ill. Any information with the Editor of the *Sentinel*, will be promptly communicated."

An example of a family's quest for a lost heirloom appeared in the July 30 issue:

> Lost: A large side double case gold watch with a link chain belonging to Captain W. L. Magruder, C.S.A., who was killed at Gettysburg, July 3; and thought to have been placed in possession of Captain W. D. Nau, Co. B, 11th Miss. Regt., who died, July 13th, at 1st Army Corps, 2d Division Hospital, and who, it is supposed, gave it to some one previous to his death for safe keeping. The full value of the watch will be given for its return and the information gratefully received. Apply to Mrs. Mary C. Magruder, 64 Cortland Street, Baltimore.

In the July 27 issue of the *Compiler* a notice appeared seeking information on the burial site of a fallen soldier: "Any person giving information at
this office where the grave of the Corporeal Wm. Strong, of the 2d
Delaware regiment, can be found will confer a great favor on his wife, who
had been searching in vain for his body during the past week." Strong's
body was located, and he was later reinterred in the Delaware section of
the National Cemetery. It is not known if the newspaper notice led to the
discovery of his body.

Visits to the battlefield and the various hospitals persisted throughout
this return to normalcy. By now, however, some county residents were gain-
ing a reputation for stinginess and greed.

"Thousands visited the battle, yet for days I did not see the first act of
charity from the people. Finally Secretary Cameron did bring and distrib-
ute (6) six lemons to the men of the hospital, and carried an officer away
in his carriage," Michigan surgeon Cyrus Bacon Jr. wrote in his daily register. "The people seem to consider us lawful prizes, and are not only extor-
tionate but give to us little real sympathy. A man comes after a bit with a
few bundles of straw. $1.00 for a loaf of bread. Such items makes one
indignant for the honor of this country."[7] Bacon acknowledged the difference between the townspeople and the county's farmers: "However, the
people of the city of Gettysburg in some measure redeem this character of
the country residents. They take the wounded into their houses and care
for them."

Bacon was not the only one to criticize the county residents for their
lack of charity. The power of the pen related similar stories of greed and
stinginess experienced by a visiting newspaper editor. Charles P. Cole,
editor of the Cortland, New York, weekly *Gazette & Banner* traveled to
Gettysburg after learning that his friend, Maj. Andrew Jackson Grover, had
been killed in action on July 1. At the request of Grover's widow, Cole
came to Gettysburg to retrieve the body.

By July 6 Cole had made his way to Gettysburg and managed to visit
one of the field hospitals where members from the Seventy-sixth New York
were being treated. He was able to learn the details of the thirty-two-year-
old major's death, but it was his trip to Gettysburg that provides some
insight of the mannerisms of the area farmers.

Cole stopped at a farm several miles above the Mason-Dixon Line. He asked the farmer if he could buy something to eat. The farmer replied that he had bread and meat, which Cole then requested. A short time later, a woman appeared "with a loaf of bread baked in a pint basin, and about three ounces of boiled ham, the smell of which clearly indicated that it had not had the best of care while being cured. We asked for a drink of water, and for a pail of water for the horse. After we had finished this sumptuous meal, we asked 'what was the charge?'"

The farmer said that the bread was a dollar and a half, the ham was a dollar, the pail of water was twenty-five cents, and the drink of water was ten cents. "Sir," Cole repled, "is not this an outrage for you, here in this loyal State of Pennsylvania; here where three days ago the sound of the enemy's cannon shook your very hills; where the army of the Union drove the invaders from your soil? I have come hundreds of miles in search of the remains of an officer who fell while defending your homes and broad acres from pillage, and you have the meanness to make this demand of me."

The man replied, "Well, if you succeed in getting the remains of your friend, the bread and meat is worth that, ain't it?"[8]

Cole recounted the conversation in his newspaper, which was read by Uberto Burnham of the Seventy-sixth New York. He concurred with the commonness of the scene, writing a letter on July 31 to his parents: "The editor gives a good and correct picture of things which he saw."[9]

Cole described the foul air and the great mounds of debris he encountered around Gettysburg:

We had proceeded but a short distance further when the terrible stench apprised us that we were not far from the scenes of the carnage of the first three days of July, 1863. It was nauseating in the extreme, so much so, that at times it was almost impossible for a person to breathe. Evidences of the battle-field soon became visible. Dead men and horses, pieces of shell, solid shot, grape, muskets, broken wagons, clothing, cartridge boxes, knapsacks, and everything that pertains to an army were strewn around for miles in great profusion.

Likewise, Cole described the scene at the local hotel: "The landlord informed us that he had nothing for man or beast. We finally got a place for our horse to remain under shelter, and procured a faithful soldier of one of the New Jersey regiments to guard him until morning." Cole and his companion each paid a dollar to sleep on the floor of a house in town.

The next day Cole was able to find Grover's grave without much difficulty. He had been buried on Thursday by men from his regiment who had been taken prisoner, and the grave had been marked. The situation, however, was not conducive to bringing the body to New York:

> After becoming satisfied that there could be no mistake as to the identity of the body, and convinced that it would be impossible to have the body removed in the condition it was then in, at this season of the year,—we returned to the town again, and made arrangements to have the body exhumed, placed in a coffin, and buried where his friends could regain him at a more suitable season of the year for such purposes. He is buried in the cemetery of the Reformed Dutch Church.[10]

Cole rode over to the battlefield and commented on the sight: "Horror of horrors! We are unable to describe the scenes which we witnessed. We saw men rebels—piled up in heaps, who were yet unburied. Many of them were in such a state of decomposition that their appearances were nauseating in the extreme, while their bloated and blackened corpses were disgusting to the sight."

His chronicle included a brief description of the damage at the Evergreen Cemetery:

> The once beautiful "Evergreen Cemetery," presented a sad appearance. From its commanding site, it was found necessary to post certain of our batteries on the summit of the eminence on which the city of the dead is located. It was one of the best positions we occupied, and the fire of the enemy's artillery was constantly directed upon it with a view of driving us back from the crest.
>
> The ground about our guns was literally strewn with shot and shell; tombstones erected over the remains of beloved relations were thrown from their positions and broken into fragments; graves were turned up by plunging shot; tasteful railings and other ornamental work around the lots were badly shattered, and even the beautiful archway over the entrance to the sacred

enclosure was splintered and penetrated. One thing remained untouched, which was the placard at the entrance reading: "All persons are prohibited from disturbing any flower or shrub within these grounds."

On the basis of the wreckage around him, Cole commented:

> The battle took its toll on Gettysburg, and its residents probably suffered more from the rapacity of the rebels than those of any other town in Pennsylvania. Stores were ransacked and emptied of their contents. Anything they could not use the rebels destroyed.
>
> Dwellings too were entered, and where men's clothing could not be procured, that of women and children was taken into the streets and roads, torn into fragments and cast aside. The houses of the professors in the educational institutions shared the same fate; and from one store here even the clocks were taken out and destroyed. Everything eatable and drinkable was secured by the rebels, and such was their unlimited stealing that they did not even extend the courtesy of offering Southern shinplasters. Visitors to the battlefield will fare badly if they do not provide themselves before leaving with such articles of food and luxury as may be necessary during their sojourn in that section.

It was these losses described by Cole that the townspeople were beginning to put behind them. Each day, despite the damages and shortages, the wounded still lingering in hospitals, and the sickening odors fouling the air, life in and around Gettysburg was returning to normal.

Cole, however, was not impressed with what he termed the "selfishness of the people" of Gettysburg:

> The conduct of a majority of the male citizens of Gettysburg, and the surrounding county of Adams, is such as to stamp them with dishonor and cravenhearted meanness. And these are the unanimous sentiments of the whole Army of the Potomac—an army who fought as men never fought before, and who feel that the doors from which they drove a host of robbers, thieves and cut-throats, were not worthy of being defended. The male citizens mostly ran away and left the women and children to the mercy of their enemies.

Cole lashed out at the Pennsylvanians who had profiteered from the battle:

On their return, instead of lending a helping hand to our wounded, and opening their houses to our famished officers and soldiers, they manifested indecent haste to present their bills to the military authorities for payment of losses inflicted by both armies. On the streets the burden of their talk was in regard to their losses, and whether the government could be compelled to pay for this or that.

One man said the stench from dead horses on his farm was very offensive, but he would not bury them himself unless some officer of the government would guarantee that he should be paid for it. On Thursday, a bill of seventeen hundred dollars was presented to Gen. [Oliver O.] Howard for damage to the cemetery during the fight. One man presented Gen. Howard a bill of thirty-seven cents for four bricks knocked off the chimney of his house by our artillery.

Our wearied, and in many instances wounded soldiers, found pumps locked so that they could not get water. A hungry officer asked a woman for something to eat, and she first inquired how much he would pay. Another begged for a drink of milk, and the female wished to know if he had any change.

These persons, it should be remarked, were not poor, but among the most substantial citizens of the town and vicinity, around whom, upon either hand, are fertile lands of yellow wheat pining for the sickle, and tall maize nodding obeisance to the wind and to numerous passersby.

We saw a poor wounded soldier in the city of Gettysburg pay a dollar for a bandage about two inches wide and a yard long. Pies baked in saucers, were sold for a dollar a piece, and milk was dealt out to the wounded and thirsty defenders of the soil of Pennsylvania at twenty-five cents a quart.

Cole contrasted the Pennsylvanians with the warm hospitality of Marylanders: "No doors were closed upon the weary soldiers, nor pumps chained up against them." He added that women and children "appeared at the doors of their dwellings with delicacies and cold spring water for the soldiers."

We spent the night of Tuesday at the mansion of one of the substantial farmers, who was surrounded by all that wealth could give him. His family had taken every sheet and pillow case from their beds, and the wife and three daughters had taken every garment of their underclothes and tore them into bandages, and sent them to the Union soldiers, free of charge. Their supply of provisions was nearly exhausted, and their sumptuous table of ten days before, had given places to bread and bacon. But such as they had was freely provided, and no remuneration would be received. Let us from all quarters have a little less lip—patriotism which is ready to show itself in deeds and sacrifices, too, if they are called for.

There are other instances of the Adams County farmers profiting from the wounded. Soldiers, still recovering from the work of the surgeon's knife and saw, needed transportation from the field hospitals to the railroad depot. "Many hired farmers' wagons, as hard as the farmers' fists themselves, and were jolted down to the railroad, at three or four dollars the man," Georgeanna Woolsey observed.[11]

It took months for the debris of battle to be cleared. Area farmers suffered losses to their crops, livestock, and property, such as fences and buildings. Some now had cemeteries on their farmland. The residents of Gettysburg suffered economic losses, including damaged or stolen personal property, buildings marked by projectiles, and business losses. Stores had been looted or ransacked. Private homes had been entered and searched, and many items had been stolen or confiscated. Government warehouses were raided and the contents taken by the Confederate army. Yet as the days moved on, daily commerce resumed.

An influx of relief workers impacted the townspeople but also offered economic opportunity. The hotels overflowed. Many stayed in private homes, mostly gratis. More people came to Gettysburg: Sanitary and Christian Commission workers and nurses, relatives in search of loved ones, and lastly, those who came to sightsee, gawk, or profit from the debris left on the battlefield.

During these tense weeks, only one case of violence against a citizen by military personnel was reported. During the evening of July 5, Maj. Michael Burns of the Seventy-third New York drew his sword and attacked the Reverend Walter Alexander of the Christian Commission in the home of Mary Wade on Breckinridge Street. Mary Wade had just buried her daughter, Ginnie, the day before, and Alexander was visiting to offer his condolences. Burns left a a gashing wound on the reverend's head. Burns was arrested, and Alexander was treated for his wound.

The Fahnestock home on the west side of Baltimore Street hosted an entire delegation from Ohio, including the state's governor. "Our beds and tables were filled for weeks afterwards," Elizabeth McClean commented.[12] Both the Sanitary and Christian Commissions helped to sustained the Fahnestock business by purchasing supplies. The family store also served as temporary headquarters for the Sanitary Commission. The Christian Commission made its headquarters at John L. Schick's store in the Stoever building on the west side of Baltimore Street. The work of these two commissions quickly improved the living conditions of wounded soldiers, both Union and Confederates.

As John Burns was recuperating on his porch on Chambersburg Street, photographers from Mathew Brady's studio took his picture. Brady brought back Burns's story to Washington, and soon the War of 1812 veteran emerged as one of the more interesting personalities from the battle. The volunteer soldier's story inspired thousands, and his legend grew. In the next several months, he was a national hero.

Burns later served as a battlefield guide. A hard-nosed Unionist, he accused anyone in the county he did not like of being a traitor. Burns lived for nearly a decade after the battle. He was buried in Evergreen Cemetery.[13]

Meanwhile, regimental bands helped the injured men to pass the time by playing patriotic selections at the hospitals, also hoping to lift the spirits of the wounded. There were fewer amputations, but there were still secondary surgeries going on.

The number of field hospitals declined with the opening of Camp Letterman. The wounded, when they could tolerate the trip, were transported by horse-drawn ambulance to the new general hospital along the York road about a mile east of town. Together the bumpy roads and the creaky ambulances promised any wounded soldier a pain-filled ride.

Some of the townspeople provided long-term care to specific wounded soldiers. One such case was described by Tillie Pierce: "A few days after the battle, several soldiers came to our house and asked mother if she would allow them to bring their wounded Colonel to the place, provided they would send two nurses along to help wait on him, saying they would like to have him kept at a private house." The family consented.

Tillie noted: "The wounded officer was carried to the house on a litter, and was suffering greatly. After they got him up stairs, and were about placing him on the bed, it was found to be too short, so that the foot-board had to be taken off and an extension added. The Colonel was a very tall man and of fine proportions."

He had been severely wounded in the right ankle and a shoulder, which extended to his spine. The surgeons were going to amputate his foot, saying it was necessary to save his life, but the colonel objected, and reportedly said that if his foot must go, he would go, too.

"Mother waited on him constantly, and the nurses could not have been more devoted," Tillie recalled. "He was highly esteemed by all his men, many of whom visited him at the house, and even wept over him in his suffering and helplessness. They always spoke of him as one of the bravest men in the army."

The colonel's sister came to Gettysburg. Tillie remembered that her "tender care and cheering words no doubt hastened his recovery."

"Several months elapsed before he was able to be removed; when, on a pair of crutches, he left for his home in St. Paul. As he was leaving the house he could hardly express fully his thanks and appreciation for all our kindness; and on parting kissed us all, as though he were bidding farewell to his own kith and kin. We, on our part, felt as though one of our own family were leaving. He promised that whenever able he would come back to see us," Tillie noted. The story, however, did not end there:

> About three years after the battle, I was standing on the front pavement one day, when a carriage suddenly stopped at the front door. A gentleman alighted, and kissed me without saying a word. I knew it was the Colonel by his tall, manly form. He ran up the front porch, rang the bell, and on meeting the rest of the family, heartily shook hands, and greeted mother and sister with a kiss. We were all glad to meet each other again, and we earnestly desired him to stay. He however said his time was limited, and his friends were waiting in the carriage to go over the battlefield. So we were forced to again say farewell.

The officer was Col. William Colvill of the First Minnesota. He was wounded at the Wheatfield on July 2 when the columns had become mixed with each other because of the dense smoke. The fighting was intense and desperate. Only 47 of the 262 men of the regiment survived the charge.

As the wounded were transferred to Camp Letterman, the town's churches emptied also. Church services resumed shortly afterward.

As visitors to town searched for loved ones, those fortunate enough to have time, a wagon, and a horse profited quickly while operating a makeshift taxi. Leander Warren explained: "Every barn south and east was a hospital. People wanted someone to take them, so I made good use of our team." The resident of Railroad Street added what was often the cold reality of the trips: "Often the return trip brought along a body wrapped in a muddy Army blanket."

A new technology and new business was soon available in Gettysburg. Embalmers arrived and set up embalming parlors. One was situated on the Mummasburg road in a brick schoolhouse, and another was set up in town, beside David Wills's building on York Street.

Some of the townspeople assisted in the body-processing business. It became a good business in short order. "A number of our citizens made a quite good thing out of this gruesome business, taking up bodies and assisting in preparing them for shipment home," John C. Will observed. "Men engaged in this work bought whiskey in great quantities."[14]

Embalming in America began during the war. Dr. Thomas Holmes is generally considered the father of modern embalming. He experimented with preservative chemicals while working as a coroner's assistant in New York. Abraham Lincoln was also keenly interested in embalming. The president directed the Quartermaster Corps to utilize embalming to allow the return of Union dead to their hometowns for a proper burial. Holmes received a commission as a captain in the medical corps and was stationed at Washington, D.C. During his assignment there, he reportedly embalmed more than four thousand men.

Holmes resigned his commission and began offering embalming commercially. His process injected a fluid into a body to preserve it for an extended period. Making an incision in the carotid artery, the deceased's veins were pumped full of a liquid to prevent further decay, thus making it possible to ship the body home. The incision was then sewn shut. His fee was one hundred dollars. Holmes also sold instruments and fluids and instructed others on the embalming process. Soon others saw the opportunity and began offering embalming services. These embalming surgeons charged less, usually fifty dollars for an officer and twenty-five dollars for an enlisted man. As the profession of embalming began, some embalmers advertised their services by displaying their work. Using an unclaimed soldier's body, the embalming surgeon would dress it in a new suit and place it in a fine coffin, where it was displayed in a front window. This crude form of advertising soon proved to have a negative influence on the army, and Maj. Gen. Benjamin F. Butler ordered embalmers to cease this method of self-promotion and advertising, especially around large military operations.

If embalming was not chosen to preserve a body, ice was utilized to ward off decomposition long enough for a funeral.

At the time of the battle of Gettysburg, there were no embalmers or undertakers in Adams County. Coffins were made only as needed by local cabinetmakers and carpenters. As a result, Henry Garlach kept busy at his cabinet-making shop on the west side of Baltimore Street.

As embalming became accepted in America, there was still a need for other services, such as arranging for transportation of the deceased, ordering a coffin, and dressing the dead for burial. As time went on, the embalmer was asked to undertake, or arrange, for these items and services, and soon they were called undertakers.

Embalming surgeons flocked to Adams County, knowing there was a dire demand for their services. Sometimes embalmers were also doctors or surgeons, supplementing their income with embalming services. A doctor near Hanover reportedly earned one thousand dollars from embalming bodies in July and August 1863.

J. Howard Wert remembered that embalmers' tents were pitched all around the county for weeks after the battle. Dr. Cyrus N. Chamberlain embalmed bodies at Camp Letterman.

Embalmers in the 1860s did not always drain all the body's fluids, and decay occurred, but not as rapidly as if the body had not been embalmed. Following embalming, the body was placed in a coffin, usually lined in zinc.

Personal effects would be placed in the coffin, and the name of the deceased was written on the outside of the wooden box as well as the address of the parents or spouse receiving the remains. The body was then shipped by railroad.

Embalmers were used even when a body had been buried for some time. It was a regular practice to embalm a body that was decomposing after being disinterred. Loved ones wanted to make sure the body they received was that of their loved one. So it was customary for the embalmers who set up their embalming parlors or tents near Gettysburg to embalm decayed remains.

Employed as an agent of the U.S. Sanitary Commission, Frederick Olmstead wrote on July 19, after visiting Gettysburg, that the dead "are all buried, and a great business is being done in disinterring bodies for embalming and shipment North. There are half of dozen diff[erent] embalmers competing for it."

Because of the fear of disease, the disinterment of corpses was stopped in August and September. On July 30 General Orders No. 2 was issued by the Department of the Susquehanna: "During the months of August and September, 1863, no corpses will be allowed to be disinterred from any of the burial grounds, cemeteries, or battleground of Gettysburg. The health of the wounded soldiers and citizens of the community requires the stringent enforcement of this order, and any violation of it reported to these headquarters will meet with the summary and severe punishment."

At about the same time, the initial wave of souvenir hunters and profiteers subsided. Several newspapers recounted where they had come from: "Hundreds of our citizens . . . visited the battlefield, at Gettysburg during the past week, to witness the destruction and desolation committed by the middles of death. No tongue can tell the miseries and sufferings experienced by the thousand of our brave troops lying wounded on the field of battle, many of whom with the last agonies of death."[15]

Young boys kept busy collecting lead from the battlefield. In 1863 ammunition manufacturers paid thirteen cents a pound for recovered lead. Unexploded shells, however, were a lethal problem, and several people were killed when they came across live ordnance. Seventeen-year-old James Culp died at Gettysburg while trying to salvage lead from unexploded shells.

Each passing day after the battle was a day closer to normalcy. As food and medical supplies arrived and the wounded were transferred from private homes and public buildings, life slowly returned to the way it was before Jubal Early's men marched through town. In addition to the ongoing relief efforts visible around town, there were many other reminders that the country was at war. Stragglers continued to turn up, family members still continued to search for missing loved ones, and more and more sightseers came to see where the battle had happened.

At first the railroad remained busy moving the wounded out of town to better hospital facilities. On July 11 the first wounded Confederates, seventy-six Southerners, were removed by rail. The rickety ride had to be an emotional one for those wounded soldiers. As the locomotive spat sparks and thick smoke, the recovering men looked out at the rolling hills of south central Pennsylvania. Many considered themselves fortunate to be alive. The warm breeze and the speed of the train had to feel good as they traveled away from the place of so much spilled blood toward an uncertain future.

• 18 •

CREATING A NATIONAL CEMETERY

The world will little note, nor long remember what we say here; while it can never forget what they did here.

ABRAHAM LINCOLN

SHORTLY AFTER THE SMOKE cleared at Gettysburg and the task of recovery began, talk started of the need for a new cemetery just for the men who fell during the battle. The countryside was filled with thousands of shallow graves on farms and in the areas near the many field hospitals that had cropped up during the three days of battle.

New York surgeon Theodore S. Dimon arrived in Gettysburg soon after the two armies marched away. In his journal he noted the disposition of many New Yorkers' graves as well as soldiers' graves in general: "While engaged in the various duties . . . I was constantly solicited for pecuniary aid in the expense attending the exhumation, disinfecting, coffining and transportation of our dead soldiers to their former homes. . . . It seemed wrong to leave the soldier 'buried like a dead horse,' when in another year all marks of his grave would be obliterated by the owner of the soil."[1]

Dimon's awareness of the transitory nature of soldiers' graves weighed against the singular importance of the battle that had raged across this land was not unique. Many others observed the poorly marked Union graves, the crop of boards crudely marked in pencil with the names of the fallen. They might only need to last until a family member could discover and recover the remains, but the markers would not last very long. By the end of July, Gettysburg newspapers noted that as many as seven hundred coffins had been made by the town's carpenters to transport remains claimed from the battlefield.[2] Vast numbers of the fallen, however, still lay in shoddy graves across the countryside.

The state of Pennsylvania paid the costs of exhumation, a zinc-lined coffin, and transportation for any soldiers from the state whose remains were claimed and conveyed to a hometown within the state. Other states, though, did not match this gesture for their citizens. Pennsylvania even provided transportation costs for families of the deceased. A notice in a Gettysburg newspaper elaborated that the state was bearing the cost for "the removal of all Pennsylvanians killed in the late battles, furnishing transportation for the body and one attendant."[3]

Most Northern families lacked the means to pay the costs involved in recovering their dead husbands, fathers, and sons. Soldiers' families from areas farthest from Gettysburg obviously had a heavier financial burden.

Dimon had no intention of allowing the identities of the fallen men from New York to be lost forever. He ordered that the New Yorkers' grave markers be re-marked with black paint. He also prepared detailed notes and maps of the graves.

At the same time that Dimon was preserving the identities of the New York dead, Col. John B. Bachelder addressed a proposal to Governor Curtin to re-mark all the graves:

I have been engaged since the battle at this place in making drawings of its various phases for historical pictures. I am now occupied upon a general view representing something over twenty square miles, on which I show each road, house, field and forest, in a word everything that could effect the tide of battle or be of interest to the public. I propose to publish a supplementary sheet, with proper reference to the general view, giving the name of every soldier whose grave is marked and showing, its position. . . . I am obliged to carefully canvass every rod of the ground, to get all the names. I find that a large proportion of them were written with lead pencil and by the rains beating the fresh earth upon them have already become nearly effaced. And before the coming autumn many will be entirely obliterated. Massachusetts sent a committee on here to remark the names of her sons that had fallen in battle; they spent several days but finding they had the whole ground to canvass they have left the remainder with me. As I said before I visit every enclosure and take every name. I now propose to the Executives of different States for a fair compensation to good men to go with me and remark every name that may need it, and when necessary put up new headboards. The expense will be but a trifle, and though entirely distinct from my business I will see it well done if left in my charge. I commenced to remark them gratuitously, but find it will take me about three times as long to go over the ground. Yet I cannot bare to leave a name un-marked which another rain may blot out from its friends forever.[4]

Sometime in late July, at a meeting in the law office of David Wills, the idea of a soldiers cemetery was discussed. Theodore Dimon summarized the proceedings in a letter:

At my request . . . a meeting was held at the office of David Wills, Esquire, agent of the State of Pennsylvania. At this meeting I presented a proposition that a portion of the ground occupied by our line of battle on Cemetery Hill should be purchased for a permanent burial place for the soldiers of our army who lost their lives in this battle, or who died here of their wounds. And that their bodies should be gathered from the fields in which they were interred and deposited in this burial place by regiments and States with proper marks designating their graves. It was proposed, also, that this should be done by joint action on the part of the Executives of the States interested. The proposition met with approval. . . . Mr. Wills entered into negotiations for the purchase of the land, and I am since informed that Governor Seymour of New York has addressed Governor Curtin, of Pennsylvania, engaging to join him, and the Executives of the other states, in purchasing this land and carrying out the proposed undertaking.[5]

There were other alternatives, such as doing nothing or leaving the problem to the various states or the soldiers' families. Instead, the rapidly deteriorating condition of the graves in the fields spurred the development of the plan to acquire a burial ground where the Union dead could be properly reburied and their graves marked and cared for.

Dimon implied that he proposed the creation of the soldiers cemetery. Two other men claimed it was their idea. Both were Gettysburg lawyers, but their plans differed slightly. Attorney David McConaughy was concerned with the poor state of the solders' graves and their pell-mell placement with no regard for water runoff or drainage. He placed the matter before the townspeople.

David Wills was the Pennsylvania agent for Gettysburg and a Republican lawyer. On July 24 he proposed the idea for a soldiers cemetery to Governor Curtin:

> There is one spot very desirable for this purpose. It is the elevated piece of ground on the Baltimore Turnpike opposite the [Evergreen] Cemetery. It is the place where our army had about 40 pieces of artillery in action all Thursday & Friday and for their protection had thrown up a large number of earthworks for the artillerists. It is the point on which the desperate attack was made by the Louisiana Brigades on Thursday evening when they succeeded in reaching the guns, taking possession of them and were finally driven back by the infantry assisted by the artillery men with their handspikes and rammers. It was the key to the whole line of our defences,—the apex of the triangular line of battle. It is the spot, above all others, for the honorable burial of the dead who have fallen on these fields. There are two lots of ground, together making eight acres, about 3½ acres belonging to Mr. [Peter] Raffensperger and 4½ to Mr. [Edward] Menchy and I called on them for the purpose of ascertaining whether it could be bought. They would not sell it for any other purpose, but offer to sell it for the purpose named for $200—per acre each. This is not much out of the way and I think it should be secured at once and the project started. I refer the matter to you for your careful consideration and decision. In examining the Act of 26th Feb. 1862, Pa L. 1862 pp 550-1 I think that both sections of that act are broad enough to cover this matter and that the act contemplates such an arrangement as I have suggested.

Our dead are lying on the fields unburied, (that is, no grave being dug) with small portions of earth dug up alongside of the body and thrown over it. In many instances arms and legs and sometimes heads protrude and my attention has been directed to several places where the hogs were actually rooting out the bodies and devouring them. And this on Pennsylvania soil and in many cases the bodies of the patriotic soldiers of our state! Humanity calls on us to take measures to remedy this and I think that it was in the contemplation of the Legislature of 1862 to remedy such matters by making provision for the honorable burial of the dead of our state who may fall on the field.

My idea is for Pennsylvania to purchase the ground at once so as to furnish a place for the friends of those who are here seeking places for the permanent burial of their fallen ones to inter them at once and also be a place for the burial of the hundreds who are dying in the hospitals. The other states would certainly through their Legislatures in cooperation with our own Legislature contribute towards defraying the expenses. . . . The graves that are marked on the field would of course be properly marked when removed to the cemetery and the bodies should be arranged as far as practicable in order of companies, regiments, divisions and Corps.

Dr. [Gordon] Winslow of the U. S. Sanitary Commission tells me that the U. S. Gov. furnish coffins and did heretofore furnish a large amount of walnut or locust headboards on which the name &c. was burnt into the wood. If the U. S. Gov. would furnish these, I think the bodies could be disinterred and buried in this place for about $3.50 or $4.—each.

I hope you will feel justified in authorizing the immediate purchase of this ground and the removal of the Penn[sylvani]a dead in the field to it. I think that an arrangement can be made with the other states at once for the removal of all the dead known & unknown. We have a man here who superintended the burial of our dead for General [Marsena R.] Patrick and knows where they are and where the Rebel graves are. So that there would be no mistake in taking up the bodies.

I know the soldiers in the field would feel most grateful for such a proper mark of respect, on the part of our Chief Executive, for his fallen comrades, and the multitude of friends of the fallen dead, at home, would rejoice to know that the bodies of their brave kindred had been properly cared for by our Governor.

You will please favor me with an early answer. If the matter is delayed I am afraid the owners of the land might be operated on by speculators.[6]

In the meantime, McConaughy began to acquire land surrounding the Evergreen Cemetery. He had a larger vision beyond a soldiers cemetery that included preserving part of the battlefield as a memorial. Some of the property was on McKnight's Hill (also known as Steven's Knoll), East Cemetery Hill, Cemetery Hill, and Little Round Top. With the property on Cemetery Hill, McConaughy envisioned a central burial site. The additional land would accommodate the battlefield dead to be reinterred in an expanded Evergreen Cemetery. This would benefit the struggling Evergreen Cemetery Association, of which McConaughy was president. He too wrote to Curtin and proposed "the most liberal arrangements" with "our Cemetery, for the burial of our own dead" as well as the dead of "all the loyal states, whose sons fell in the glorious strife." His letter to the governor was dated a day later than Wills's letter:

I have purchased & now hold all the land upon Cemetery Hill which encircles the Ever Green Cemetery Grounds, & which was occupied by the Artillery and forces on the centre of our line of battle, on the ever memorable 1st 2d & 3d of July inst.

In doing so I have had two purposes, viz. to enlarge the area of our Cemetery, of which I am the President, and (2d) to secure so as to be held in perpetuity, the most interesting portions of this illustrious Battlefield, that, we may retain them in the actual form & condition they were in, during the battles, the most eloquent memorials of their glorious struggles and triumphs.

In that connection, I have also purchased the Granite Spur of Round-top, on our left (some 30 acres) the position held by our Pennsylvania Reserves, with the wonderful stone defences constructed by them, & which shall remain undisturbed, as their own monument of their heroic labors & valor. I am also in successful negotiation for about the same extent of Wolf Hill [meaning Culp's Hill], on our right, embracing the extensive timber breast works, & the equally wonderful exhibition of the withering effects of our musketry fire. And pervading this all, is the fixed purpose that this Battlefield shall be held by the sons of Pennsylvania and not by those of other states. At the same time the most liberal arrangements can be had with our Cemetery, for the burial of our own dead, & not of our State only but of all the loyal states, whose sons fell in the glorious strife, on this the great Battle-field of Pennsylvania.

I propose to make a public offer, to patriotic citizens of our state, that they may participate in the tenure of the sacred grounds of this Battlefield, by con-tributing to its actual cost, (the minimum sum to be 10- and the maximum $100.00 from any one citizen). Shall I have the pleasure of enrolling your name first as one of the holders of this glorious patrimony?

Again, may we not have the assurance from you, that Pennsylvania, will, out of her common Treasure, bury her noble dead within Ever Green Ceme-tery, which furnished the very centre and impregnable apex of the battle field? We have already buried nearly one hundred, at the cost (for ground & burial) of $5 each; and we have abundant room for all who fell here, or have died since the battles. We are also ready to enter into arrangements with our state and with all the other loyal states, to bury the dead in such manner as shall be most agreeable to them & to arrange our grounds accordingly.

Our Cemetery has also initiated a movement for the erection of a noble National Monument in memory of the battles & the dead. The plan is the $1-subscription, similar to that of the Washington monument. Shall we enroll you & to what amount?[7]

David Wills was probably aware that McConaughy was one of those "speculators" who was trying to control the land he was seeking. The two men lived near each other, but there was little communication between them as they presented their plans to the governor. In fact, there was little contact between the two men prior to this; they had not served on the same committees or boards in the town. Their different philosophies over the future of the proposed cemetery led to a conflict between the two lawyers, and for a brief time it appeared that the cemetery was doomed to failure.[8]

Edward Fahnestock and David Buehler, both prominent citizens and friends of Wills and McConaughy, acted as mediators between the two. A primary issue for McConaughy was how Evergreen Cemetery would be per-ceived in comparison to the new cemetery. It would be to the cemetery association's advantage to have the two properties appear as a single burial ground, and the nondistinction would most likely help in the sale of burial plots at the Evergreen Cemetery. So McConaughy argued that there should be no clear demarcation between the two cemeteries, no fence separating the two properties.

In short order the state of Pennsylvania stepped in, and the governor endorsed Wills's proposal: Evergreen Cemetery would not be the final resting place for the reinterment of the battlefield dead.

Once he learned that the state did not want the local association to control the new cemetery, McConaughy agreed to sell the land he had bought and dropped his argument about not separating the two cemeteries. Instead, the sale involved only one stipulation: that an "open railing enclosure of ordinary height" would separate the two cemeteries. McConaughy eventually sold the land he had acquired adjacent to the Evergreen Cemetery to the state for two hundred dollars an acre—the price he had paid for it.

Newspapers touted the news of the new cemetery: "Arrangements have been made to purchase a part of the battle-field at Gettysburg for a cemetery, in which it is proposed to gather the remains of our dead. The ground embraces the point of the desperate attack made upon the left centre of our army. Eight other states have already united with Pennsylvania in this project. The removal of the dead from the battle-field of Gettysburg is forbidden during the months of August and September."[9]

Wills went to work immediately developing the newly acquired land. Landscape architect William Saunders designed the burial ground. A landscape gardener who worked with the Department of Agriculture from an office in Philadelphia, Saunders was respected for his designs of many formal grounds and city parks in Philadelphia and other cities.

"I was pleased with the site," the architect noted after touring the area of the cemetery. "On my first visit I studied the ground thoroughly and thought of various methods of treatment. It occurred to me . . . and I felt it all important under the plan that the remains of the soldiers from each State should be laid together in a group."

Saunders created a simple design. The plots were arranged by state in a semicircular pattern around a central site where a large monument was to be erected. Curved granite markers inscribed with names and regiments would be used as headstones. His plan made no distinction between officers and enlisted men; the remains were buried under identical stones in no special order.

Wills worked determinedly with Saunders and agents from other states who had been sent to Gettysburg to investigate the common cemetery and to report on the proper disposition of their dead. Initially, the plan was to have all the dead buried in one general area, but Saunders determined to follow his plan that each state would be allotted a plot and the dead would be buried by state.

Work commenced on the seventeen-acre site, and Wills continued to move the project forward, including plans for a dedicatory ceremony. Although the cemetery would not be completed at the time of its dedication on October 23, Wills fixed that date for the dedication.

As was the custom of the day, an orator would speak at length to the crowd. Several speakers were available, and all had an ability to mesmerize a crowd with powerful sermonic presentations. Wills first approached Henry Wadsworth Longfellow, John Greenleaf Whittier, and William Cullen Bryant, but each declined. On September 23 Wills contacted Edward Everett, the foremost orator in the country.

The sixty-nine-year-old Everett accepted the invitation but indicated that one month was not sufficient time to prepare an appropriate address. He persuaded Wills to reschedule the ceremony for November 19.

With a speaker engaged and a definite date for the ceremony, Wills finalized plans for the rest of the celebration. Invitations were extended to various musical groups and dignitaries while work on the cemetery progressed slowly. Almost as an afterthought, Wills sent an invitation to the White House:

> The Several States having Soldiers in the Army of the Potomac, who were killed at the Battle of Gettysburg, or have since died at the various hospitals which were established in the vicinity, have procured grounds on a prominent part of the Battle Field for a Cemetery, and are having the dead removed to them and properly buried.
>
> These Grounds will be Consecrated and set apart to this Sacred purpose, by appropriate Ceremonies, on Thursday, the 19th instant. Hon Edward Everett will deliver the Oration.

I am authorized by the Governors of the different States to invite you to be present, and participate in these Ceremonies, which will doubtless be very imposing and solemnly impressive.

It is the desire that, after the Oration, you, as Chief Executive of the Nation, formally set apart these grounds to their Sacred use by a few appropriate remarks.

It will be a source of great gratification to the many widows and orphans that have been made almost friendless by the Great Battle here, to have you here personally; and it will kindle anew in the breasts of the Comrades of these brave dead, who are now in the tented field or nobly meeting the foe in the front, a confidence that they who sleep in death on the Battle Field are not forgotten by those highest in Authority; and they will feel that, should their fate be the same, their remains will not be uncared for.

We hope you will be able to be present to perform this last solemn act to the Soldiers dead on this Battle Field.

Wills also opened his home to the president for his stay in town:

As the Hotels in our town will be crowded and in confusion at the time referred to in the enclosed invitation, I write to invite you to stop with me. I hope you will feel it your duty to lay aside pressing business for a day to come on here to perform this last sad rite to our brave Soldier dead on the 19th instant.

Governor Curtin and Hon Edward Everett will be my guests at that time and if you come you will please join them at my house.

Lincoln accepted the thirty-two-year-old attorney's invitations and made plans for the trip to Gettysburg. The president traveled by train from Washington to Hanover to Gettysburg. His entourage was small, and he rode in a regular coach car with other passengers.

At Hanover word spread that the president would be traveling through. Hundreds of people gathered at the depot to get a look at the chief executive. When he emerged from the passenger car onto the rear platform, the crowd applauded their greeting. He shook hands and made a brief impromptu speech.

"Well, you have seen me, and, according to general experience, you have seen less than you expected to see," Lincoln quipped to the amusement of the people. "I trust when the enemy was here, the citizens of Hanover were loyal to our country and the stars and stripes. If you are not all true patriots in support of the nation, you should be." His stop lasted only eight minutes.

At 6 P.M. on November 18 the president's train arrived at the Gettysburg depot. A large crowd, numbering many thousands, cheered and bands played patriotic songs when the president emerged. Lincoln was then escorted to the Wills home, the largest house on the town square. After dinner a crowd gathered outside the house and called for Lincoln. He made an appearance but said nothing, then he retired to a bedroom and edited his remarks for the ceremony.

The weather was unusually warm and mild for late November. Many people stayed in the streets throughout the night and into the early morning. Influencing some in this regard was the lack of accommodations. Even William Saunders, the architect of the cemetery and an honored guest at the ceremony, had to sleep in a chair in a crowded parlor.

For weeks the townspeople of Gettysburg had prepared for this latest invasion. "Our old town roused up to action," Harry Sweeney recalled. Town meetings had addressed the matters of housing and feeding the expected visitors. "Churches, public schools, town halls, all the private dwellings, barns, etc. were thrown open to receive them."

During the night, while Lincoln stayed in his room, the Wills home filled to capacity with dignitaries and prominent citizens. By the time Governor Curtin arrived, all the bedrooms were taken, and he was forced to sleep a few hours on a chair in the parlor.

The weather was bright and clear the next morning. At 10 A.M. the booming of cannons on Cemetery Hill—the signal to begin the procession—was heard throughout the packed town. The processional ended at a special platform in the new cemetery. The area was soon filled to capacity.

Lincoln reviewed a spate of telegrams from the War Department then joined the procession. Shortly before noon, he arrived in the cemetery and took his seat on the platform. Bands played while the crowd swelled to more than ten thousand.

Everett was introduced. He looked over the hushed congregation and began to speak. His voice thundered, filled with passion and emotion. He spewed the history of the setting and compared this honor for the deceased Union sons to the funerals held for the heroes of ancient Greece. The aged speaker recalled the events of the great battle, an account of current European affairs, and his view of the eventual outcome of the war. He spoke for more than two hours. Near the point of exhaustion himself, he closed with a strong appeal to once again raise the Stars and Stripes over the Southern capitols.

After a brief musical interlude, the president rose from his seat and faced the crowd. He took two pieces of folded paper from his coat pocket and spoke for just three minutes, interrupted five times by applause, then he returned to his chair. Some were stunned that his speech was so short. Lincoln himself allegedly remarked to aide Ward Lamon, "That speech won't scour. It is a flat failure." Yet his words accomplished their purpose for the dedicatory moment and at the same time generated a new understanding of the war effort.

When the ceremony was concluded, the Marine Band and other members of the military escorted Lincoln back to the center of town. After dinner at the Wills house, the president greeted the other dignitaries and guests at an informal reception. In the hallway of the home he met seventy-year-old John L. Burns, who was still recovering from his battle wounds. Later that night Lincoln went to the train station and departed for Washington.

His speech had been brief but to the point. Its purpose was clear: unification of the Northern people to support the Union cause and see the war through to the end. Democratic newspapers ridiculed the shortness of his speech. Others mostly hailed his Gettysburg Address for its simplicity. The greatest compliment came from the day's orator, Edward Everett, who wrote the president the next day, "I should be glad if I could flatter myself that I came as near to the central idea of the occasion in two hours, as you did in two minutes."

Although Lincoln supposedly was not impressed with his speech and thought its delivery a failure, his simple words were destined to become a part of the national fabric as important as the Declaration of Independence and the Constitution. Contrary to popular opinion, he did not compose the speech on the back of an envelope. There are five copies of the speech in Lincoln's handwriting, all written on regular-size stationery. The copy he used at Gettysburg is in the Library of Congress.

The simple, eloquent words he used that day in Gettysburg became immortal. While many would not understand much about the battle, they would learn his speech and hear the words repeatedly.

Four score and seven years ago our fathers brought forth, upon this continent, a new nation, conceived in liberty, and dedicated to the proposition that "all men are created equal."

Now we are engaged in a great civil war, testing whether that nation, or any nation so conceived, and so dedicated, can long endure. We are met on a great battle field of that war. We come to dedicate a portion of it, as a final resting place for those who died here, that the nation might live. This we may, in all propriety do. But, in a larger sense, we can not dedicate—we can not consecrate—we can not hallow, this ground—The brave men, living and dead, who struggled here, have hallowed it, far above our poor power to add or detract. The world will little note, nor long remember what we say here; while it can never forget what they did here.

It is rather for us, the living, we here be dedicated to the great task remaining before us—that, from these honored dead we take increased devotion to that cause for which they here, gave the last full measure of devotion—that we here highly resolve these dead shall not have died in vain; that the nation, shall have a new birth of freedom, and that government of the people by the people for the people, shall not perish from the earth.

•19•
CREATING A NATIONAL PARK

As the autumn of 1863 approached, the summer heat gave way to cooler days and colder nights. By October it was time to begin reburying the Union soldiers. The gory work entailed unearthing and moving the remains to new graves in the Soldiers National Cemetery. By the time of the cemetery's dedication on November 19, workers had completed only a small portion of the task. It would take six months to finish the job. When they were done, 3,512 bodies had been interred in the cemetery grounds. More than one-fourth of those buried were unknowns.[1]

The task of exhuming the bodies provided economic opportunity for many African Americans in Gettysburg. Leander Warren described the work: "Basil Biggs had the contract to raise the dead and put them into coffins. He had a two-horse team and hauled six at a time. Every particle of the body was gathered up by them and the grave neatly closed over and leveled. The bodies were found in various stages of decomposition. They were generally covered up with a small portion of earth dug up from along side the body."[2]

For months Biggs exhumed the bodies. Exactly what he earned for his labor is not known, but Franklin W. Biesecker, the contractor for whom Biggs worked, was paid $1.59 per body.[3]

Life in the town and county returned to its normal pace, but the scars of battle remained. Farmers harvested their crops and readied their farms for winter. Still, routine life could be interrupted suddenly with tragic news. On Friday, November 20, Allen Frazer was killed at the Solomon Powers home on High Street.

The tragic episode involved Russell Briggs, a grief-stricken father, who had come from Philadelphia for the dedication of the cemetery and to retrieve the remains of his son—Cpl. George E. Briggs of the Seventy-second Pennsylvania who had died at a field hospital on July 18. Briggs was staying at the Powers home. On the battlefield he found a shell and decided to unload it. He managed to remove the cap then began striking the shell on a stone in a crude attempt to remove the powder. Allen Frazer noticed what was going on and approached Briggs to warn him that hitting the shell was a "very dangerous thing to do." At that instant the shell exploded.[4]

"I heard a terrible explosion," Albertus McCreary recalled. "There I saw a young school-mate lying on his back with his bowels blown away. He looked at me for a second, and then closed his eyes in death. Near him was a man almost torn to pieces, his hands hanging in shreds."[5]

Briggs barely survived his wounds. Doctors amputated his hands and a leg. Allen Frazer was buried the next day at the Evergreen Cemetery.

Incidents like this occurred too frequently. Years later, residents who were youths at the time recalled several deaths caused by unexploded ordnance. Hugh M. Ziegler recollected that he and some other boys "wandered over the battlefield and several of them were killed by tampering with shells that [had] failed to explode." Ziegler was ten years old at the time of the battle. He recalled, "There were several farmers and their teams killed by plow point coming in contact with unexploded shells."[6]

Trophy hunting pretty much ended as winter approached. From mid-July there had been a steady flow of relic searchers. This group of people seemed to think nothing of taking whatever they could find on the battlefield. It was fair sport to yank buttons off dead Confederates or take any-thing they found as a souvenir.

Of particular interest were cannonballs and bullets. Their finders kept them as trophies. It also seemed that trees, fence posts, or similar lumber with a bullet or shell embedded in it was a prized object. Such items quickly disappeared. Scavengers nabbed bayonets, swords, muskets, and other mili-tary items.

IN 1864 the U.S. Navy converted a captured steamship into a gunboat and recommissioned the vessel the USS *Gettysburg*. Naming the ship after the July 1863 battle was one of the earliest recognitions of the great struggle that had occurred there. The navy used the side-wheel steamship intermit-tently for years until it was decommissioned in 1879 and sold overseas.

A YEAR after the battle of Gettysburg, Confederate Gen. Jubal Early com-manded another Confederate incursion into Pennsylvania, this time to avenge the destruction of the Virginia Military Institute and David Hunter's raiding in the Shenandoah in June 1864. Early sent Gen. John McCausland's cavalry above the Mason-Dixon Line. Gettysburg prepared for the invaders much as it had the previous year.

McCausland's cavalry arrived in nearby Chambersburg instead. At the time the town was the seat of Franklin County and an important supply base. McCausland demanded one hundred thousand dollars in gold or five hundred thousand in U.S. greenbacks from the town as compensation for Hunter's recent campaign in the Shenandoah. If the town failed to pay the ransom, the Rebel cavalry commander threatened to torch the town. "I informed them that I would wait six hours, and if they would then comply with the requirements their town would be safe; but if not, it would be destroyed in accordance with my orders from General Early," McCausland later explained.[7]

When the people did not pay, McCausland evacuated the three hun-dred townspeople and torched the business district. The massive fire destroyed more than five hundred buildings. The Confederates rode south and crossed the Potomac near Hancock, Maryland, and never again returned to the North.

Tension built up in Gettysburg as the town filled with refugees from Franklin County and southern Adams County. Although they braced for another invasion, calm returned when the threat subsided. Gettysburg's people collected goods and money to send to their neighboring community. Still, for several weeks during the summer of 1864, the residents of Adams County were anxious over the possibility of the returning Confederate cavalry.

Sanitary Fairs were held in the North to raise funds for the Sanitary Commission. Gettysburg residents supplied artifacts—moss baskets, wreaths, shell medallions, shell pieces, and other relics from the battlefield—to a fair in Philadelphia.

Sarah Broadhead oversaw the printing of seventy-five copies of her diary from June 15 to July 15, becoming the first Gettysburg resident to share her recollections of what had happened before, during, and after the battle. The copies were offered for sale at the fair in Philadelphia. Broadhead, however, made it clear that she was printing, not publishing, her memoirs for her "kindred and closest friends." She was concerned over the criticism she might receive for rushing her words into print, which was a problem for proper ladies in the nineteenth century. Many other townspeople followed Broadhead's lead by putting their memories to paper, creating manuscripts that would later be scoured by historians and scholars.

Many years passed before the county recovered from the long-term effects of the battle. Some farmers never recovered their losses, but some managed to rebuild their livelihoods. Some sold their property, packed up their belongings, and left the wrecked land that held only gruesome memories. Those who stayed saw their sleepy hamlet change radically as a direct result of the battle.

Residents of Adams County filed damage claims amounting to $552,383. Claims from Franklin County totaled $838,162. In 1868 the state received the claims, which included about $270,000 in damages or loss to private property. More than 800 horses, 1,000 cattle, 400 sheep, and 200 hogs were lost.[8]

A total of 813 residents filed claims, which probably was only a portion of the actual losses suffered. Damage claims included crop losses, fences, clothing, and grain. The claims also sought reimbursement for items stolen by the Confederates: saddles and bridles, clothing, tools, and food. The claim process was laborious. Few ever received settlements, and those who did were woefully underpaid.

Some citizens sought to preserve the battlefield. On April 30, 1864, the Gettysburg Battlefield Memorial Association was founded by attorney David McConaughy. The charter of the new organization was simple: "To hold and preserve the battleground at Gettysburg." In May 1864 the Pennsylvania legislature recognized the group. Gov. Andrew Curtin and Gettysburg attorneys David McConaughy and David Wills headed the board, which included directors from across Pennsylvania. They developed plans to open avenues along the Union lines but lacked funds to do much of anything.

Fourteen years later, in 1878, the association oversaw the erection of a fifty-foot observation platform on the eastern side of Cemetery Hill. That tower stood until 1895.

From 1864 to 1895 the Gettysburg Battlefield Memorial Association acquired 522 acres of land. The first acquisition included portions of Culp's Hill, a wooded section of Little Round Top, and the site where John F. Reynolds was killed.

In 1865 workers set the foundation for the Soldiers Monument, the main memorial in the Soldiers Cemetery. The cornerstone was placed during a dedication on July 4, 1865. The monument, designed as a national memorial of sorrow with marble statues surrounding the base of the tall monument, represented the backgrounds of the men who fought at Gettysburg. Workers completed the cemetery in 1869, and a small ceremony recognized the completion of the monument. The federal government assumed the administration of the national cemetery in 1872.

The Gettysburg Battlefield Memorial Association hired Nicholas G. Wilson, a former sergeant of the 138th Pennsylvania Infantry, to serve as superintendent of the grounds. The first battlefield memorials were erected during his caretakership. He supervised the placement of more than two hundred monuments and memorials.

The New York State Monument was not placed on the battlefield. Rather, officials decided to erect it in the northern end of the Soldiers National Cemetery because of that state's sacrifice during the Gettysburg campaign. More soldiers from New York than from any other Union state died or were injured during the battle. Ceremonies dedicating the monument occurred on July 2, 1893, thirty years after the battle.

Confederate dead remained in their field graves and the temporary cemetery at the site of Camp Letterman for years after the end of the war. By 1870 a movement was under way to remove the Southern soldiers from Pennsylvania and return them to Southern soil as their final resting place. Southern newspapers printed stories of how the Adams County farmers gave notice that if someone does not remove the Southerners' bodies, their graves would be plowed up, and the bones would be ground up for fertilizer.[9]

Stirred by these inflammatory reports, ladies' societies from several Southern states began to raise funds for a program to have the remains of Southern soldiers exhumed and brought south. In 1877 gravediggers disinterred the first Confederate remains from their graves at Gettysburg for reburial. Eventually the ladies' societies transferred a large number of the Confederates to the Hollywood Cemetery in Richmond, Virginia. Other disinterments followed, sending the remains to Savannah, Georgia; Charleston, South Carolina; and Raleigh, North Carolina.

For many years after the battle, officials received reports of discoveries of soldiers' remains in the area. There, no doubt, were many more findings that were never reported.[10] Visitors spotted many partial remains. Further examination of any report usually revealed more remains and perhaps a button or piece of a uniform, which might offer a clue to the identity of the unknown soldier. Whenever officials were notified of such discoveries, the general policy was to rebury the soldier in the same place but in a deeper grave. Discoveries of bones continued throughout the twentieth century.

When the war ended in the spring of 1865, the mood of the country was to get on with life and leave the war behind. Reconstruction set the mood in the South, the West beckoned many of the war weary, and reconciliation between the Northern and Southern states slowly took root. For decades after the war there was little national desire to visit the great battlefields of the Civil War much less preserve them. Gettysburg, however, was different.

From time to time during the latter half of the nineteenth century, visitors came to see the battlefield. Many were veterans returning with their families to show them the place where the war was won and and the place that forever after influenced his life. Interest in the battle slowly grew.

In 1873 Col. John B. Bachelder, an early historian of the battle, published the first guidebook to the area, *Gettysburg: What to See and How to See It.* Many other Gettysburg books followed. As a result, many people came to Gettysburg to see the sights about which they were reading so much.

Interest grew in the battle and the many places where the fighting occurred—the Peach Orchard, Devil's Den, Little Round Top. Merchants found a profitable market for stereoviews of the battlefields and pictures of the battle.

As visitors increased in number, a new industry was created: professional tour guides. Perhaps begun by some unemployed men who lounged about town in hotel lobbies under the guise of looking for work, the guides hired themselves out to visitors who might be looking for a relative's grave. By 1880 many people in the town were making a living as "hackers" and offering to guide visitors to various places on the battlefield. They made themselves available at the railroad station, hotel lobbies, and livery stables.

In 1878 the Grand Army of the Republic's Pennsylvania Division held its annual summer encampment at Gettysburg. For a week the Union veterans encamped on East Cemetery Hill. For many this was their first time back at Gettysburg since the battle. Two of the member posts of the GAR—Gen. Strong Vincent, Post No. 67 of Erie, and Col. Fred Taylor, Post No. 19 of Philadelphia—used the occasion to place memorial stones at the positions where their namesakes were killed or mortally wounded during the battle.

During this time some of the veterans took an interest in taking control of the nearly dormant Gettysburg Battlefield Memorial Association. Within two years they accomplished just that. At the same time, they interested other veterans groups in making Gettysburg a permanent memorial. Throughout the decade of the 1880s regimental associations traveled to Gettysburg to mark the field with a variety of monuments. With each new arrival, the residents offering guide services had opportunities to acquire new knowledge and stories from a wide variety of sources.

In 1884 the Gettysburg and Harrisburg Railroad completed its line into town, making Gettysburg more accessible by rail travel. Thus travelers from New York, Philadelphia, and other major cities could more conveniently travel to the Pennsylvania town and see the battlefields. The railroad promoted battlefield tourism, even publishing a tour book and informing readers of the availability of tour guides—who saw good business as a result.

Livery stables near the railroad station were soon renting wagons and carriages for battlefield tours. The excursions were generally all-day affairs. In the morning the tour guides transported the visitors to the battlefields of Day 1. They returned to town for lunch then toured the battlefields of Days 2 and 3 during the afternoon. Naturally, the drivers of the wagons and surreys frequently halted and shared stories about the area. Gettysburg's tourism industry was born. By 1890 more than 150,000 people annually visited the battlefield.

In the late 1880s track was laid for the Round Top Extension, allowing Sunday excursion trains to travel through the town and south across the battlefield to a station on Little Round Top. There visitors found picnicking and other recreational facilities. They could visit the Round Tops and Devil's Den. They were encouraged to walk north toward the High Water Mark. Another train took interested parties to Oak Ridge, where they could hike to various sites associated with the first day's battle.

Although much of the battlefield was still privately owned in 1893, and therefore inaccessible, the Gettysburg Electric Railway laid tracks through the area. Controversial construction soon offered convenient trolley transportation from town to the Round Tops and Devil's Den. Entrepreneurs established amusement parks along the trolley line, which took visitors to Wheatfield Park, also known as Wible's Grove. Other parks included Tipton's Park, which covered about thirteen acres east of Devil's Den. Round Top Park was just northeast of Little Round Top. These parks offered restaurants, bandstands, dance pavilions, photo galleries, and relic and souvenir stands.

On August 15, 1910, two trolleys on the line collided near Tipton Park. No one was killed, but several passengers were seriously injured.

The advent of the automobile derailed the trolley in 1917. Today a few rail beds and bridges are still visible, but the buildings of the old parks are long gone.

WHILE BATTLEFIELD visitation grew by leaps and bounds during the last decades of the nineteenth century, and entrepreneurs did what they could to attract, inform, and entertain them, not much was being done to preserve and manage the Gettysburg battlefield. Yet perhaps the most outspoken advocate for a battlefield park was Daniel E. Sickles. He had lost a leg on the battlefield on July 2, and now the one-legged New York congressman stumped like no one else to establish a federal park to preserve the battlefield. On February 11, 1895, his bill to establish the Gettysburg National Military Park as a memorial dedicated to the two armies became law.

On May 12, 1895, the board of directors of the Gettysburg Battlefield Memorial Association prepared to relinquish all holdings to the federal government. The War Department took over the park.

A specially appointed commission of Civil War veterans administered the new park. Two priorities were the preservation of important features of the battlefield and recognizing the wishes of veterans in marking the battlefield. The commission began by designing and constructing bridges, avenues, unit markers, and landscape work across the battlefield.

Officials quickly moved to make the battlefield more accessible to the public. One of the first goals was to remove the tracks of the railroad and trolley lines, which scarred the battlefield and antagonized the veterans who saw entertainment stands where comrades had fallen. A twenty-year court battle ensued with the Gettysburg Electric Railway, but before the case could be resolved, the trolley went out of business. Still, the tracks were not finally removed until after World War II.

As more and more visitors came to Gettysburg, it became apparent that some of the tour guides were less than knowledgeable or professional. Complaints arose concerning poor service, overaggressive solicitation, open conflicts in the streets between guides, and a tendency on the part of some guides to shortchange visitors by abbreviating tours but still charging full prices. Gettysburg was getting a bad reputation just when the town stood at the threshold of a larger tourism industry. Finally, the park management required that all guides had to be licensed. The process began in 1914 and continues to the present.

• 20 •

GETTYSBURG TODAY

What has been done and is still doing on the battlefield of Gettysburg, shows how devoted is the heart of the American nation to the memory of those brave men, who through their loyalty were willing to suffer and to lay down their lives in order that the precious institutions of our land might not perish.

TILLIE PIERCE

I N 1875 EDDIE PLANK was born in Gettysburg. He attended Gettysburg Academy, but back then no one dreamed what he would accomplish in his lifetime. Plank became one of the most dominant baseball pitchers of the twentieth century. He was known as "Gettysburg Eddie" and compiled a record of 326-194 over a seventeen-year career (1901–17), mostly with the Philadelphia Athletics. He won twenty or more games eight times and helped the A's win six pennants and three world championships. Plank returned to Gettysburg after he retired from baseball, and he died in his hometown in 1926. He was elected to the Baseball Hall of Fame in 1946.

During the time that Eddie Plank was proving himself on the diamond, the fiftieth anniversary and remembrance was held in Gettysburg. It was the largest combined reunion of Civil War veterans.

Pennsylvania hosted the celebration and extended invitations to all surviving veterans of the war, both Union and Confederate. The event was scheduled to be an exceptional encampment, a combined reunion of the Grand Army of the Republic and the United Confederate Veterans. Their response was overwhelming.

More than fifty thousand veterans traveled to Gettysburg to be a part of the big event. The veterans settled into a great camp that was set up on the battlefield. The former opponents who had changed the face of a nation now walked together over the hallowed ground and relived the terrible days when so many comrades were lost. Their cotton-white hair and scraggly beards bespoke their age. The creases of their leathery faces testified that these men had been eyewitnesses to the great battle.

Pennsylvania Gov. John K. Tener insisted that the Keystone State be the sole host of the reunion. State funds provided free rail transportation to all of Pennsylvania's veterans. Tener urged other states to also pay for their veterans' travel expenses. Some did. The Virginia chapter of the United Daughters of the Confederacy played a role in the celebration and supplied UCV uniforms to those Virginians who needed them.

As plans changed and the event grew, the cost of the reunion increased. Tener had to seek assistance from the federal government, which resulted in funds to feed and shelter the veterans during the encampment. With this assurance of federal aid, the Pennsylvania legislature approved five hundred thousand dollars toward the cost of the reunion.

Two years before the event, planning began for a camp large enough to accommodate the prospective guests and military support personnel. When the federal government became involved in 1912, personnel from the quartermaster and engineer corps joined the planners.

Army engineers surveyed the area adjacent to the fields of Pickett's Charge and chose that site for the Great Camp. They divided the camp into separate areas for Union and Confederate veterans. The army installed utility systems, erected hundreds of tents to house the veterans, and built picnic tables, benches, and boardwalks throughout the site.

By June 1, 1913, the sprawling Great Camp occupied 280 acres. It included more than 47 miles of avenues and company streets. More than 500 arc lights illuminated the area, and 32 water fountains were installed. The army dispatched more than 2,000 cooks and bakers to operate 173 field kitchens. They prepared three hot meals a day for everyone in attendance.

The American Red Cross and the army medical corps provided health care. Several hundred Boy Scouts served as escorts to the veterans and acted as aides and messengers in the hospitals and for officials at the event. The army dispatched two battalions from the Fifth Infantry to guard the camps and supply depots and provide security. These troops were supported by a detachment from the Fifteenth U.S. Cavalry.

Pennsylvania also provided medical staff. A detachment of the state police and the National Guard were also sent to support the reunion activities.

The first veterans arrived in Gettysburg on June 25. The youngest veteran was 61 years old; the oldest claimed to be 112. Each man was assigned to a cot in a tent that held eight men. Kitchens were placed at the end of every company street. The first meals included fried chicken, pork roast sandwiches, and ice cream.

In spite of the brutal summer heat and dusty conditions, nothing could keep the aged veterans in the Great Camp. Hundreds wandered the battle-field. Many visited the ground where they and their comrades were positioned fifty years ago. Some wiped back tears; others wept at the memories. Confederate veterans were particularly pleased to see that park officials had positioned old cannons to mark the sites where their batteries had been during the battle.

A highlight of the fiftieth reunion was a meeting of the Pickett's Division Association and the Philadelphia Brigade Association at the High Water Mark, a reenactment of Pickett's Charge. Virginians advanced across the field as they had fifty years before; Union veterans stood behind the stone wall that had marked their line a half century before. The men of Robert E. Lee's army stopped at the stone wall and traded ceremonial flags and shook hands with the men who had shot at them so long ago.

A large tent was erected on the field of Pickett's Charge. Each day there were programs and speeches. The old men talked to the current soldiers and spoke about how much things had changed over the past fifty years. Governors from several states made speeches.

At the last minute, President Woodrow Wilson arrived and addressed the veterans on July 4: "These venerable men crowding here to this famous field have set us a great example of devotion and utter sacrifice. They were willing to die that the people might live. But their task is done. Their day is turned into evening. They look to us to perfect what they have established. Their work is handed unto us, to be done in another way but not in another spirit. Our day is not over; it is upon us in full tide."

By the end of the reunion, more than 688,000 meals had been served. The days were hot and miserable, typical July weather for south-central Pennsylvania. On July 2 the temperature reached 100 degrees. Medical personnel treated more than 9,980 patients, many for heat exhaustion and physical fatigue. Nine died during the weeklong reunion.

For years it seemed that the Great Reunion was to be the last gathering of the UCV and the GAR. The goodwill articulated at Gettysburg dulled when the nation entered the Great War in Europe. A decade later the nation fell into the Great Depression.

In the mid-1930s social programs of the New Deal made substantial and lasting contributions to the Gettysburg National Military Park's development. Agencies authorized by New Deal programs created jobs and employed scores of young men who lived in camps at Pitzer's and McMillan's Woods. These youths worked with park staff on new avenue construction projects at Benner's Hill, Jones's Battalion, Oak Hill, and Granite Schoolhouse Lane. Snow removal, tree repair, landscaping, monument cleaning, farm-building repairs, and water line and drain installation were some of the tasks assayed by these young laborers.[1]

As the seventy-fifth anniversary of the battle approached, it appeared that another Gettysburg reunion was unlikely. For five years Gettysburg native Paul Roy pursued the matter with the leadership of the UCV and GAR, finally convincing both to have one last meeting on the old battleground. In 1938 only about eighteen hundred veterans traveled to Gettysburg for this last reunion, but the gathering of old men and survivors of a seventy-five-year-old battle was of little interest to the world. Even though the veterans of Gettysburg were dying, fading in memory, the country was more concerned with the economic hardships of the Depression and the storm clouds of war gathering in Europe.

THERE IS no evidence today of the Great Camp of the 1913 reunion. The ground returned to growing crops soon after the grand reunion. Instead of monuments to the reunion, there are corn and wheat fields.

In 1917 the War Department established Camp Colt near the site of the Great Camp. It was the first army camp designed to train the fledgling Tank Corps during World War I. In command of the post was Capt. Dwight D. Eisenhower. All traces of Camp Colt have vanished except for a commemorative marker and a tree planted near the Emmitsburg road in the general location of the camp.

The Second World War brought another army camp to Adams County. A temporary holding compound held approximately three hundred German prisoners of war. The camp was in a field on the west side of the Emmitsburg road for about six months in 1944. The prisoners were used as general labor to pick fruit, cut lumber, and to make road improvements in Adams County. Like Camp Colt, all traces of this camp have faded away.

After World War II tourists rediscovered Gettysburg. Amusement parks offered family entertainment, and the National Park Service supervised the Gettysburg National Military Park.

Gettysburg became the home of a future president. In 1950 Dwight and Mamie Eisenhower, looking toward retirement, purchased the Allen Redding farm adjoining Gettysburg National Military Park. It was the only home the Eisenhowers ever owned. The original 189-acre farm was transformed by stages into the 230-acre country estate of the thirty-fourth president of the United States. During his presidency, the president used the farm as a weekend retreat, a refuge in time of illness, and a comfortable meeting place for world leaders. On adjoining farms Eisenhower raised a prize-winning herd of Angus cattle. Here he entertained Premier Nikita Khrushchev of the Soviet Union in September 1959. From 1961 until Eisenhower's death in 1969, the farm was his home. In 1967 the Eisenhowers deeded the farm to the nation to be administered by the National Park Service as the Eisenhower National Historic Site.

In the 1950s Vice President Richard M. Nixon visited the Soldiers National Cemetery and his great-grandfather's grave. Pvt. George Nixon, Company B, Seventy-third Ohio Infantry, is interred in the Ohio section.

Vice President Lyndon Johnson visited Gettysburg on May 30, 1963. During remarks on Memorial Day, he said, "On this hallowed ground, heroic deeds were performed and eloquent words were spoken a century ago. We, the living, have not forgotten—and the world will never forget—

the deeds or the words of Gettysburg. We honor them now as we join on this Memorial Day of 1963 in a prayer for permanent peace of the world and fulfillment of our hopes for universal freedom and justice."

The park headquarters over the Gettysburg post office were woefully inadequate to accommodate the growing numbers of visitors needing direction and assistance. The celebrated Paul Philippoteaux cyclorama of the third day's battle was now in need of conservator's treatment as well as new quarters. It had been housed in a circular brick building on Baltimore Street since 1913. In 1941 the park acquired the cyclorama.

The National Park Service constructed a new cyclorama building and visitors center. The new building with its huge drum protecting the revitalized painting opened in 1962 in preparation for the centennial observance of the battle. Ten years later, the former Rosensteel National Museum, complete with its unique collection of battle artifacts and electric map, was acquired by the National Park Service. It complemented the cyclorama building as the new visitors center.

In addition to the farms and landmarks acquired by the War Department, the National Park Service has been active in protecting and preserving additional sites, such as the Rose, Sherfy, Patterson, Spangler, Wills, McClean, Blocher, Warfield, Snyder, and Cobean farms. In some of these efforts the park has been ably assisted by a groundswell of public support through such organizations as the Gettysburg Battlefield Preservation Association. The association is the oldest battlefield preservation organization at Gettysburg, founded in 1959 by President Eisenhower and television personality Cliff Arquette (Charley Weaver). The Gettysburg Battlefield Protection Association was created to carry on the work of the defunct Gettysburg Battlefield Memorial Association. More than one hundred historic or farm-related buildings require constant preservation by the National Park Service on Adams County farms that were used as battlefields. The National Park Service also supervises almost eight miles of defense works, more than thirteen hundred monuments and markers, twenty-four miles of historic fencing, buildings, defense works, woodlands, orchards, open agricultural fields, and more than seventy thousand artifacts.

In the mid-1960s the Gettysburg Battlefield Preservation Association and the Military Order of the Loyal Legion of the United States (MOLLUS) donated more than 175 acres to the park. The 3,865-acre park was listed in the National Register of Historic Places.

In 1975 the 11,820-acre Gettysburg Battlefield Historic District was listed in the National Register of Historic Places. Additional documentation was added to the registry in 1985. In the late 1980s the Gettysburg Battlefield Preservation Association donated the 31-acre Taney farm to the park after an act of Congress authorized the park to accept this tract.

It was also at this time that the Friends of the National Parks at Gettysburg was incorporated and established as a nonprofit organization. Since its conception, the Friends have acquired various lands associated with the park and turned them over to the National Park Service. They have also succeeded in making park improvements, such as having utility poles removed. Through fund-raising efforts, they continued to support the park.

Today more than 4,223 acres of the 11,581-acre area that constituted the Gettysburg battle are protected. Yet the area surrounding the town is experiencing rapid economic growth. Residential and commercial development has occurred along the borders of the park. The growing community is a constant threat to the battlefield and areas that contribute to its historic setting.

Funds are always needed to maintain the massive park. The Civil War Sites Advisory Commission designated Gettysburg as one of the fifty most threatened Civil War battlefields in the country. Much work needs to be done to maintain the monuments, the battlefields, and the park.

The site of Camp Letterman, easily identified with a marker on the south side of Route 30 about a mile east of Gettysburg, is for sale at the time of this writing. Most likely, by the time these words are read, the area will have been developed. The fields where tents stood and wounded men bled will be developed. Modern commercial buildings will stand on this land, joining restaurants, motels, and retail stores already constructed. Blacktop will cover the hallowed ground of what was Camp Letterman and Hospital Woods. A concrete slab will be laid, and another steel box will be erected to house another commercial store. Any remains of those who served and died at the camp will be forever covered when the land is sold and developed for commercial uses.

Nearly two million visitors visit Gettysburg each year. Movies and television stir public interest. Reenacting has become its own industry, and Gettysburg seems often to be a favorite destination. Shops and stores offer all types of uniforms, hats, boots, and accoutrements. Reenactors descend onto Gettysburg every year for a variety of events, including the annual battle reenactment in July. Thousands of visitors tour Gettysburg and Adams County each week. Because of its close proximity to major tourist areas in south-central Pennsylvania—Hershey and Lancaster County— Gettysburg easily maintains a high tourist traffic.

Of course, the town of Gettysburg has its share of souvenir stores, museums, and antique shops. Tours are still available from licensed guides. In addition to the regular hospitality industry—lodging, restaurants, and attractions—another interesting industry has taken root. Now visitors can embark on ghost tours of the town or battlefield. One service even offers a meter to measure paranormal activity.

"The carnage and desolation, the joys and sorrows therein depicted, have all long since passed away," Tillie Pierce observed more than a century ago.

Instead of the clashing tumult of battle, the groans of the wounded and dying, the mangled corpses, the shattered cannon, the lifeless charger, and the confusion of arms and accouterments, a new era of joy and prosperity, harmony and unity prevails. Where once the bloody hand of Mars blighted and killed the choicest of Nature's offspring, there Peace, with her smiles and arts has transformed the desolation into a Paradise of beauty and bloom. Where once I saw a terrible chaos I now behold a pleasing order.

NOTES
SELECTED BIBLIOGRAPHY
INDEX

NOTES

Chapter 1: The Borough of Gettysburg

1. Matilda J. "Tillie" Pierce Alleman, *At Gettysburg, or What a Girl Heard and Saw of the Battle* (New York: W. Lake Borland, 1889).
2. *Gettysburg Compiler*, June 24, 1908.
3. *1886 History of Adams County, Pennsylvania* (Chicago: Warner, Beers & Co., 1886), 7.
4. From an advertisement in the *Gettysburg Compiler*, September 22, 1862.
5. *Gettysburg Compiler*, May 12–June 23, 1863.
6. Robert L. Bloom, *A History of Adams County, Pennsylvania, 1700–1990* (Gettysburg: Adams County Historical Society, 1992), 28–29.
7. *1886 History of Adams County*, 333.
8. *The Underground Railroad*, Historic Pennsylvania Leaflet published by the Pennsylvania Historical and Museum Commission.

Chapter 2: The Rebels Are Coming!

1. On April 18, 1861, officials established Camp Curtin in Harrisburg. It was the first regular army camp formed in the North. Before the end of the month, the army sent twenty-five regiments to the front from Pennsylvania. The camp was originally named Camp Union, but officials changed the name to honor the state's governor, Andrew G. Curtin. Many Pennsylvania volunteers who served at Gettysburg had been at Camp Curtin for orientation.
2. *Philadelphia Press*, June 26, 1863.
3. Sarah M. Broadhead, *A Diary of a Lady of Gettysburg* (n.p.: privately printed, n.d.).
4. Based on transcriptions of the diaries of Salome "Sallie" Myers Stewart. The original diaries disappeared from the Adams County Historical Society in the 1960s.
5. Daniel A. Skelly, *A Boy's Experiences During the Battle of Gettysburg.* (n.p.: privately printed, 1932).
6. Peter C. Vermilyea, "The Effect of the Confederate Invasion of Pennsylvania on Gettysburg's African American Community," Adams County Historical Society, Gettysburg, Pa.

7. Albertus McCreary, "Gettysburg, A Boy's Experience of the Battle," *McClure's Magazine*, July 1909.
8. James C. Mohr, ed., *The Cormany Diaries: A Northern Family in the Civil War* (Pittsburgh: University of Pittsburg Press, 1982).
9. Jemima K. Cree, letter, in *Kittochtinny Papers, 1905–1908* (Chambersburg, 1908), 94.
10. McCreary, "Gettysburg, A Boy's Experience of the Battle."
11. Alleman, *At Gettysburg*.
12. Fannie Buehler, *Recollections of the Great Rebel Invasion and One Woman's Experiences During the Battle of Gettysburg* (N.p.: privately published, 1896).
13. Mary Warren Fastnacht, *Memories of the Battle of Gettysburg, Year 1863* (New York: Princely Press, 1941), 3.
14. Charles M. McCurdy, *Gettysburg: A Memoir* (Pittsburgh: Reed and Wittin, 1929), 13.

Chapter 3: The Rebels Are Here

1. Sarah M. Broadhead, *A Diary of a Lady of Gettysburg* (n.p.: privately printed, n.d.).
2. Matilda J. "Tillie" Pierce Alleman, *At Gettysburg, or What a Girl Heard and Saw of the Battle* (New York: W. Lake Borland, 1889).
3. Daniel A. Skelly, *A Boy's Experiences During the Battle of Gettysburg.* (n.p.: privately printed, 1932).
4. Broadhead, *Diary*.
5. Gates D. Fahnestock, Speech, National Arts Club of New York, February 12, 1934.
6. Alleman, *At Gettysburg*.
7. Sarah King, "A Mother's Story," *Gettysburg Compiler*, July 4, 1906.
8. Alleman, *At Gettysburg*.
9. John C. Will, "Reminiscences of the Three Day Battle of Gettysburg at the Globe Hotel," Adams County Historical Society, Gettysburg, Pa.
10. Charles M. McCurdy, *Gettysburg: A Memoir* (Pittsburgh: Reed and Wittin, 1929), 13.
11. Will, "Reminiscences."
12. Elizabeth M. Thorn, "Mrs. Thorn's War Stories," Gettysburg National Military Park, Gettysburg, Pa.
13. Ibid. The dead Union soldier was most likely Gettysburg native George Sandoe.

Chapter 4: The Federals Arrive

1. When the townspeople of Frederick complained of the public display of Talbot, Buford stated that he hanged him rather than send him to Washington for fear that "they would make him a Brigadier General." Buford's remark was

an allusion to the June 28 promotions to brigadier general of Capts. Wesley Merritt, Elon J. Farnsworth, and George A. Custer.

2. Daniel A. Skelly, *A Boy's Experiences During the Battle of Gettysburg* (n.p.: privately printed, 1932).

Chapter 5: July 1

1. Henry Heth, *The Memoirs of Henry Heth*, ed. James L. Morrison Jr. (Westport, Conn.: Greenwood Press, 1974).

2. A. P. Hill, Report, June 3–August 1, 1863, in United States, War Department, *The War of the Rebellion: A Compilation of the Official Records of the Union and Confederate Armies*, 128 vols. (Washington, D.C.: Government Printing Office, 1880–1901), The Gettysburg Campaign Official Records, ser. 1, vol. 27/2, S #44.

3. There is no consensus on when the first shot was fired at the battle of Gettysburg. The First Shot Marker records the time as 7:30 A.M. In 1886 this marker was erected by the three men involved in firing the first shot.

4. Many question that Buford and Reynolds met at the seminary. Some suggest that the meeting occurred at the Blue Eagle Tavern in Gettysburg.

5. Reynolds's body was taken to the George house, a small stone house on Steinwehr Avenue. Original wood boards stained with the general's blood are still visible.

6. William C. Davis, *Battlefields of the Civil War* (Norman: University of Oklahoma Press, 1996), 298–99

7. J. T. Trowbridge, "The Field of Gettysburg," *Atlantic Monthly*, November 16, 1865.

8. Agnes Barr, "Account of the Battle of Gettysburg," Adams County Historical Society, Gettysburg, Pa.

9. Basil Biggs, private family file, Adams County Historical Society, Gettysburg, Pa.

10. Daniel A. Skelly, *A Boy's Experiences During the Battle of Gettysburg* (n.p.: privately printed, 1932).

11. Lance Herdegen and W. Beaudot, *In the Bloody Railroad Cut at Gettysburg* (Dayton, Ohio: Morningside, 1990), 220.

12. Mary McAllister, "An Interview," *Philadelphia Inquirer*, June 26–29, 1938. This is an excerpt from the memoirs of McAllister. Her original memoir is in the collection of the Adams County Historical Society.

13. Howell was the only chaplain killed during the battle of Gettysburg.

14. A monument was placed at the foot of the church steps in 1889 in memory of Howell.

15. Based on transcriptions of the diaries of Salome "Sallie" Myers Stewart, Adams County Historical Society, Gettysburg, Pa.

16. Had Stewart lived, he would have become Sallie Myers's brother-in-law.

17. *Twice Told Tales of Michigan and Her Soldiers in the Civil War* (Lansing: Michigan Civil War Centennial Observation Commission, 1966), 30–31.

18. *1886 History of Adams County, Pennsylvania* (Chicago: Warner, Beers & Co., 1886).

19. Peter C. Vermilyea, "The Effect of the Confederate Invasion of Pennsylvania on Gettysburg's African American Community," Adams County Historical Society, Gettysburg, Pa.

20. Numbers & Losses Files, Gettysburg National Military Park, Gettysburg, Pa.

21. John D. Vautier, "At Gettysburg: The Eighty-Eighth Pennsylvania Infantry in the Battle," November 10, 1886, in *Gettysburg Newspaper Clippings*, 124–26.

22. Elizabeth M. Thorn, "Mrs. Thorn's War Stories," Gettysburg National Military Park, Gettysburg, Pa.

Chapter 6: July 2

1. Sarah M. Broadhead, *A Diary of a Lady of Gettysburg* (n.p.: privately printed, n.d.).

2. Catherine Foster, "The Story of the Battle," *Gettysburg Compiler*, June 6, 1904.

3. Robert McClean, "A Boy in Gettysburg," *Gettysburg Compiler*, June 30, 1909.

4. Mary McAllister, "An Interview," *Philadelphia Inquirer*, June 26–29, 1938.

5. John C. Will, "Reminiscences of the Three Day Battle of Gettysburg at the Globe Hotel," Adams County Historical Society, Gettysburg, Pa.

6. Anna Garlach Kitzmiller, "Mrs. Kitzmiller's Story," *Gettysburg Compiler*, August 9, 23, 1905.

7. The McCreary table is on display at the museum at the Gettysburg National Military Park, Gettysburg, Pa.

8. M. L. Culler, "Interesting Incidents Connected with the Battle of Gettysburg," *Gettysburg Compiler*, July 19, 1911.

9. Based on transcriptions of the diaries of Salome "Sallie" Myers Stewart, Adams County Historical Society, Gettysburg, Pa.

10. William McClean, "Days of Terror," *Gettysburg Compiler*, July 1, 1908.

11. Nellie Aughinbaugh, *Personal Experiences of a Young Girl During the Battle of Gettysburg* (n.p.: privately printed, 1941).

12. McAllister, "Interview."

13. Mary Elizabeth Montford, "How a 12 Year Old Girl Saw Gettysburg," *Doylestown (Pa.) Daily Register*, May 30, 1959.

14. Peter C. Vermilyea, "The Effect of the Confederate Invasion of Pennsylvania on Gettysburg's African American Community," Adams County Historical Society, Gettysburg, Pa.

15. Will, "Reminiscences."

16. Michael Jacobs, *Notes on the Rebel Invasion of Maryland and Pennsylvania and the Battle of Gettysburg, July 1st, 2nd, and 3rd, 1863*. Philadelphia, 1864.

Chapter 7: July 3

1. Cindy L. Small, *The Jennie Wade Story* (Gettysburg: Thomas Publications, 1991). The author reports that Wade secured her brother's release. Tillie Pierce states that her mother secured Sam's release.
2. Speculation continues as to where the bullet came from that killed Ginnie Wade. Most contend the fatal bullet originated from the Rupp tannery. Recently, some have theorized that the bullet came from the area of the Farnsworth House.
3. Agnes Barr, "Account of the Battle of Gettysburg," Adams County Historical Society, Gettysburg, Pa.
4. Robert McClean, "A Boy in Gettysburg," *Gettysburg Compiler*, June 30, 1909.
5. Sarah King, "A Mother's Story," *Gettysburg Compiler*, July 4, 1906.
6. Sarah M. Broadhead, *A Diary of a Lady of Gettysburg* (n.p.: privately printed, n.d.).
7. King, "A Mother's Story."
8. William T. Simpson, "The Drummer Boys of Gettysburg," *Philadelphia North American*, June 29, 1913.
9. John D. Imboden. "The Confederate Retreat from Gettysburg," in *Battles and Leaders of the Civil War*, ed. Robert U. Johnson and Clarence C. Buel, 4 vols. (1888; reprint, Secaucus, N.J.: Castle, 1983), 3:420–29.
10. *1886 History of Adams County, Pennsylvania* (Chicago: Warner, Beers & Co., 1886), 172. Meade's decision greatly disappointed Lincoln. On hearing the news, Lincoln wrote to Meade, "My dear general, I do not believe you appreciate the magnitude of the misfortune involved in Lee's escape. He was within your easy grasp, and to have closed upon him would, in connection with our other late successes, have ended the war. As it is, the war will be prolonged indefinitely. If you could not safely attack Lee last Monday, how can you possibly do so south of the river, when you can take with you very few more than two thirds of the force you then had in hand? It would be unreasonable to expect, and I do not expect you can now effect much. Your golden opportunity is gone, and I am distressed immeasurably because of it."
11. Matilda J. "Tillie" Pierce Alleman, *At Gettysburg, or What a Girl Heard and Saw of the Battle* (New York: W. Lake Borland, 1889).
12. *1886 History of Adams County Pennsylvania*, 171.
13. Joseph K. Barnes et al., *The Medical and Surgical History of the War of the Rebellion, 1861–1865*, 3 vols. (Washington, D.C.: Government Printing Office, 1870–88), vol. 3.

14. Mary McAllister, "An Interview," *Philadelphia Inquirer*, June 26–29, 1938.

15. John C. Will, "Reminiscences of the Three Day Battle of Gettysburg at the Globe Hotel," Adams County Historical Society, Gettysburg, Pa.

16. Elizabeth Stoever, "A Woman's Story of the Town," *Gettysburg Compiler*, June 24, 1909.

17. Will, "Reminiscences."

Chapter 8: July 4

1. *1886 History of Adams County, Pennsylvania* (Chicago: Warner, Beers & Co., 1886).

2. Mary McAllister, "An Interview," *Philadelphia Inquirer*, June 26–29, 1938.

3. Daniel A. Skelly, *A Boy's Experiences During the Battle of Gettysburg* (n.p.: privately printed, 1932).

4. Sarah M. Broadhead, *A Diary of a Lady of Gettysburg* (n.p.: privately printed, n.d.).

5. Agnes Barr, "Account of the Battle of Gettysburg," Adams County Historical Society, Gettysburg, Pa.

6. Skelly, *A Boy's Experiences*.

7. Jennie McCreary, letter to her sister Julia, July 22, 1863, published in the *Philadelphia Evening Bulletin*, July 2, 1938.

8. There are many estimates of the length of this wagon train, but most scholars agree it was at least fifteen miles long.

9. John D. Imboden. "The Confederate Retreat from Gettysburg," in *Battles and Leaders of the Civil War*, ed. Robert U. Johnson and Clarence C. Buel, 4 vols. (1888; reprint, Secaucus, N.J.: Castle, 1983), 3:420–29.

10. "The Days of Terror in 1863," in *Gettysburg Newspaper Clippings*, 6:155.

11. Autobiography of Carl Schulz, from the reprint version published by Reprint Services Corp.

Chapter 9: The Wounded

1. Leonard Marsden Gardner, "The Carnage at Gettysburg As Seen by a Minister," *Civil War Times* 3, no. 4 (July 1961): 14.

2. Mary Elizabeth Montford, "How a 12 Year Old Girl Saw Gettysburg," *Doylestown (Pa.) Daily Register*, May 30, 1959.

3. Roland R. Maust, *Grappling with Death: The Union Second Corps Hospital at Gettysburg* (Dayton, Ohio: Morningside, 2001).

4. *Chelsea Telegraph and Pioneer*, March 5, 1864.

5. Jonathan Letterman, October 3, 1863, in United States, War Department, *The War of the Rebellion: A Compilation of the Official Records of the Union and Confederate Armies*, 128 vols. (Washington, D.C.: Government Printing Office, 1880–1901), The Gettysburg Campaign Official Records, ser. 1, vol. 27/1, S #43.

6. John Shaw Billings, Papers, Adjutant General's Office Records (RG 94), National Archives, 1861–95.

7. Matilda J. "Tillie" Pierce Alleman, *At Gettysburg, or What a Girl Heard and Saw of the Battle* (New York: W. Lake Borland, 1889).

8. Dr. John S. Billings, Medical Reminiscences of the Civil War, a speech given April 5, 1905.

9. John Gregory Bishop Adams, *Reminiscences of the 19th Mass. Regiment* (Boston: Wright & Potter, 1899).

10. William T. Simpson, "The Drummer Boys of Gettysburg," *Philadelphia North American*, June 29, 1913.

11. Claims Files, Gettysburg National Military Park, Gettysburg, Pa.

12. Excerpted from J. R. Boyle's diary. His surgery was performed on July 2.

13. John C. Brinton, *Memoirs* (1891).

14. U.S. Christian Commission, Second Report of the Committee of Maryland.

15. Janet King, "Civil War Medicine," *Vermont of the Civil War*, March 2, 1999.

16. Joseph K. Barnes et al., *The Medical and Surgical History of the War of the Rebellion, 1861–1865*, 3 vols. (Washington, D.C.: Government Printing Office, 1870–88), vol.1, pt. 1.

17. Bell I. Wiley, *The Life of Johnny Reb* (Baton Rouge: Louisiana State University Press, 1994).

18. J. D. Billings, *Hardtack and Coffee* (Boston: George M. Smith, 1887).

19. Gerald R. Bennett, *Days of "Uncertainty and Dread"* (Littlestown, Pa.: Plank's Suburban Press, 1997), 78–79.

20. An inflammatory disorder of the lower intestinal tract, usually caused by a bacterial, parasitic, or protozoan infection and resulting in pain, fever, and severe diarrhea, often accompanied by the passage of blood and mucus.

21. Disturbed digestion; indigestion.

22. Inflammation of the intestinal tract, especially of the small intestine.

23. Linus P. Brockett and Mary C. Vaughan, *Woman's Work in the Civil War: A Record of Heroism, Patriotism and Patience* (Philadelphia: Zeigler, McCurdy & Co., 1867), 335.

Chapter 10: The Second Week of July

1. Many times the Daughters of Charity based in Emmitsburg, Maryland, were known as the Sisters of Charity. The corporate title is Sisters of Charity of Saint Joseph's. The correct title after 1850 is Daughters of Charity. The proper title, however, was and remains Daughters of Charity of Saint Vincent de Paul.

2. Archives of Saint Joseph's Provincial House 7-5-1-2, #8, Betty Ann McNeil, DC, ed., *Daughters of Charity in the Civil War* (Emmitsburg: Saint Joseph's Provincial House, 2002), 67.

3. Now the Gettysburg Hotel, located in the same location on the town square as McClellan's Hotel.

4. Archives of Saint Joseph's Provincial House, 68.

5. Ibid., 73.

6. Ibid., 69.

7. The sisters later documented their pastoral activities at Gettysburg for Father Burlando, who was preparing a report to the Major Superiors in Paris.

8. Archives of Saint Joseph's Provincial House, 76.

9. The nuns used the supplies in hospitals throughout Adams County. In addition to the many field hospitals, the Daughters of Charity served at the temporary hospitals set up at Saint Francis Xavier Church, the Methodist church, and the Pennsylvania College.

10. John Shaw Billings, papers, Adjutant General's Office Records (RG 94), National Archives, 1861–95.

11. Fannie Buehler, *Recollections of the Great Rebel Invasion and One Woman's Experiences During the Battle of Gettysburg* (N.p.: privately published, 1896).

12. Jonathan Letterman, October 3, 1863, in United States, War Department, *The War of the Rebellion: A Compilation of the Official Records of the Union and Confederate Armies*, 128 vols. (Washington, D.C.: Government Printing Office, 1880–1901), The Gettysburg Campaign Official Records, ser. 1, vol. 27/1, S #43.

13. Mary C. Gillett, *The Army Medical Department, 1818–1865* (Washington, D.C.: Center of Military History, 1987).

14. William Warren Potter, "Reminiscences of Field-Hospital Service with the Army of the Potomac," *Buffalo Medical and Surgical Journal* (October-November 1889): 15–16.

15. Richard H. Shryock, "A Medical Perspective on the Civil War," in *Medicine in America: Historical Essays* (Baltimore: Johns Hopkins Press, 1966), 91.

16. Theodore S. Dimon, "From Auburn to Antietam—The Civil War Journal of a Battlefield Surgeon Who Served with the Army of the Potomac, 1861–1863," Gettysburg National Military Park, Gettysburg, Pa.

17. Camp Letterman General Hospital file, Gettysburg National Military Park, Gettysburg, Pa.

18. Their monument is a modest dual square design.

19. Elizabeth M. Thorn, "Mrs. Thorn's War Stories," Gettysburg National Military Park, Gettysburg, Pa.

Chapter 11: Help for Gettysburg

1. *Lewistown (Pa.) Gazette,* July 15, 1863.

2. Charles J. Stillé, *History of the United States Sanitary Commission* (Philadelphia: J. B. Lippincott & Co., 1866).

Chapter 12: Burying the Dead

1. Quoted in Gregory A. Coco, *A Strange and Blighted Land, Gettysburg: The Aftermath of Battle* (Gettysburg: Thomas Publications,1995), 6.
2. John B. Linn, diary, July 6–11, 1863.
3. *Adams County Sentinel*, July 7, 1863.
4. Matilda J. "Tillie" Pierce Alleman, *At Gettysburg, or What a Girl Heard and Saw of the Battle* (New York: W. Lake Borland, 1889).
5. *Gettysburg Compiler*, July 20, 1863.
6. Linn, diary.
7. Quoted in Earl J. Coates, "A Rendezvous at Gettysburg: Identification of a Group of Unknown Union Dead," Gettysburg National Military Park, Gettysburg, Pa.
8. Daniel A. Skelly, *A Boy's Experiences During the Battle of Gettysburg* (n.p.: privately printed, 1932).
9. Skelly later learned the grave was that of Col. Joseph Wasden, Twenty-second Georgia Infantry. He was killed on July 2.
10. Roland R. Maust, *Grappling with Death: The Union Second Corps Hospital at Gettysburg* (Dayton, Ohio: Morningside, 2001).
11. Anna Morris Holstein, *Three Years in Field Hospitals of the Army of the Potomac* (Philadelphia: J. B. Lippincott, 1867).
12. Thomas M. Aldrich, *The History of Battery A, First Regiment Rhode Island Light Artillery in the War to Preserve the Union, 1861–1865* (Providence: Snow & Farnham, 1904), 221.
13. *Lancaster (Pa.) Intelligencer*, July 7, 1863.
14. Pennsylvania, Gettysburg Battlefield Commission, *Pennsylvania at Gettysburg: Ceremonies at the Dedication of the Monuments Erected by the Commonwealth*, 4 vols. (Harrisburg: W. S. Ray, 1914), 1:224–25.
15. J. C. Williams, *Life in Camp* (Claremont, N.H.: Claremont, 1864).
16. In 1866 a school known as the National Homestead at Gettysburg was established for soldiers' orphans. Among its first students were Alice, Frank, and Frederick Humiston, the children of Sgt. Amos Humiston. Philinda Humiston was the school's first matron. Approximately two hundred students attended before the school closed in 1877.
17. *Franklin Repository*, July 8, 1863.
18. C. W. Eliot, ed., *American Historical Documents*, The Harvard Classics, vol. 43 (New York: P. F. Collier & Son, 1910), 14.
19. Skelly, *A Boy's Experiences*.
20. William T. Simpson, "The Drummer Boys of Gettysburg," *Philadelphia North American*, June 29, 1913.

21. Liberty A. Clutz Hollinger, *Some Personal Recollections of the Battle of Gettysburg* (Gettysburg: privately printed, n.d.).

22. *Adams Sentinel,* July 14, 1863.

23. Skelly, *A Boy's Experiences.*

24. John C. Will, "Reminiscences of the Three Day Battle of Gettysburg at the Globe Hotel," Adams County Historical Society, Gettysburg, Pa.

25. *Cortland (N.Y.) Gazette & Banner,* July 16, 1863.

Chapter 13: Military Medical Care

1. They were called contract surgeons and were listed as acting assistant surgeons in the official records.

2. Adams, George W., *Fighting for Time,* in *The Image of War, 1861–1865,* ed. William C. Davis, vol. 4 (Garden City, N.Y.: Doubleday, 1983).

3. Jonathan Letterman, October 3, 1863, in United States, War Department, *The War of the Rebellion: A Compilation of the Official Records of the Union and Confederate Armies,* 128 vols. (Washington, D.C.: Government Printing Office, 1880–1901), The Gettysburg Campaign Official Records, ser. 1, vol. 27/1, S #43.

4. Linus P. Brockett and Mary C. Vaughan, *Woman's Work in the Civil War: A Record of Heroism, Patriotism and Patience* (Philadelphia: Zeigler, McCurdy & Co., 1867), 408.

5. Lt. William Wheeler, Thirteenth New York Battery, to family, July 26, 1863, Gettysburg National Military Park, Gettysburg, Pa.

6. William Robert Houghton, *Two Boys in the Civil War and After* (Montgomery, Ala.: Paragon Press, 1912), 33.

7. The roadway is now marked as Route 30, sometimes known as the Lincoln Highway. Camp Letterman was on the south side of the highway, between the town and Route 15, a bypass that generally runs north and south around Gettysburg.

8. Roland R. Maust, *Grappling with Death: The Union Second Corps Hospital at Gettysburg* (Dayton, Ohio: Morningside, 2001).

Chapter 14: Prisoners of War

1. United States, War Department, *The War of the Rebellion: A Compilation of the Official Records of the Union and Confederate Armies,* 128 vols. (Washington, D.C.: Government Printing Office, 1880–1901), The Gettysburg Campaign Official Records, ser. 1, vol. 27/1, S #44.

2. William B. Hesseltine, ed., *Civil War Prisons* (Kent, Ohio: Kent State University Press, 1962), places the numbers at Northerners 212,000, Southerners 463,000.

3. Quoted in Gregory A. Coco, *A Strange and Blighted Land, Gettysburg: The Aftermath of Battle* (Gettysburg: Thomas Publications, 1995), 257.

4. *Staunton (Va.) Spectator*, August 4, 1863.

5. Franklin Horner quoted in Mark Nesbitt, *35 Days to Gettysburg: The Campaign Diaries of Two American Enemies* (Harrisburg, Pa.: Stackpole Books, 1992).

6. Matilda J. "Tillie" Pierce Alleman, *At Gettysburg, or What a Girl Heard and Saw of the Battle* (New York: W. Lake Borland, 1889).

7. *Harper's New Monthly Magazine* 27, no. 160 (September 1863): 558.

Chapter 15: Life As a Nurse

1. Beverly Sanders, *Women During and After the Civil War, 1860–1890*, Women in American History, no. 3 (Minneapolis: Education Development Center; 1986).

2. Dorothy Clarke Wilson, *Stranger and Traveler: The Story of Dorothea Dix, American Reformer* (Boston: Little, Brown, 1975).

3. *Chelsea Telegraph and Pioneer*, March 5, 1864.

4. Roland R. Maust, *Grappling with Death: The Union Second Corps Hospital at Gettysburg* (Dayton, Ohio: Morningside, 2001).

5. Linus P. Brockett and Mary C. Vaughan, *Woman's Work in the Civil War: A Record of Heroism, Patriotism and Patience* (Philadelphia: Zeigler, McCurdy & Co., 1867), 408.

6. Anson D. Randolph, "Three Weeks at Gettysburg," 1863, Gettysburg National Military Park, Gettysburg, Pa.

Chapter 16: Total Casualties

1. Total casualty figures were compiled from various sources, including: Edwin B. Coddington, *The Gettysburg Campaign: A Study in Command* (New York: Charles Scribner's Sons, 1968); Numbers & Losses Files, Gettysburg National Military Park, Gettysburg, Pa.

2. Numbers quoted are from various sources but in particular from Burke Davis, *The Civil War: Strange and Fascinating Facts* (New York: Fairfax Press, 1982).

3. Stewart M. Brooks, *Civil War Medicine* (Springfield, Ill.: C. C. Thomas, 1966).

4. Figures presented here come from materials at the Gettysburg National Military Park, Gettysburg, Pa., various encyclopedias, diverse resource books, and other sources included in the bibliography.

5. United States, War Department, *The War of the Rebellion: A Compilation of the Official Records of the Union and Confederate Armies*, 128 vols. (Washington, D.C.: Government Printing Office, 1880–1901), 299.

Chapter 17: Returning to Normalcy

1. Lydia Catherine Ziegler Clare, "A Gettysburg Girl's Story of the Great Battle," Adams County Historical Society, Gettysburg, Pa.

2. Nellie Aughinbaugh, *Personal Experiences of a Young Girl During the Battle of Gettysburg* (n.p.: privately printed, 1941).

3. Sarah King, "A Mother's Story," *Gettysburg Compiler*, July 4, 1906.

4. "The Days of Terror in 1863," in *Gettysburg Newspaper Clippings*, 6:155.

5. Linus P. Brockett and Mary C. Vaughan, *Woman's Work in the Civil War: A Record of Heroism, Patriotism and Patience* (Philadelphia: Zeigler, McCurdy & Co., 1867), 408.

6. *Franklin Repository*, July 22, 1863.

7. Cyrus Bacon Jr., daily register, Gettysburg National Military Park, Gettysburg, Pa.

8. *Cortland (N.Y.) Gazette & Banner*, July 16, 1863.

9. Burnham's letter was published in the *Cortland (N.Y.) Gazette & Banner*, August 13, 1863.

10. The following October, Grover's remains were transported to Cortland, N.Y., for reburial.

11. Brockett and Vaughan, *Woman's Work*, 329.

12. Elizabeth McClean, "The Rebels Are Coming," *Gettysburg Compiler*, July 8, 1908.

13. The Gettysburg hero was immortalized in the battlefield when a monument was erected in his honor. A sculpture was placed upon a boulder taken from the battlefield. The memorial was dedicated on July 1, 1903, the fortieth anniversary of the battle.

14. John C. Will, "Reminiscences of the Three Day Battle of Gettysburg at the Globe Hotel," Adams County Historical Society, Gettysburg, Pa.

15. *Lancaster (Pa.) Intelligencer*, July 14, 1863.

Chapter 18: Creating a National Cemetery

1. Theodore S. Dimon, "From Auburn to Antietam—The Civil War Journal of a Battlefield Surgeon Who Served with the Army of the Potomac, 1861–1863," Gettysburg National Military Park, Gettysburg, Pa.

2. *Adams Sentinel*, July 21, 1863.

3. Ibid., July 28, 1863.

4. John B. Bachelder to Gov. Andrew G. Curtin, August 10, 1863, Gettysburg National Military Park, Gettysburg, Pa.

5. Theodore S. Dimon to John F. Seymour, August 1, 1863, Gettysburg National Military Park, Gettysburg, Pa.

6. David Wills to Gov. Andrew G. Curtin, July 24, 1863, Gettysburg National Military Park, Gettysburg, Pa.

7. David McConaughy to Gov. Andrew G. Curtin, July 25, 1863, Gettysburg National Military Park, Gettysburg, Pa.

8. Kathleen R. Georg, "This Grand National Enterprise," Gettysburg National Military Park, Gettysburg, Pa.

9. *Lancaster (Pa.) Intelligencer,* August 4, 1863.

Chapter 19: Creating a National Park

1. According to the Gettysburg National Military Park, Gettysburg, Pa., 979 unknowns are buried in the Soldiers National Cemetery.

2. Leander Warren, Adams County Historical Society, Gettysburg, Pa.

3. Gary Wills, *Lincoln at Gettysburg: The Words That Remade America* (New York: Simon and Schuster, 1992), 9.

4. *Gettysburg Compiler,* November 23, 1863.

5. Albertus McCreary, "Gettysburg, A Boy's Experience of the Battle," *McClure's Magazine,* July 1909.

6. Hugh M. Ziegler, unpublished manuscript, Adams County Historical Society, Gettysburg, Pa.

7. *Confederate Veteran* 11, no. 10 (October 1903).

8. Gregory A. Coco, *A Strange and Blighted Land, Gettysburg: The Aftermath of Battle* (Gettysburg: Thomas Publications,1995), 361.

9. *Hawkinsville (Ga.) Dispatch,* July 6, 1871.

10. A list of these findings is on file at the library of the Gettysburg National Military Park, Gettysburg, Pa.

Chapter 20: Gettysburg Today

1. Kathleen J. Georg, "A Fitting and Expressive Memorial: The Development of Gettysburg National Military Park," Gettysburg National Military Park, Gettysburg, Pa..

SELECTED BIBLIOGRAPHY

1886 History of Adams County Pennsylvania. Chicago: Warner, Beers & Co., 1886.

Adams County Sentinel. July 21, 28, 1863.

Adams, John Gregory Bishop, *Reminiscences of the 19th Mass. Regiment.* Boston: Wright & Potter, 1899.

Aldrich, Thomas M. *The History of Battery A, First Regiment Rhode Island Light Artillery in the War to Preserve the Union, 1861–1865.* Providence: Snow & Farnham, 1904.

Alleman, Matilda J. "Tillie" Pierce. *At Gettysburg, or What a Girl Heard and Saw of the Battle.* New York: W. Lake Borland, 1889.

Andrist, Ralph K. *The American Heritage History of the Confident Years.* New York: American Heritage, 1969.

Annual Reports of the GNMP Commission, 1895–1920. Gettysburg National Military Park, Gettysburg, Pa.

Approvals of Requests, 1895–1918. Gettysburg National Military Park, Gettysburg, Pa.

Aughinbaugh, Nellie. *Personal Experiences of a Young Girl During the Battle of Gettysburg.* N.p.: privately printed, 1941.

Bachelder, John B. Letter to Gov. Andrew G. Curtin, August 10, 1863. Gettysburg National Military Park, Gettysburg, Pa.

————. Papers. New Hampshire Historical Society. Microfilm, reel #3, letters. Gettysburg National Military Park, Gettysburg, Pa.

Barr, Agnes. "Account of the Battle of Gettysburg." Adams County Historical Society, Gettysburg, Pa.

Bates, Samuel P. *History of the Pennsylvania Volunteers, 1861–65.* Harrisburg, Pa.: B. Singerly, 1869–71.

Bennett, Gerald R. *Days of Uncertainty and Dread.* Littlestown, Pa.: Bennett, 1997.

Betty Ann McNeil, DC, ed. *Daughters of Charity in the Civil War.* Archives of Saint Joseph's Provincial House 7-5-1-2, #8. Emmitsburg, Md.: Saint Joseph's Provincial House, 2002.

Biggs, Basil. Private family file. Adams County Historical Society, Gettysburg, Pa.

Billings, John Davis. *Hardtack and Coffee.* Boston: G. M. Smith, 1888.

Billings, John Shaw. "Medical Reminiscences of the Civil War." Speech given April 5, 1905. Gettysburg National Military Park, Gettysburg, Pa.

————. Papers. Adjutant General's Office Records (RG 94). National Archives, 1861–95.

Bloom, Robert L. *A History of Adams County, Pennsylvania 1700–1990*. Gettysburg: Adams County Historical Society, 1992.

Boritt, Gabor S., ed. *The Gettysburg Nobody Knows*. New York: Oxford University Press, 1997.

Boyle, Frank A. *A Party of Mad Fellows*. Dayton, Ohio: Morningside, 1996.

Broadhead, Sarah M. *A Diary of a Lady of Gettysburg*. N.p.: privately printed, n.d.

Brockett, Linus P., and Mary C. Vaughan. *Woman's Work in the Civil War: A Record of Heroism, Patriotism and Patience*. Philadelphia: Zeigler, McCurdy & Co., 1867.

Buehler, Fannie. *Recollections of the Great Rebel Invasion and One Woman's Experiences During the Battle of Gettysburg*. N.p.: privately published, 1896.

Buel, Clarence, and Robert U. Johnson, eds. *Battles and Leaders of the Civil War*. 4 vols. 1888. Reprint, Secaucus, N.J.: Castle, 1983.

Chamberlain, Thomas. *History of the One Hundred and Fiftieth Regiment, Pennsylvania Volunteers, Second Regiment, Bucktail Brigade*. Philadelphia: F. McManus, 1905.

Chelsea (Mass.) Telegraph and Pioneer, March 5, 1864.

Clare, Lydia Catherine Ziegler. "A Gettysburg Girl's Story of the Great Battle." Adams County Historical Society, Gettysburg, Pa.

Clark, Champ, ed. *Gettysburg, The Confederate High Tide*. Alexandria, Va.: Time-Life Books, 1985.

Clark, Walter. *Histories of the Several Regiments and Battalions from North Carolina in the Great War, 1861–1865*. 5 vols. Raleigh: E. M. Uzzell, 1901.

Coates, Earl J. "A Rendezvous at Gettysburg: Identification of a Group of Unknown Union Dead." Gettysburg National Military Park, Gettysburg, Pa.

Coco, Gregory A. *Gettysburg: The Aftermath of a Battle*. Gettysburg: Thomas Publications, 1994.

————. *Wasted Valor: The Confederate Dead at Gettysburg*. Gettysburg: Thomas Publications, 1990.

Coddington, Edwin B. *The Gettysburg Campaign: A Study in Command*. New York: Charles Scribner's Sons, 1968.

Coffin, Charles Carleton. *Marching to Victory*. New York: Harpers & Brothers, 1889.

Confederate Veteran, vol. 11, no. 10 (October 1903).

Cortland (N.Y.) Gazette & Banner. July 16, 1863.

Cree, Jemima K. Letter. In *Kittochtinny Papers, 1905–1908*. Chambersburg, 1908.

Culler, M. L. "Interesting Incidents Connected with the Battle of Gettysburg." *Gettysburg Compiler*, July 19, 1911.

Cumberland Township Tax Records, 1799–1895. Adams County Historical Society, Gettysburg, Pa.

Davis, William C. *Battlefields of the Civil War*. Norman: University of Oklahoma Press, 1996.

Dawes, Rufus R. *Service with the Sixth Wisconsin Volunteers*. Marietta, Ohio: E. R. Alderman, 1890.

Deed Books B, L, Z, and AA. Adams County Courthouse.

Dimon, Theodore S. "From Auburn to Antietam: The Civil War Journal of a Battlefield Surgeon Who Served with the Army of the Potomac, 1861–1863." Gettysburg National Military Park, Gettysburg, Pa.

————. Letter to John F. Seymour. August 1, 1863. Gettysburg National Military Park, Gettysburg, Pa.

Doylestown (Pa.) Daily Register. May 30, 1959.

Elmore, Thomas L. "Courage Against the Trenches: The Attack and Repulse of Steuart's Brigade on Culp's Hill." *Gettysburg Magazine*, no. 7 (July 1992): 83–97.

Fastnacht, Mary Warren. *Memories of the Battle of Gettysburg, Year 1863*. New York: Princely Press, 1941.

Foote, Shelby. *Stars in Their Courses: The Gettysburg Campaign, June–July 1863*. New York: Modern Library, 1994.

Foster, Catherine. "The Story of the Battle." *Gettysburg Compiler*. June 6, 1904.

Fox, William Freeman. *Regimental Losses in the American Civil War, 1861–1865*. Albany, N.Y.: Albany Publishing Co., 1889.

Franklin (Pa.) Repository, July 8, 1863.

Frassanito, William A. *Gettysburg: A Journey in Time*. New York: Charles Scribner's Sons, 1975.

Freeman, Douglas S. *R. E. Lee: A Biography*. 4 vols. New York: Charles Scribner's Sons, 1934–45.

Gardner, Leonard Marsden. "The Carnage at Gettysburg As Seen by a Minister." *Civil War Times*, July 1961.

Garlach, Anna. *See* Kitzmiller, Anna Garlach.

Georg, Kathleen R. "A Fitting and Expressive Memorial: The Development of Gettysburg National Military Park." January 1988. Gettysburg National Military Park, Gettysburg, Pa.

————. "This Grand National Enterprise." May 1982. Gettysburg National Military Park, Gettysburg, Pa.

Gettysburg Borough Tax Records, 1857–1863. Adams County Historical Society.

Gettysburg Compiler. September 22, 1862; November 23, 1863; April 9, 1895; June 28, 1905; August 9, 23, 1905; July 4, 1906; June 24, 1908; July 1, 1908.

Glatfelter, Charles. "Extracts from the Road Docket and Quarter Sessions Docket, Lancaster and York Counties, Pennsylvania." 1974. Adams County Historical Society, Gettysburg, Pa.

Godcharles, Frederic A. *Pennsylvania Political, Governmental, Military and Civil.* Military Volume. New York: American Historical Society, 1933.

Gordon, John Brown. *Reminiscences of the Civil War: Electronic Edition.* New York: Charles Scribner's & Sons, 1964.

Gould, Benjamin Apthorp. *Investigations in Military and Anthropological Statistics of American Soldiers.* New York: Hurd & Houghton, 1869.

Hage, Anne A. "The Battle of Gettysburg As Seen by Minnesota Soldiers." *Minnesota History,* July 1963.

Hall, Hillman A., et al. *History of the Sixth New York Cavalry.* Worcester, Mass.: Blanchard, 1908.

Harper's New Monthly Magazine, September 1863.

Hartwig, D. Scott. "The 11th Army Corps on July 1, 1863." *Gettysburg Magazine,* January 1990.

Haskell, Frank A. *American Historical Documents.* The Harvard Classics. New York: P. F. Collier & Son, 1909.

Hassler, Warren W., Jr. *Crisis at the Crossroads.* Gettysburg: Stan Clark Military Books, 1991.

Hawkinsville (Ga.) Dispatch. July 6, 1871.

Herdegen, Lance, and W. Beaudot. *In the Bloody Railroad Cut at Gettysburg.* Dayton, Ohio: Morningside, 1990.

Hess, Earl. *Pickett's Charge: The Last Confederate Attack at Gettysburg.* Chapel Hill: University of North Carolina Press, 2001.

Hesseltine, William B, ed. *Civil War Prisons.* Kent, Ohio: Kent State University Press, 1962.

Heth, Henry. *The Memoirs of Henry Heth.* Edited by James L. Morrison Jr. Westport, Conn.: Greenwood Press, 1974.

Hollinger, Liberty A. Clutz. *Some Personal Recollections of the Battle of Gettysburg.* Gettysburg: privately printed, n.d.

Holstein, Anna Morris. *Three Years in Field Hospitals of the Army of the Potomac.* Philadelphia: J. B. Lippincott, 1867.

Horner, Franklin. Quoted in Mark Nesbitt, *35 Days to Gettysburg: The Campaign Diaries of Two American Enemies.* Harrisburg, Pa.: Stackpole, 1992.

Houghton, William Robert. *Two Boys in the Civil War and After.* Montgomery, Ala.: Paragon Press, 1912.

Hubler, Simon. "Just the Plain, Unvarnished Story of a Soldier in the Ranks: Exactly What a Corporal in the 143rd Pennsylvania Infantry Did, Thought, and Saw During the Three-Days' Battle." *New York Times,* June 29, 1913.

Hunsecker, Catherine. "Civil War Reminiscences." *Christian Monitor.* January 1924.

Imboden, John "The Confederate Retreat from Gettysburg" in *Battles and Leaders of the Civil War*. Edited by Clarence Buel and Robert U. Johnson. 4 vols. 1888. Reprint, Secaucus, N.J.: Castle, 1983. 3:420–29.

Imholte, John Quinn. *The First Volunteers*. Minneapolis: Ross & Haines, 1963.

Jacobs, Michael. *Notes on the Rebel Invasion of Maryland and Pennsylvania, and the Battle of Gettysburg, July 1st, 2nd, and 3rd, 1863*. Philadelphia: J. B. Lippincott, 1864.

Jordan David M. *Winfield Scott Hancock: A Soldier's Life*. Bloomington: Indiana University Press, 1988.

King, Sara B. "A Mother's Story." *Gettysburg Compiler*. July 4, 1906.

Kitzmiller, Anna Garlach. "Mrs. Kitzmiller's Story." *Gettysburg Compiler*. August 9, 23, 1905.

Kunhardt, Philip B., Jr. *A New Birth of Freedom: Lincoln at Gettysburg*. Boston: Little, Brown and Co., 1983.

Lancaster (Pa.) Intelligencer. August 4, 1863.

Lewistown (Pa.) Gazette. July 15, 22, 1863.

Malone, Dumas, ed. *Dictionary of American Biography*. 11 vols. New York: Scribner, 1946–58.

Marbaker, Thomas B. *11th New Jersey: History of the Eleventh New Jersey Volunteers from Its Organization to Appomattox—To Which Is Added Experiences of Prison Life and Sketches of Individual Members*. Trenton, N.J.: MacCrellish and Quigley, 1898.

Marye, John L. "The First Gun at Gettysburg: With the Confederate Advance Guard." *American Historical Register* (July 1895).

Maust, Roland R. *Grappling with Death: The Union Second Corps Hospital at Gettysburg*. Dayton, Ohio: Morningside, 2001.

McAllister, Mary. "An Interview." *Philadelphia Inquirer*. June 26–29, 1938.

McClean, Elizabeth. "The Rebels Are Coming." *Gettysburg Compiler*, July 8, 1908.

McClean, Robert. "A Boy in Gettysburg." *Gettysburg Compiler*, June 30, 1909.

McClean, William. "Days of Terror." *Gettysburg Compiler*, July 1, 1908.

McConaughy, David. Letter to Andrew Curtin, July 25, 1863. Gettysburg National Military Park, Gettysburg, Pa.

McCreary, Albertus. "Gettysburg, A Boy's Experience of the Battle." *McClure's Magazine*, July 1909.

McCreary, Jennie. Letter to her sister Julia. July 22, 1863. *Philadelphia Evening Bulletin*, July 2, 1938.

McCurdy, Charles M. *Gettysburg: A Memoir*. Pittsburgh: Reed and Wittin Co., 1929.

McPherson, Edward. Claims file. Gettysburg National Military Park, Gettysburg, Pa.

———. "Local History." *Adams County Star and Sentinel,* May 14, 1895.

———. Papers, Extracts. Microfilm. Library of Congress.

McPherson, James M. *Battle Cry of Freedom.* New York: Ballantine Books, 1988.

———. *Ordeal by Fire: The Civil War and Reconstruction.* New York: Knopf, 1982.

Meinhard, Robert W. "The First Minnesota at Gettysburg." *Gettysburg Magazine* (July 1991).

Metzger, Frank R. "The Honorable Edward McPherson, Citizen of Gettysburg." 1933. Adams County Historical Society.

Miers, Earl Schenk, and Richard A. Brown. *Gettysburg.* New Brunswick: Rutgers University Press, 1948.

Minnesota in the Civil War and Indian War. 2 vols. St. Paul: Pioneer Press, 1883.

Moe, Richard. *The Last Full Measure: The Life and Death of the First Minnesota Volunteers.* New York: Henry Holt, 1993.

Mohr, James C., ed. *The Cormany Diaries: A Northern Family in the Civil War.* Pittsburgh: University of Pittsburg Press, 1982.

Montford, Mary Elizabeth. "How a 12 Year Old Girl Saw Gettysburg." *Doylestown (Pa.) Daily Register.* May 30, 1959.

Myers, Sallie. *See* Stewart, Salome "Sallie" Myers.

Nesbitt, Mark. *35 Days to Gettysburg: The Campaign Diaries of Two American Enemies.* Harrisburg, Pa.: Stackpole, 1992.

New York Monuments Commission. *New York at Gettysburg.* 3 vols. Albany: J. B. Lyon, 1900.

Nicholson, John P. Journal, 1893–1921. Gettysburg National Military Park, Gettysburg, Pa.

Numbers & Losses Files. Gettysburg National Military Park, Gettysburg, Pa.

Palmer, Michael A. *Lee Moves North: Robert E. Lee on the Offensive.* New York: John Wiley & Sons, 1998.

Pennsylvania, Gettysburg Battle-field Commission. *Pennsylvania at Gettysburg: Ceremonies at the Dedication of the Monuments Erected by the Commonwealth.* 4 vols. Harrisburg, Pa.: W. S. Ray, 1914– .

Pfanz, Harry W. *Gettysburg: Culp's Hill and Cemetery Hill.* Chapel Hill: University of North Carolina Press, 1993.

———. *Gettysburg: The First Day.* Chapel Hill: University of North Carolina Press, 2001.

———. *Gettysburg: The Second Day.* Chapel Hill: University of North Carolina Press, 1987.

Philadelphia Press. June 26, 1863.

Philadelphia Inquirer. June 26–29, 1938.

Philadelphia Times. November 1876.

Pierce, Tillie. *See* Alleman, Matilda J. "Tillie" Pierce.

Randolph, Anson D. "Three Weeks at Gettysburg." 1863. Gettysburg National Military Park, Gettysburg, Pa.

Receipt Book, September 6, 1918. Gettysburg National Military Park, Gettysburg, Pa.

Robbins, William Mack. Journal. Gettysburg National Military Park, Gettysburg, Pa.

Sanders, Beverly. *Women During and After the Civil War, 1860–1890.* Women in American History, no. 3. Minneapolis: Education Development Center, 1986.

Schildt, John W. *Eyewitness to Gettysburg.* Shippensburg, Pa.: Burd Street Press, 1997.

———. *Roads from Gettysburg.* Shippensburg, Pa.: Burd Street Press, 1998.

Sheads, J. Melchior, and J. Roger Dunn. "Historian's Report: Old McPherson Farm House." Gettysburg National Military Park, Gettysburg, Pa.

Shue, Richard S. *Morning at Willoughby Run, July 1, 1863.* Gettysburg, Pa.: Thomas Publications, 1995.

Simpson, William T. "The Drummer Boys of Gettysburg." *Philadelphia North American.* June 29, 1913.

Skelly, Daniel A. *A Boy's Experiences During the Battle of Gettysburg.* N.p.: privately printed, 1932.

Slentz, John. Claims file. Gettysburg National Military Park, Gettysburg, Pa.

Smith, Donald L. *The Twenty-Fourth Michigan of the Iron Brigade.* 1962. Reprint, Gaithersburg, Md.: Old Soldier Books, 1987.

Southern Historical Society Papers, vol. 5. January–February 1877.

Staunton (Va.) Spectator. August 4, 1863.

Stewart, George R. *Pickett's Charge: A Microhistory of the Final Attack at Gettysburg, July 3, 1863.* Dayton, Ohio: Morningside, 1980.

Stewart, Salome "Sallie" Myers. Diary (from a transcript; the original diaries disappeared from the Adams County Historical Society in the 1960s). Adams County Historical Society, Gettysburg, Pa.

Stillé, Charles J. *History of the United States Sanitary Commission.* Philadelphia: J. B. Lippincott, 1866.

Stoever, Elizabeth. "A Woman's Story of the Town." *Gettysburg Compiler.* June 24, 1909.

Swann, John S. "Prison Life at Fort Delaware." 1998. Library of Congress, Manuscript Division. Miscellaneous Manuscripts.

Taylor, Frank Hamilton. *Philadelphia in the Civil War, 1861–1865.* Philadelphia: City of Philadelphia, 1913.

Thorn, Elizabeth. "Evergreen Gatehouse Account." *Gettysburg Compiler.* July 26, 1905.

Trowbridge, J. T. "The Field of Gettysburg." *Atlantic Monthly*, November 16, 1865.

Tucker, Glenn. *High Tide at Gettysburg: The Campaign in Pennsylvania.* New York: Bobbs-Merrill Co., 1958.

The Underground Railroad. Historic Pennsylvania. Pennsylvania Historical and Museum Commission.

U.S. Census for 1800, Pennsylvania, York County, Cumberland Township. Gettysburg National Military Park, Gettysburg, Pa.

U.S. Census for 1810–1850, Pennsylvania, Adams County, Cumberland Township and Gettysburg Borough. Adams County Historical Society, Gettysburg, Pa.

U.S. Census for 1860, Pennsylvania, Adams County, Cumberland Township. Gettysburg National Military Park, Gettysburg, Pa.

U.S. Direct Tax for 1798, Pennsylvania, York County, Cumberland Township. Gettysburg National Military Park, Gettysburg, Pa.

United States, War Department. *The War of the Rebellion: A Compilation of the Official Records of the Union and Confederate Armies.* 128 vols. Washington, D.C.: Government Printing Office, 1880–1901. Series 1, 27, 3 parts.

Vautier, John D. "At Gettysburg: The Eighty-Eighth Pennsylvania Infantry in the Battle." November 10, 1886. In *Gettysburg Newspaper Clippings,* 124–26.

Vermilyea, Peter C. "The Effect of the Confederate Invasion of Pennsylvania on Gettysburg's African Americans." Adams County Historical Society, Gettysburg, Pa.

Walker, J. A. "Some Stirring Incidents." *Philadelphia Times.* March 17, 1882. In *Gettysburg Newspaper Clippings.*

Warren, Leander. Account of Leander Warren. Adams County Historical Society, Gettysburg, Pa.

Welcher, Frank J. *The Union Army, 1861–1865: Organization and Operations,* Volume 1: *The Eastern Theater.* Bloomington: Indiana University Press, n.d.

Wert, Jeffrey D. *Gettysburg Day Three.* New York: Simon and Schuster, 2001.

Wheeler, Richard. *Gettysburg, 1863.* New York: Penguin Putnam, 1999.

———. *Voices of the Civil War.* New York: Meridian Books, 1990.

Will Book F. Adams County Courthouse, Gettysburg, Pa.

Will, John C. "Reminiscences of the Three Day Battle of Gettysburg at the Globe Hotel." Adams County Historical Society, Gettysburg, Pa.

Wills, Gary. *Lincoln at Gettysburg: The Words That Remade America.* New York: Simon and Schuster, 1992.

Wilson, Dorothy Clarke. *Stranger and Traveler: The Story of Dorothea Dix, American Reformer.* Boston: Little, Brown & Co., 1975.

Young, James Bowman. *The Battle of Gettysburg.* New York: Harper & Brothers, 1913.

Ziegler, Hugh M. Unpublished manuscript. Adams County Historical Society, Gettysburg, Pa.

INDEX